SHADOW VOYAGE

Also by Peter Huchthausen

Echoes of the Mekong
Hostile Waters (with Igor Kurdin and R. Alan White)
Frye Island, 1748–1998
K19: The Widowmaker
October Fury
America's Splendid Little Wars

SHADOW VOYAGE

THE EXTRAORDINARY WARTIME ESCAPE OF THE LEGENDARY SS *BREMEN*

PETER A. HUCHTHAUSEN

Copyright © 2005 by Peter A. Huchthausen. All rights reserved
Maps by John Lane

Published by John Wiley & Sons, Inc., Hoboken, New Jersey
Published simultaneously in Canada

For general information about our other products and services, please contact our Customer Care Department within the United States at (800) 762-2974, outside the United States at (317) 572-3993 or fax (317) 572-4002.

Wiley also publishes its books in a variety of electronic formats. Some content that appears in print may not be available in electronic books. For more information about Wiley products, visit our web site at www.wiley.com.

Library of Congress Cataloging-in-Publication Data:

Huchtausen, Peter A., date.
    Shadow voyage : the extraordinary escape of the legendary SS Bremen /
Peter A. Huchthausen.
        p. cm.
    Includes bibliographical references and index.
    ISBN 0-471-45758-2 (Cloth: alk paper)
    1. Bremen (Ship) 2. World War, 1939-1945—Naval operations, German. I. Title.
    VM383.B7H88   2005
    940.53—dc22
                                                2004014948

Printed in the United States of America

10 9 8 7 6 5 4 3 2 1

To my son, Paul Duncan Huchthausen

They that dwell under his shadow shall return.

Hosea 14:7

CONTENTS

Acknowledgments

I am sincerely grateful to Irmgard Benco for leading me to my good friend Dr. Hannes Zimmermann who launched me on the right track in research and for finding three former *Bremen* sailors and introducing me to the staff of the Bremerhaven Deutsches Schiffahrtsmuseum. There, I found the *Bremen* deck log and other pertinent data and manuscripts with the invaluable assistance of Archives Director Klaus-Peter Kiedel, Library Assistant Simon Kursawe, and Photo Archivists Klaus Fuest and Norbert Rebs. I am deeply indebted to Imke Schwarzrock, a longtime student of Norddeutscher Lloyd, a spirited enthusiast of the history of the liner *Bremen*, and especially for her assistance finding Frau Renate Wilm, daughter of Commodore Adolf Ahrens and Frau Maris Eberling, daughter of *Bremen*'s Leading First Officer Eric Warning.

I am sincerely grateful for the assistance of Janice Robinson in finding the crew list and log of the HMS *Salmon* and leading me around the British Archives, former Public Record Office, at Kew. I am thankful also for the assistance of the staff at the British Submarine Museum at Gosport for their help finding the late commander E. O. Bickford's patrol report and endorsements and to Horst Harms, son-in-law of the first *Bremen* chief engineer Julius Hundt, and to Erwin Drechsel, son of former New York chief marine superintendent William Drechsel. And thanks to Herr Barth of Nordsee Zeitung. Special thanks to former crew members Wilhelm Bohling, Ernst Henningsen, and Heinz Slominski for graciously offering me their time and memories.

PRELUDE

In still, sweltering heat, in the afternoon of August 30, 1939, as war in Europe grew inevitably closer, the one-time speed-record-holding German passenger liner SS *Bremen* slipped her moorings on Manhattan's West Side and sailed out of New York Harbor. A dark bank of clouds approached the Verazzano Narrows, promising relief to the week of stickiness that had exacerbated the long process of getting the ship cleared for departure and underway on her voyage into the unknown. The majestic liner swung her bow south for the narrows and steamed defiantly past Ellis Island and the Statue of Liberty.

Just as the Staten Island Ferry crossed *Bremen's* wake, a knot of Germans gathered on the liner's stern in the stifling late afternoon heat. After suffering three days of frustrating sailing delays, the *Bremen* crewmen and a handful of employees from German businesses and embassy and consular staffs, reduced to only essential personnel, were finally heading home to Germany as the clouds of war gathered over Europe. A well-known German photographer recorded the crew on *Bremen's* towering stern as they sang the Nazi "Horst Wessel" march and national anthem and gave the "Heil Hitler" salute with right arms outstretched, paying their final farewell to the United States before beginning their extraordinary flight from New York.

1

Their departure launched the liner on a three-and-a-half-month life-and-death race with British warships. *Bremen*'s master, sixty-year-old Adolf Ahrens, knew from radio intercepts relayed to him from Berlin over the prior two days, that a Royal Navy search force consisting of two cruisers was lurking somewhere in the North Atlantic to intercept the liner along her normal great-circle return track to Bremerhaven. There was little doubt to the master and crew aboard the liner that the recent actions by the New York City collector of the port, the Federal Bureau of Investigation, and U.S. Customs had been concocted to intentionally delay their departure. It was obvious that these delaying tactics were part of a not-so-subtle U.S. effort to buy time to allow British warships to form a naval cordon to strangle Nazi Germany's trade with the Western Hemisphere and to position themselves along the usual track of the eastbound liner to intercept and seize her as a prize if war broke out.

After clearing Sandy Hook, with a blinding rain beginning to fall, the liner feinted to the south with topside lighting glowing normally. Then, after steaming through the fading light for ten minutes, the majestic 52,000-ton liner abruptly extinguished all her lights, cranked on 29 knots, turned north, using the foul weather as cover to throw off any would-be pursuers, and commenced an epic escape to avoid capture by Royal Navy warships searching for her as a coveted high-speed troop transport. *Bremen*'s return voyage to Germany would terminate three and a half months after becoming a worldwide sensation in an episode that challenged the rules for unrestricted warfare at sea. Both Germany and Britain claimed *Bremen*'s epic escape run through the Royal Navy blockade as a major propaganda victory. This symbol of hope for a new Germany and a resurgent maritime power gained world attention during the final event-packed days presaging Europe's plunge into World War II.

At first glimpse, this event seems merely a yarn of superior seamanship and good fortune, but on closer scrutiny, it evolves into an epic maritime adventure pitting daring ship handling and intricate German planning during *Bremen*'s sprint from Murmansk through the British naval blockade obstructing the path to her homeport of Bremerhaven, an event that seriously questioned Great Britain's grip on naval supremacy. "Helene," the detailed operation prepared by the German Navy High Command, discovered recently by researchers in the Freiburg naval archives, reveals the importance the Germans placed on the safe return of *Bremen*. The plan governing the security of *Bremen's* dash from the northern Russian port of Murmansk south to her homeport of Bremerhaven, through the Norwegian Sea into the North Sea penetrating the net cast by the Royal Navy, reveals the exceptional coordination designed for the endeavor by the German Navy High Command. The early rules for the Atlantic submarine war, which very nearly strangled the embattled British, were set by a single Royal Navy submarine commander when his decision regarding *Bremen* unintentionally became a benchmark for Allied, and for a time also, German behavior. This is a story of cunning and deception on the part of the Germans, and of great courage and magnanimity of the Royal Navy.

INTRODUCTION

There still exists today a grand mystique of the luxury liners of the past, their graceful lines, towering superstructures, castlelike salons, swaying dining rooms, thundering whistles, and raw power, all designed to whisk passengers across the Atlantic in comfort and ease. Despite the efforts of modern cruise lines in the last decades to recapture the breathtaking aura and excitement of yesterday's transatlantic express liners, their ships don't come close to duplicating the vitality of the old liners. Perhaps it was that the express liner combined the best way to travel, the most elegant, as well as the most efficient, while today those superlatives are spread among the different jet air carriers. The express liners of the 1920s and 1930s were a means of transportation for businessmen, pleasure seekers, statesmen, artists, and ordinary travelers alike who demanded swift and efficient crossings to and from the continent yet in a dignified manner befitting every passenger's belief in his or her own importance. The image of these sleek floating castles looming in the darkness of wartime oceans, steaming stealthily into fog banks, and disappearing with lights doused in tossing seas to deliver extraordinary cargoes of men or equipment into the armed struggle is the thing of grand imagination and terrifying memories. Think of a huge luxury liner, bereft of lights, no radar, and stripped of visual navigation aides, disappearing from the routine transatlantic lanes into iceberg-infested waters and skulking away from searching warships and pursuing aircraft. Imagine that scene in the dark prewar days of 1939 and you have this story.

World War I interrupted the thrilling period of luxurious sea travel, turning the once peaceful Atlantic into a graveyard of ships. During that war, German shipping companies had sustained major losses to their fleets including superliners *Vaterland* and *Kronprinzessin Cecilie*, key ships lost to allied internment. The industry eventually bounced back, yet the decade immediately following the war were lean years for international North Atlantic luxury passenger liner service. The only significant fast liners to join the international fleet in the years right after the armistice were the French ships *Ile de France* and *Paris*. Thus in 1926, when the Bremen-based German firm Norddeutscher Lloyd ordered two new express liners, *Bremen* and *Europa*, they promised a fresh start to contest the lucrative North American passenger business. The highly competitive race for superiority during what would become the final heyday of luxury liners restarted in earnest in the mid-1920s and continued until 1939 and the outbreak of World War II.

The return of Germany to the transatlantic passenger competition was reminiscent of another venture in the late nineteenth century. In 1889, the new kaiser Wilhelm II was so intimidated by Britain's maritime prowess after witnessing Queen Victoria's fleet review in the Solent and touring the new British liner *Teutonic* armed as a commerce raider that he promptly ordered Norddeutscher Lloyd to build and arm the superpassenger liner *Kaiser Wilhelm der Grosse* to outclass the British in size, comfort, and speed. This 649-foot behemoth was launched in May 1897 in Stettin and soon won the coveted Blue Riband, the award for achieving the fastest crossing, on her maiden voyage. This surge into the passenger liner trade by the world's second largest merchant fleet was designed also to catapult the kaiser's navy from a distant fifth in the world to a position nearer the Royal Navy, still a distant first. This presaged a parallel buildup of the heavy combatants of the new kaiser's navy, the large castles of steel that saw final defeat and ignoble death by scuttling in 1919. Again in the 1920s, a recovering Germany would burst full strength into the maritime limelight

Norddeutscher Lloyd's *Bremen*. (Courtesy of Deutsches Schiffahrtsmuseum, Bremerhaven)

with the end goal of surpassing the British. And again, their success would be highly dramatic but short lived.

Popular luxury travel between the Americas and Europe was focused during this epoch on the rapid crossings achieved by the express service of British, French, and German liners between New York and the major European ports of Southampton, Cherbourg, Bremerhaven, and Hamburg. Germany snatched a substantial but brief lead in this race in 1929 with the new oil-burning, steam-turbine twins *Bremen* and *Europa*. The rapid pace of these new purebreds demanded a third ship to meet the strenuous requirements of the express route. The older 32,350-ton *Columbus*, whose keel had been laid during World War I, and retained by Germany through a loophole in the Treaty of Versailles, modified her stacks to resemble her running mates and increased Norddeutscher Lloyd's New York express to a trio. By 1932 the three express liners had captured more than 12 percent of the North Atlantic passenger service. During this same period, the forward-thinking Norddeutscher Lloyd also prepared for the advent of transatlantic air travel by sponsoring the first airship company, Deutsche Zepplin-Reederei, which operated the passenger-carrying *Graf Zeppelin* and ill-fated *Hindenburg*. (*Bremen*'s second master, Captain Adolf

Ahrens, was on hand in Lakehurst, New Jersey, with a crew of twelve of his ship's line handlers to assist docking the airship *Hindenburg* when she exploded and burned on that fateful day in May 1937.)

Bremen was built by the A. G. Weser shipyard in Bremen, while *Europa* was built by Blohm and Voss in Hamburg. *Europa* was scheduled to be completed earlier but suffered a fire while fitting out, so *Bremen* was ready first. Per contract, the average speed of the two was to be 27 knots in order to make their regular crossings in five days. *Bremen* easily took the Blue Riband speed award on her maiden crossing in July 1929, sailing from Cherbourg breakwater to New York's Ambrose Channel Lightship in the record time of 4 days, 17 hours, and 42 minutes, with an average speed of 27.9 knots, thus capturing the record from the British *Mauretania*. The old lady *Mauretania*, which had taken the Blue Riband from the Germans in 1907, was quadruple-screw, then still coal fired with 324 firemen and trimmers. To clinch her reputation, *Bremen* made a record return crossing from New York to Plymouth (Eddystone Light) in 4 days, 14 hours, and 30 minutes, with an average speed of 27.92 knots, completing her maiden round-trip voyage with two record-breaking crossings, a feat never before accomplished in Blue Riband history. Sister ship *Europa* easily took the speed prize the following year.

The two new German ships were designed to incorporate simple beauty and emphasized a more pure form of modern grandeur, freeing the traveler from decades of suffocation under the more traditional *grand ampleur* luxury of their predecessors. According to passenger liner expert John Maxtone-Graham, "Norddeutscher Lloyd were primarily concerned with speed rather than size; they sought an interior décor ending the Wagnerian Teutonic phase of La Belle Epoque. *Bremen* was to have purity of form, beauty of line and superior quality of the material." The new German ships were designed to be functional as well as luxurious. While *Mauretania*'s lines had frequently been compared to a cruiser, the new German twins, low in silhouette and streamlined, with raked bows and stubby stacks, resembled oversized destroyers.

Deck plan of *Bremen*. (From *Marine Engineering and Shipbuilding Age*, July 1930)

9

German engineers disclosed, following *Bremen*'s first crossing, that her record-breaking speed was attained using less than her full design power capability, which was claimed to be 92,500 shaft horsepower (shp). It was later estimated by U.S. and British engineers to be nearer to 160,000 shp. Engineers boasted that *Bremen* had reached 32 knots in short bursts of speed during sea trials. Sister ship *Europa* was slightly more powerful with an estimated total of 170,000 shp, and was a few inches longer. (Germans experts today claim *Bremen*'s actual shaft horsepower was 130,000 shp and *Europa*'s was 134,400 shp.) Both new ships incorporated the new bulbous bow, designed by American admiral David Taylor, which improved flow and enhanced speed. *Bremen* displaced 51,656 tons, which allowed a remarkable load of 9,500 tons of fresh water with a draft of 32 feet. The availability of abundant fresh water is key to a luxury liner, which is naturally configured in all respects for the maximum comfort of the passengers. *Bremen* had more than enough water for her 1,000 separate cabins for passengers organized into four classes. She had quadruple propellers, machined for minimal cavitation, was driven by steam turbines with power provided by twenty watertube boilers, and was linked by single, direct-drive reduction gears. Her newly tested bulbous bow and forward overlapping, instead of aft overlaying hull plating presumably increased her speed an additional half knot. Her sturdy airfoil-section Oertz rudders, which were filled with a lightweight material, weighed only sixty-two tons. The builders built in positive stability under all loading conditions and designed her to sustain the total flooding of any two adjacent compartments in case of collision. *Bremen* carried sixteen hundred tons of fuel in a double hull. She was equipped with the most modern safety systems including a fire protection system designed to New York Port Authority standards. She possessed lifeboats with capacity for two hundred more than the total complement of passengers and crew. *Bremen* was also equipped with a Heinkel floatplane, which was catapulted from a revolving rail located between the stacks and could be launched up to six hundred miles from the destination port to deliver priority mail. In 1935, with the improvement of wireless and telephone communications, the floatplanes were discontinued and the catapult was replaced by a large garage used for storing automobiles and excess baggage. Many of her design aspects were unique; for example, the swimming pool was built directly above the keel below G deck surrounded by two boiler rooms, keeping it sufficiently warm to use in winter. An alternative first-class restaurant was placed between the stacks on the sun deck, boasting a glorious panoramic view of the sea.

Bremen's long relationship with the city of New York was a complex affair of close social affection, which had grown from the early days of the liner's success. When *Bremen* was due on her maiden voyage, on July 22, 1929, thousands of New Yorkers had gathered by midday on the streets, roofs, and anywhere else they might find a view to observe her arrival. In addition, it was not unusual to see celebrities such as W. Somerset Maugham, leading screen actors, European royalty, and captains of industry, like Henry Ford, John D. Rockefeller, and William Randolph Hearst, writing glowing words in the personal guest book of *Bremen's* first master, Commodore Leopold Ziegenbein. It was also popular for New York luminaries to receive gilded invitations to splendid arrival dinners aboard *Bremen*, flown in aboard the mail floatplane a full day before the ship arrived. *Bremen's* crewmen competed for, and several times won, the North Atlantic soccer trophy at matches against the other famous liners in an ongoing New York YMCA-sponsored competition for the international crews.

When Norddeutscher Lloyd resumed hauling passengers to and from New York in the early 1920s, their liners proved too long for the old pier in Hoboken, New Jersey, and were forced to use the Brooklyn army piers until adequate piers became available. Due to the crowning success of the new express liners, Hoboken also proved too distant from Manhattan for efficient passenger service. During this time, Hamburg-Amerika had been Norddeutscher Lloyd's rival company. Finally in 1934, during a brief union of the two German lines, following a long and complex battle with competing shipping firms and politicians from New York's Tammany Hall, the German giants finally moved to the lengthened Hapag Piers 84 and 86 on Manhattan's West Side. This success was due in no small measure to the hard work of their intrepid chief marine superintendent, Captain William Drechsel, a former passenger ship master himself and a man who would play a pivotal role in the history of *Bremen*'s love affair with New York until her final voyage. Drechsel was named chief superintendent of the new Hapag-Lloyd North Atlantic Union, whose masters were advised that, when in U.S. waters, they would be under his authority. Some unique German traditions spread in New York during these happy days. In December 1930 *Bremen* arrived in New York with lighted Christmas trees atop both masts, thus starting a tradition observed to this day by many ships and yachts. So successful was *Bremen* in capturing the image of a top liner that Norddeutscher Lloyd proclaimed proudly, "No liner in modern times has so caught the imagination of the public. Already she has become a legend and a classic. Her name gleams like a new planet."[1] A little-known impact of these two liners on America's future was that the designer of the post-war SS *United States*, the fastest passenger liner ever built, used the concept of *Bremen* and *Europa* configured as one-ship naval task forces in case of the military need for high-speed transports. Captain William Drechsel provided the U.S. Navy with the full blueprints and details of *Bremen*'s operations in the late 1930s; they eventually inspired the design of the SS *United States*.

In the mid-1930s, *Bremen*'s social exploits were interrupted by intermittent outbursts of growing anti-Nazi furor and a major spy scandal.

Bremen was the first liner in any shipping company to employ a full-time ship's special passenger service hostess. Since *Bremen*'s maiden voyage, Dr. Gertrude Ferber had served aboard doubling as hostess and personal secretary to the ship's first and beloved master, Commodore Ziegenbein. Ferber later wrote the book *Eight Glass* using the pen name Tintoretta, describing life aboard the luxury liner during the period leading up to World War II. Her story relates the complex yet discreet struggle on board with *Bremen*'s officers and crew fighting to preserve the ship's popularity with international travelers despite the adverse Nazi political grip on German ships. Ferber assisted aged and infirm passengers, and sometimes quietly helped Jewish passengers on their way to free-

Passengers relaxing in a first-class cabin. (Hanns Tschira—courtesy of Deutsches Schiffahrtsmuseum, Bremerhaven)

dom, unknown to the Nazi SA Bordsturm trooper cadres implanted in *Bremen*'s crew of one thousand men and women.

The reputation of the German passenger ships as the epitome of North Atlantic luxury travel began to deteriorate shortly after Adolf Hitler came to power, and significantly so when he sought to spread Nazi political influence abroad with cadres of Nazi Party Sturm Abteilung (SA; Storm Troopers). These SA Bordsturm, as they were called, were a part of Hitler's policy to "insure the Party reached every German cottage and ship throughout the world." The first maritime SA Bordsturm was established in Hamburg in 1931, and by 1939 more than thirty thousand SA personnel were assigned aboard German merchant ships. From 1936 onward, all German ships were purged of foreign crewmembers and the political cadres were firmly ensconced within the crews of the passenger ships, usually in the service field, as stewards, waiters, and galley staff, the vital heart of a passenger ship's workforce. The members of the SA Bordsturm were intended to anchor the authority of the master and the ship's officers, all of whom were required, at least on paper, to be party members.

When open anti-Semitism and racial cleansing began in earnest in German society, German shipping companies were ordered to release all Jewish crewmembers. By 1938, when the firms were required to be free of Jews, the Norddeutscher Lloyd management quietly disregarded the Nazi Party order and successfully retained some of their highly qualified and experienced crewmen who happened to be Jewish. Norddeutscher Lloyd then further encouraged many of their most seasoned Jewish crewmen to change their identities in the records and largely ignored the purging order.

The Nazi racial bias irked most German sailors, who, like their foreign maritime counterparts, were primarily men of the sea and true internationalists. As the climate in Germany grew more fanatically Nazi, however, individual cases of hardship occurred. For example, Machinist Mate Fritz Obermeier from the Norddeutscher Lloyd ship *Argo* was dismissed for hiding his Jewish identity. He was fired as a crewman, then his astonished wife divorced him for deceiving her. The following year he was deported to a concentration camp and murdered by Nazi guards.[2] As the influence of the SA Bordsturm and the Gestapo (secret police) grew, the personal evaluation cards of crewmen facing reprimand for infractions of discipline were handed over to the Gestapo for action. Already in 1933 the Gestapo was banning American magazines, such as *Harper's, Current History,* and *Life,* from *Bremen's* library, the same year they confiscated a copy of Erich Remarque's *All Quiet on the Western Front* from a popular sailors' hangout in Bremerhaven as anti-German propaganda.[3]

When *Bremen's* commander, Commodore Ziegenbein, personally financed a celebration in a Bremerhaven park for three thousand of his crew and their families and friends, his goal was to enhance the spirit of family and society and to bolster the leadership bond among his junior officers and staff. In resentful response, the local Nazi Party, initially reluctant to openly confront the popular and socially influential commanding officer, initiated an annual series of Christmas concerts at the Columbus Pier called "Green Is the Meadow," at which a uniformed band from the Strength through Joy (Kraft durch Freude; KdF) organization

Leopold Ziegenbein,
Bremen's first master.
(Courtesy of Deutsches Schif-
fahrtsmuseum, Bremerhaven)

played nationalist songs and led sailors and their friends in patri-
otic songs.[4]

Bremen's onboard Nazi SA Bordsturm was composed of fifteen
cells that were industrious in maintaining control of the more
politically reluctant crew. This sometimes-not-so-subtle Nazi infes-
tation led to some dramatic yet discreet struggles aboard Norddeutscher Lloyd ships as the new German regime sought to replace
the more independent-minded and internationally accepted masters and crewmen with more obedient party Germans. Such a
struggle festered aboard *Bremen* as Commodore Ziegenbein continued to resist the Nazis until 1936, when, after steadfastly refusing to end his correspondence with the required salutation, Heil
Hitler, the popular first commander of *Bremen* took early retire-
ment after forty-seven years at sea, at the age of sixty-two. He stated
that he could not in good conscience represent "that party" abroad.
His replacement, Captain Adolf Ahrens, was an experienced master of several Norddeutscher Lloyd ships, most recently *Columbus*,

and had several times replaced Ziegenbein as a supernumerary master of *Bremen*. Later, as the permanent commander, Captain Ahrens and his brilliant seamanship would prove essential to *Bremen*'s future.

The anti-Nazi feelings also grew in the management of Norddeutscher Lloyd. Captain William Drechsel, their New York chief inspector, spoke out publicly in support of one celebrated maritime Nazi victim, Arnold Bernstein, a World War I Iron Cross recipient, who had purchased the old German Red Star line in 1935. He had converted the line into a low-cost carrier of tourist class and cargo only, catering to the increasing flow of refugees leaving Europe. The Nazis seized the line in 1937 and threw Bernstein into a concentration camp until his U.S. supporters eventually bought his freedom in 1939. He later became a U.S. citizen and formed the American Banner Line, also a one-class, low-cost line.

By 1934, the second year of Hitler's regime, the German propaganda machinery began to focus on the large German American community in the United States. Many thousands of German emigrants who had settled in the United States had joined the core of the U.S. economic success story. Their achievements in industry, especially in the engineering and scientific fields, had contributed to the exponential growth of U.S. industrial might. Hitler's Propaganda Ministry trumpeted the key role that ethnic Germans were playing as the leading brains in U.S. business. At the same time, Hitler's embryonic human intelligence services began to target Americans of German descent, especially those who worked in defense industries, as prime targets for exploitation. The restrictions on German military construction and development in industry, dictated by the Versailles Treaty following World War I, provided the burgeoning Nazi intelligence services the impetus to focus their collection efforts against the leading-edge technology in the defense industries, especially in the rapidly developing U.S. aircraft and shipbuilding arenas. A large segment of the successful business society of the United States was made up of well-to-do citizens of German origin, who still participated openly in various German American friendship organizations: the German American Bund, the German American Friendship Guild, the Friends of the New Germany, and the Steuben Society.

The ideal vehicle for transporting the German intelligence services' harvest were the grand express passenger ships, namely the star liner *Bremen*, her sister ship *Europa*, and the lesser-known *Columbus*. Also used for this purpose were *New York*, *St. Louis*, *Reliance*, and their sister ships. These ships were routinely berthed on Manhattan's West Side, immersed in the business of preparing for their weekly voyages laden with passengers heading for Europe. The German ships, with their high ratio of crew to passengers, provided an excellent arena for absorbing intelligence couriers and agent handlers, whose presence on secure territory of the German-flagged ships seemed impenetrable. By 1934 the crews of each of the express liners were fully augmented with SA Bordsturm Brown Shirts, and who, although seldom aboard in uniform, provided excellent security for the intelligence work by the agents operating undercover as crewmen. By 1935 the number of SA staff integrated into *Bremen*'s crew reached a total of 150.

The leader of *Bremen*'s SA Bordsturm detachment was Erwin Schulwitz, a stocky veteran of the Great War, whose name, to his consternation, did not appear on the list of key ship's officers and passengers printed in the pamphlet distributed to all travelers on each crossing. He had seen significant combat on the eastern front and had been captured by the Russians during the Battle of Tannenberg. He spent three years as a prisoner of war in Murmansk and prided himself for his virulent hatred of all communists, Russians in particular. He ran his 150-man SA detachment as a military unit, even though they were prohibited from wearing their brown-shirt uniforms and were scattered throughout many of the ship's divisions. Nevertheless, Schulwitz wore his civilian clothing as if he were in uniform, and he tended to march instead of walk. He held miniature rallies below decks in the crew recreation area, where he would give political talks, show propaganda films, and end the session with "Horst Wessel," a popular song sung by the Nazi Party. Captain Ahrens had asked First Officer Warning to tell Schulwitz to tone down the affairs because the director of special passenger services, Dr. Gertrude Ferber, an outspoken anti-Nazi, complained that his antics disturbed the passengers, especially the elderly. The captain also banned strutting around the ship, which Schulwitz did anyway, as it was impossible for him to merely walk casually. He apparently had difficulty passing by a mirror, of which there were many in the main first-class salon and elegant staircases between the A and B decks. He would pose and preen like a peacock, so Warning banned Schulwitz from these areas. Knowing how Captain Ahrens felt about the party activities aboard, Schulwitz made himself scarce topside and was rarely seen above the F deck, where the crew quarters and dining hall were located. Ahrens considered the SA Bordsturm more a pain in the neck than a serious menace. Warning also disliked their antics, but as a naval reserve officer and war veteran himself, he treated Schulwitz with the respect due a fellow veteran and former prisoner of war.

In 1937 an ominous event shocked the North Atlantic shipping community when the first transatlantic air service commenced. The new air travel initially did no harm to the express lines business. Nevertheless, passenger bookings on German ships fell. *Bremen* was briefly removed from the previously lucrative transatlantic run and sent on a winter cruise around South America, which the U.S. press made into a significant Nazi propaganda coup by heralding the passage of the largest ship through the Panama Canal. (*Bremen* held that record until nearly thirty-five year later when *Queen Elizabeth II* took the honor as the larger of the two.) But there were still plenty of passengers to carry across the Atlantic.

In the summer of 1938, the unmasking of a major Nazi spy ring in the United States spiced the New York history of *Bremen* and her sister, *Europa*. The most notable events revolved around the espionage adventures of Dr. Ignatz Griebl and William Lonkowski during their efforts to steal U.S. defense secrets, among them the highly prized Norden bombsight plans. The Griebl-Lonkowski net, operating since 1934 out of Wilhelmshaven—the Abwehr's (military intelligence) most productive post—under the control of Dr. Erich Pfeiffer, was already responsible for sending out a flood of intelligence from the United States. The Griebl case became a widely publicized spy story and eventually precipitated a major windfall victory for U.S. counterintelligence, but only after some glaring oversights and costly blunders.

Notwithstanding this aberration in *Bremen*'s reputation as a leading star in New York's social scene, her high life continued and the spy scandal was soon forgotten. But as the Nazis increased their appalling behavior in Europe, *Bremen* again became the focus of confrontation. Several times, when Nazi intervention in the Spanish civil war was in full swing, anti-Nazi demonstrators, made up of American communist, Roman Catholic, and Jewish citizens, marched to Pier 86 to denounce the regime. In July 1935, when two hundred New York policemen proved unable to contain the demonstrators, a handful of activists forced their way aboard *Bremen* thirty minutes prior to sailing. While the passengers and guests reveled in semisobriety, the demonstrators surged to the bow and hauled down the Nazi swastika flag from the jack staff and tossed it into the Hudson River. In the melee that followed, a New York plainclothesman shot a demonstrator in the groin and wounded several crewmen and protestors. Ten days later, appearing in court for disorderly conduct, a handful of the demonstrators was released with a warning by the judge, who by chance was Jewish. In reaction to the incident, an enraged Adolf Hitler decreed that the Nazi Party swastika flag would become the new German national standard, replacing the unpopular black, red, and gold of the Weimar Republic that had, in turn, replaced the still older black, red, and white banner of the kaiser's imperial Germany.[5]

Similar public anti-German demonstrations erupted anew in 1936 during the Berlin Olympics and soon after the German intervention in the Spanish civil war. On August 22, 1936, when *Bremen* was due to sail from Pier 36 just after midnight, more than a hundred visitors appeared aboard in evening dress feigning farewells to passengers. Once aboard, they stripped off their black jackets revealing white T-shirts emblazoned with the slogan "Hands off Spain" and began handing out anti-Nazi leaflets. When New York uniformed police and plainclothesmen arrived in force, rioting erupted, sending deck chairs and champagne bottles flying about the decks in a spectacular melee. Surprise boardings just prior to

Flying the Nazi flag in New
York Harbor. (Hann Tschira—
courtesy of Deutsches Schiffahrtsmuseum, Bremerhaven)

sailing by demonstrators continued through 1938, which twice
more managed to tear down the new Nazi flag. After returning to
Germany following one confrontation, Gestapo agents arrested
two *Bremen* officers for negligence in opposing the boarders.

During this period Norddeutscher Lloyd continued to operate
their three prime luxury liners on regularly scheduled transits,
with one ship always in Bremerhaven or New York and one underway in the North Atlantic, an achievement that had given Germany a lead in the number of passengers carried, but that began
to wane with Hitler's waxing misbehavior and notably so following
Crystal Night in 1938. German liners were rapidly losing popularity,
and, as the exodus of wealthy Europeans swamped crowded west-
bound liners, fewer chose to ride in ships flying the Nazi swastika.

The Italian liners *Rex* and then *Conte di Savoia* took the coveted Blue Riband crossing speed record in 1932, and the French

liner *Normandie* captured the record in 1935. By then Norddeutscher Lloyd was operating at a loss blamed on the devaluation of the reichsmark and the Jewish boycott of German trade. Then in 1936, the new British liner *Queen Mary* took the crossing speed honor back to Britain and held it throughout the war. While on a downward slide, Norddeutscher Lloyd canceled *Bremen*'s scheduled ninety-day world cruise for the tour company Raymond and Whitcomb, and returned her to the normal express service between Bremerhaven and New York.

In the late 1930s, Atlantic liners of all flags were conducting a brisk service hauling passengers of wealth and more modest means, often with all their worldly possessions, westward as tensions rose in Europe. During the final months prior to the German invasion of Poland, President Franklin D. Roosevelt was actively dealing under the table to keep the noisy advocates of neutrality off his back and secretly organizing a joint British-American intelligence network, with headquarters in New York and with William Stephenson, the man called Intrepid, at its head. Although the organization was not officially established until 1940, the early founders were already on the ground by August 1939 gathering maritime information and planning devious measures to counter German plans to employ commerce raiders should war break out, which seemed certain. As a former assistant secretary of the navy, Roosevelt was vitally concerned with foreign shipping, and with the memories still fresh of the renowned German surface raiders of World War I, he was determined to take early measures to protect U.S. neutrality from armed merchantmen. Famous commerce raiders, in German Hilfskreuzer (armed naval support ships), such as Count von Luckner's fully rigged *Seeadler* and the liner *Kaiser Wilhelm der Grosse*, fitted out with four five-inch guns, had wrought havoc with allied shipping in many oceans. By this time, Roosevelt was receiving intelligence that Germany was preparing to convert many of its most capable merchant ships into armed commerce raiders. Many German ships were configured for eventual use as troop transports, or as Hilfskreuzer, hospital ships, and recreation ships (Strength through Joy ships) designed as classless liners for the diversion of deserving workers. These KdF ships increased in number to include vessels such as *Stuttgart, Sierra Cordoba, Der Deutsche, Berlin, St. Louis, Sierra Morena,* and *Wilhelm Gustloff.*

Roosevelt was determined to take timely measures to protect U.S. interests. He was keenly aware of the case of the Confederate warship CSS *Alabama* during the Civil War and the damage that warship had inflicted on Union trade in the Atlantic. *Alabama,* which had been built in Liverpool and was manned primarily by British sailors, had destroyed sixty-two U.S. merchant ships between 1862 and 1864. In that war, Confederate commerce raiders destroyed 257 merchants and whalers, as their commerce raiders ran amok through the Atlantic trade lanes. Years after the war, Britain was compelled by Admiralty courts to pay more than $15 million in damages to the United States because of its role in building *Alabama* and supporting armed Confederate raiders. Roosevelt was determined not to let Germany force itself onto neutral America, nor did he want to see Britain lose the opportunity to snatch key German merchant ships and passenger liners, which might be in U.S. waters when war began. Thus, he quietly assisted British naval intelligence to locate and track important ships such as *Bremen,* and went out of his way to make sure the United States would do all it could, while remaining outwardly neutral, to help the Royal Navy make key intercepts and seizures.

The famed golden era of luxury liner travel ended on August 25, 1939, when Berlin suddenly ordered all its ships back to Germany or into neutral ports. A short time later, the German Navy High Command assumed operational control of all German ships. *Europa* was immediately recalled (it was only one day out) and returned to Bremerhaven, while *Columbus* scuttled herself off the Virginia coast to prevent her falling into British hands. *Bremen* continued to New York to disembark 1,770 passengers before turning about, sailing without passengers into the unknown. What follows is the tale of *Bremen*'s celebrated 1939 flight from New York and its extraordinary run for home.

1

Uncertain Crossing

A young seaman stood on Bremerhaven's Columbus Quay early one August morning in 1939, gazing up at *Bremen's* graceful bow. He could hear the humming of the auxiliary plant providing power inside the black-hulled giant as he contemplated the journey ahead. Wilhelm Bohling, an eighteen-year-old apprentice waiter in the first-class dining salon, treasured the early predawn hours before the pier area and large ship awoke to a beehive of activity, deck hands washing down the decks, shining the brass fittings, and readying the ship for departure. In a few hours hundreds of passengers would be arriving by train, bus, and car for embarkation. Bohling had walked the entire way from the center of town to the pier area in the early morning hours anticipating the departure, wearing his blue uniform with its triple rows of shiny gold buttons. He had overheard two passersby say in response to an unheard question, "Oh, he's a sailor off *Bremen.*" The phrase had made Bohling happy and proud to be so identified. He gazed up at the high stem of the ship with its graceful flaring bow of highly polished steel. He could make out the city crest of Bremen in relief high atop the prow, giving the ship a seal of identity and setting her apart from her sister ship, *Europa*, which looked identical with the two squat yellow funnels. The mooring lines, thick as Bohling's upper arms, stretched like a spider web to the bollards on the pier side. This was not just a ship, he thought, the largest and fastest in Germany; it was his home, it was warm and it fed well.

Wilhelm Bohling, an apprentice waiter on *Bremen*, taken in the 1950s. (Courtesy of Wilhelm Bohling)

SS *Bremen*
At sea
Tuesday, August 22 to Monday, August 28, 1939

Bremen sailed from Bremerhaven on Tuesday, August 22, at 2:00 P.M., with 1,220 passengers aboard bound for New York via Southampton and Cherbourg—officially logged as *Bremen*'s Voyage 187. In brilliant weather the next day she steamed past Dover and anchored off Southampton for two hours to embark more passengers. Many of the crew aboard were wrestling with quiet doubts and fears of the unpredictable future. Most felt an uncomfortable foreboding that events at home in Germany were spiraling out of control, and above all, feared they might lose their precious access to world travel, specifically their regular trips to New York. Indeed, at this time *Bremen* was widely viewed as a metaphor for German American esteem that had emerged and flourished following the dark days of World War I. To those who cultivated strong friendships and ties with Americans, the mutual respect and closeness took on an importance far greater than the crew's loyalty to the new German political dogma. As sailors they were primarily internationalists, but in Germany it was not prudent to openly admit it.

The *Bremen* sailed again the same day to make Cherbourg, taking on a total of five hundred additional passengers and disembarking very few. It seemed that more people were leaving Europe than going the other way. There were now 1,770 passengers embarked.

On this same day Adolf Hitler and Joseph Stalin signed the nonaggression pact with its secret clause for the division of Poland. Of course, the ship's crew learned of this only much later.

Early on Thursday morning, to punctuate their concerns for the future, the *Bremen* bridge watch sighted the French liner *Normandie* coming from Le Havre bound also for New York via Southampton. Previously, such chance encounters at sea were celebrated with excitement, waving, and exchange of salutes. This time, however, crew and passengers aboard both ships appeared uncharacteristically glum and merely stared quietly across the sea at the other ship, showing little sign of emotion, perhaps their thoughts dwelling on the gradually withering security of peacetime. The two ships were steaming on nearly parallel courses, but for some reason *Bremen* veered away to the south until she drew outside visual range, then swung back to a westerly heading. The crew guessed their captain was shunning company, especially with a French or English ship, given the tense state of affairs in Europe.

The ship's passengers were kept well aware of the current situation in Europe through the *Lloyd Post* newspaper, copied daily by wireless and run off on a mimeograph machine for all to read. Feelings aboard were tense, especially since it appeared that the standoff between Germany and Poland was reaching a climax. Most of the crew had little to say about what was happening, yet some believed the whispers of the Nazi Party SA Bordsturm people integrated aboard with the crew who were claiming the Polish

hordes were knocking at the gates of Berlin. But most sailors serving in the first-class areas, like Bohling, were too busy meeting the
demands of the passengers and scrambling for tips, which in those
times were gold mines for those men and women who had experienced the ravages of the last ten years of Germany's economic
doldrums.

The *Bremen* crew had been imbued with the code that their
single most important function was pleasing the passengers, and
they were clever enough to succeed in meeting those demands in
manners affable enough to garner handsome remuneration in the
form of U.S. dollars or reichmarks. Thus, the crew lost themselves
in the daily routine, but always kept their ears attuned to the abundant rumors circulating the ship for any tidbits that might indicate
a change to the voyage schedule.

Bohling had made friends with a second-generation German
American family in Hoboken, New Jersey, on his first trip to New
York, and on each subsequent visit spent time with them, went on
outings, and gradually became accepted as one of the fold. Ernst
Henningsen, also from Bremerhaven, the son of a sailor who had
served for many years aboard Norddeutscher Lloyd passenger
ships, was a waiter in the first-class dining room. He was especially
happy to be on this trip. Having spent two years as a waiter aboard
the sister ship *Europa* before changing to *Bremen,* the twenty-year-
old waiter had worked his way into the coveted job as a top waiter
with its many rewards. Heinz Slominski, a rough-and-tumble seaman from Bremen on the ship's deck force, was also happy to be
aboard, as this would be his second trip to New York, where he had
made fast friends with a family originally from Germany whom he
visited on every opportunity. Walter Renneberg, a twenty-two year
old from Hamburg, had shipped aboard *Bremen* as an intern cook
working directly for Leading Cook Hans Künlen, the rotund and
jovial chef with thirty years' experience aboard Bremerhaven liners.
Renneberg was especially pleased to be close to all major events in
the galley, a position that enabled him to barter with other crewmen for precious items, such as American cigarettes, French
cognac, or English toffee, in return for delicacies he could easily

Ernst Henningsen (third from right), a waiter in *Bremen's* first-class dining room. (Courtesy of Ernst Henningsen)

pilfer from the plenteous galley. Besides misappropriating food to trade, Renneberg kept a detailed memoir of his time on *Bremen*.

Thus, while hard at work during the frequent transits, many of the *Bremen* crew enjoyed their ties with American families in and around New York. The families' relations with the ships' crew provided the new Americans a fond link to their past and the nostalgic memory of German customs, food, and, especially during this time, rumors and tidbits of news from their homeland. These contacts had taken on vital importance as the printed news was gradually being filled with half-truths and outright lies pumped out by the new Berlin Propaganda Ministry. It was growing more and more difficult to know precisely what was going on at home in their towns and villages. Loyalties became more diffused with the growth of the Nazi Party, and while the crew were limited by regulations to possessing only four American dollars, there were innumerable ways to enlist the help of their many New York friends to overcome the restrictions to purchase American items, which were rare in Europe, and bring them home as gifts to their families or

Many of *Bremen*'s crew
had nurtured close ties
with American families in
and around New York.
(Hanns Tschira—courtesy of
Deutsches Schiffahrtsmuseum,
Bremerhaven)

girlfriends. The regulations were spelled out in detail in the passenger brochure for each transit:

> According to the German Regulations Governing the Control
> of Foreign Currency German coins can be accepted from pas-
> sengers in payment for services on board only during the ship's
> voyage from Bremerhaven to the first foreign port of call,
> Southampton and then only within the limits of 10 Reichs-
> marks. No German money whatever, notes or silver, will be
> accepted on the homeward bound voyage from New York to
> Europe.

Bremen's passengers on this trip were mostly Americans, heading home after cutting short vacations on the Riviera or elsewhere
in Europe, instigated by the rumors of war and abuses of certain
minorities. On this transit, there were a half-dozen high-ranking

German diplomats, five of them envoys to South American countries returning to their posts following consultations in the Foreign Ministry in Berlin. The first-class passenger list boasted important personalities such as Claudius Dornier Jr, scion of the famous aircraft manufacturer; Baroness Elisabeth von Epenstein-Mauternburg; Prince Egon zu Hohenlohe-Langenburg, and Princesses Maria Franciscaes and Elisabeth zu Hohenlohe-Langenburg— high-sounding names that may have meant something to the ship's officers but not to the normal sailor. Also aboard for this crossing were State Councilor H. E. Pabst, the Reich's wool minister, and Keizo Yamamoto, cousin of the Japanese admiral soon to become famous in the Pacific war. There were also a large number of tourists who looked as if they were hauling their life's belongings in their baggage. There was even Donna Fox, captain of the 1936 U.S. Olympic bobsled team, and another lady, a Jewish author in tourist class, who never left her cabin for fear of the German authorities.

The passengers seemed more solemn than they normally would be after embarking on a five-day luxurious voyage. There was considerably less dancing in the ballroom and the bar dispensed much more alcohol than normal, already a considerable amount. Many guests remained in the bar until the wee hours talking about the situation in Europe and could be heard discussing the most recent offers of compromise made by Prime Minister Neville Chamberlain.

The first night out of Bremerhaven a fist fight erupted in the tourist lounge on C deck between a British passenger and a German from Berlin. Bohling said the Englishman was drunk and had taken offense when the Berliner, also in the advance stages of inebriation, called him a Jew-bastard and punched him in the nose. Leading First Officer Eric Warning was called to the scene after two of the SA Bordsturm pounced on the hapless Englishman and beat him nearly to a pulp. That same evening, the crew learned that one of the night stewards, Heinrich Behrens, was missing. They searched the ship and never found him. It was rumored he was involved with a French girl in Cherbourg, and no

The first-class lounge on *Bremen*. (Hanns Tschira— courtesy of Deutsches Schiffahrtsmuseum, Bremerhaven)

one could remember seeing him since they left that port. Captain Adolf Ahrens made a log entry to that effect and reported him as missing by wireless message to the Norddeutscher Lloyd Bremerhaven office. Another rumor had it that Behrens was in trouble with the onboard SA Bordsturm troopers, who were known to do some pretty nasty things. He reported to work the first day out of Bremerhaven, after having been summoned by the SA for disciplinary action for failure to salute properly during the departure ceremony. He had acquired a black eye and showed signs he had taken the worst in a fight. He was never seen again.

Captain Ahrens was a likable man. The crew mostly saw him at a distance, but he seemed friendly enough, appearing much like a benevolent bear, with a ready smile, looking as if he was sharing a pleasant secret when he gazed at his crewmen. Born in Bremerhaven in 1879, he first shipped out at age fourteen aboard the fully rigged *Renée Rickmers*. After five years aboard sailing ships, he attended the Maritime School at Elsfurt and qualified as a quartermaster. He began serving with Norddeutscher Lloyd in 1901 and continued with their ships, achieving his first command of the SS *Columbus* in 1928. After periodically replacing the first and original captain, Commodore Leopold Ziegenbein, during vacations or sickness, Ahrens became the permanent captain of *Bremen* in 1936, in the midst of the ongoing struggle with the new Nazi effort to take control of the spiritual backbone of the German merchant fleet.[1]

On Friday, August 25, still three days out of New York, a *Bremen* radio telegrapher handed Leading Radio Officer Kurt Gerstung the message he had just copied on the typewriter while guarding the Berlin *Norddeich* merchant broadcast. It was a wireless warning message sent with the prefix key H followed by the code QWA, signifying it was for *Bremen* to copy. Gerstung took the message and read it, immediately stiffening in reaction. "Exact time of receipt?" he queried the operator sharply.

"Exactly 20:06 Greenwich time, sir," the operator answered, surprised at the officer's reaction.

Gerstung bolted for the radio room door. He had been briefed about the new emergency operational codes promulgated by the Navy High Command in Berlin to all German merchant ships two weeks before. In view of the deteriorating situation with Poland, the navy was preparing to take over operational control of all shipping, which would happen following a series of radio alert commands using the code QWA prefixed by the letter H, for Handelsmarine (merchant fleet). Gerstung now had in his hands the first message with that code. He raced one deck up from the boat deck to the bridge on the sun deck level and directly aft to Captain Ahrens's sea cabin, stopping at the door to catch his breath before knocking.

Gerstung was the ship's senior radio officer, trained in the well-known DEBEG, in Hamburg, which had for years proven their worth as one of the leaders of the world's maritime radio services.[2] Gerstung had recently attended the special Abwehr school in Wilhelmshaven, under command of military intelligence, for

Adolf Ahrens became the
captain of *Bremen* in 1936.
(Courtesy of Deutsches Schiffahrtsmuseum, Bremerhaven)

radio direction finding and communications intelligence, specializ-
ing in traffic analysis. He was fluent in English and had a reinforced
team of talented radio-intercept personnel aboard, also trained in
Berlin with the DEBEG and subsequently by the Abwehr B Service in Wilhelmshaven. Gerstung's assistant was a Bordsturm officer and several of his men were subordinate to the SA Bordsturm
party organization. Despite the integration of these SA men, Gerstung's radio room operated efficiently and his operators buried
their feelings of animosity. He and his men would play a key role
in the next months during *Bremen*'s dash into history.

Gerstung opened the door and stepped into the cabin as soon
as he heard Captain Ahrens's soft, "Enter."

Gerstung saluted, then handed the message to the captain.
"Important alert signal," he said.

Ahrens studied the message:

QWA 7—All ships deviate from scheduled tracks by 30–100
nautical miles as security precaution.

Ahrens looked up at the communicator. "Very well," he said. "Please call First Officer Warning and ask him come to my cabin. Let me know as soon as you hear anything new." He turned and walked back to his desk, looking intently at the chart laid out beneath a reading light. "And Gerstung," he added calmly, "be very alert regarding intercepts from any other vessels, especially British. I wish to know immediately if you hear any chatter from British or American warships. Understood?" He paused, then added, "Oh yes, and from now on there will be no lettergrams sent for the passengers; we are to transmit only what I give you. Tell the passengers that atmospheric conditions have made this service unavailable."

"Perhaps we should notify the passengers officially that this service is canceled," Gerstung suggested.

"Yes," Ahrens replied. "Good idea. I'll have Master Warning post a notice to that effect on the passenger bulletin board."

Gerstung clicked his heels, "Aye, Herr Captain!" He departed quickly and slid down the ladders three steps at a time thinking, This action is exactly what I love! Plus, it was good not to have to send those lettergrams; it was always a bother for his men.

A few moments later, First Officer Warning was in the captain's sea cabin. After reading the QWA alert, Ahrens pointed to the chart on his desk. "Number One, let's adjust our track to the south a hundred miles; make up the time by cranking on another half a knot. I'm not sure what the threat is, but I've alerted Gerstung to keep us informed quickly."

"I agree, Herr Captain," the first officer nodded. "The news we've been copying in the *Lloyd Post* has not been encouraging. Seems the British are taking a stand on the Poland issue." The first officer left the cabin and proceeded to the bridge to adjust the navigation track.

Warning strode forward along the promenade deck past the officers' living quarters, mounted the carpeted staircase, opened two more doors, and stepped into the grandeur of the wheelhouse. He glanced toward the array of thick plate-glass windows. Looking forward, he could observe the green ocean below and make out the ship's blunt bow ten stories down through the gleaming windows.

Bremen's grand wheelhouse offered a view to the ocean below through its gleaming windows. (Hanns Tschira—courtesy of Deutsches Schiffahrtsmuseum, Bremerhaven)

The bridge windows bulged slightly forward, and the first officer could see the glistening wheel and the four sturdy brass engine room telegraphs, proudly symbolizing their connection with the power of the four main engine rooms located nine decks below. They served as the relay between the ship's brain, the pilothouse, and the ship's heart, the engine room. To the right of the wheel was Iron Mike, the steering system designed to hold the ship on course automatically, and used only during bright and clear daylight and never at night or in poor visibility, in case its ease of use and accuracy might be used as a substitute for visual vigilance. To the left of the wheel stood two large brass-encased compasses, one magnetic, the other the main gyrocompass repeater, on which the ship's course was set and steered; the magnetic being merely a backup in case of gyro failure. The gyrocompass itself was located amidship and nine decks below in a solitary den from which it controlled the many gyrorepeaters located at key positions throughout the ship, rotating in a single plane, and electrically transmitting its resistance to the slightest movement away from that plane, thus recording all minute two-dimensional changes in the ship's heading. Mounted on the forward bulkhead of the pilothouse was the latest aid to safe navigation, the Svenska Log, functioning as the ship's speedometer. It read out the actual speed of the ship's hull through the water so accurately that even when the ship was anchored, it read the velocity of the current washing by the hull. Four large brass-encased dials, mounted on a gleaming mahogany board above the wheel, gave the exact number of revolutions per minute of each of the ship's bronze propellers. The rest of the bridge was the size of a tennis court and exuded irreproachable tidiness of brass, mahogany, and brilliant white paint surrounded by brightly shining levers, odd-shaped knobs, and batteries of over-sized telephones for communications from stem to stern.

When the ship was underway there were six men in the wheel-house or on the commander's open bridge. The supreme being was, of course, the captain, and below him the leading first officer, also called the chief officer. These two men were always found on the bridge during maneuvering, poor visibility, or fog; continuously during entry and exit from port; and in cases of key decision making. There were three additional first officers, all wearing the four gold rings of a captain and who served as the watch chiefs for each section answerable directly to the captain or leading first officer. One of the three first officers was always in the wheelhouse, in the chart room, just behind the bridge, checking the navigation plot, or on either wing of the bridge, scanning the horizon with his marine glasses for hazards to navigation. Three additional officers, the second officers, served on each watch section, roaming the ship checking remote course and depth indicators, trim gauges, barographs, and patent logs for safe navigation. One experienced quartermaster in each section, seasoned by many years in the trade, steered the ship during the four-hour watch and was assisted by a half-dozen deck seamen to answer phones, serve as lookouts, and carry out any commands that came their way from the senior officers.

Other key instruments were to be found in the chart house, which was set off from the bridge with a green curtain and a polished mahogany door. One was the fathometer, or echo sounder, which functioned by transmitting sound pulses through the water, whose echoes were timed to warn the navigator of shallow and dangerous waters and to assist him in fixing the ship's position by matching the ship's bottom with soundings shown on the hydrographic chart. There were two of these in the chart house, one for shallow depths at one frequency, and another for deeper seas transmitting at a higher frequency. Together they marked every change in depth below the keel from two to fifteen thousand feet. The newest navigational aides in the chart house were the radio direction finders fixed to a loop antenna that could be tuned toward coded radio signals keyed from transmitters dotting the shores of most countries. These measured their exact bearing, allowing the navigator to triangulate and fix his own position to the nearest mile in good conditions. Even though they could not provide a precise range, they could indicate distance based on the signal strength. A passive hydrophone receiver located on the hull similarly detected the bearing and strength of sound signals transmitted underwater from a myriad of navigational aids such as lightships, buoys, or shore stations; the navigator used these signals to more accurately fix the ship's position. In August 1939 these were the sum total of navigational aides augmenting the sextant, chronometer, and compass, the navigator's basic tools, used for centuries by sailors to plot their courses across the earth's oceans.

After correcting the ship's track, First Officer Warning left the chart house and stood for a while observing the watch on the bridge. Warning was a reserve naval officer who had seen action in World War I. Ahrens liked the efficiency of his number one, who also held the rank of kapitänleutnant (senior lieutenant) in the German Naval Reserve. Warning was born in Gross-Mölln, near Stolp in 1901, the son of a customs official. He served in the Norddeutscher Lloyd aboard *Kronprinzessin Cecile* and *Hannover* before World War I and, following duty on *Bremen*, would soon make himself famous as the prize commander of the captured Norwegian tanker *Storstad*, the seven-thousand-ton ship renamed *Passat* and converted into a commerce raider and minelayer.[3] Warning viewed the discipline aboard all merchant and passengers ships as somewhat lax and often felt the need to crank up the vigi-

First Officer Eric Warning (second from left). (Courtesy of Deutsches Schiffahrtsmuseum, Bremerhaven)

lance and responsiveness of some indifferent crewmen. But he had been cautioned by Captain Ahrens that too snappy a crew might be off-putting to the passengers, many of whom were already reluctant to travel on German ships because of the burgeoning reputation of the harsh Nazi discipline. Warning studied the watch, sighed silently, and retired below to his cabin for a cup of tea.

That same day a curious chain of events began to unfold.

**The White House
Washington, D.C.
August 25, 1939**

Concerned about the maritime situation, President Franklin D. Roosevelt sent a White House memorandum to Acting Secretary of the Treasury John W. Hanes (Secretary Henry Morgenthau Jr. was away in Europe):

Dear Mr. Secretary—

I have reason to believe that there is a possibility that merchant ships belonging to European governments, which may become involved in war, or belonging to their citizens, are carrying armaments capable of being mounted on the high seas, thus converting them into armed ships. This raises immediately the question of American responsibility for giving clearance papers to such ships unless this government is wholly certain that such armaments are not being carried.

You will, therefore, withhold clearance papers from all ships suspected of carrying armaments until a complete search has been made and you are satisfied that no armaments are aboard.

Very sincerely yours,

FDR[4]

That same day, the U.S. embassy in Berlin passed on more sinister news. Two intelligence reports arrived in Washington from the U.S. naval attaché in Berlin, causing additional concern in the White House. The first stated that the German Navy High Command had assumed control of all merchant shipping. The second was a report containing an extract from a year-old letter purloined from the German Navy High Command:

From: The Marine Kommandoamt [Naval Command
         Department]
Berlin, 16 September 1938

Subject: Operation of Naval Auxiliary Cruisers [Hilfskreuzer]
         on the High Seas

Considering that in the case of mobilization against Britain as an enemy the swift transfer within the time allowed of auxiliary cruisers stationed in home waters to the Atlantic is not ensured. The Chief of the Navy High Command has ordered a speedy examination to be made determining how quickly, during peacetime conditions, the navy can convert and equip the largest possible number of merchant vessels suitable for that purpose without essentially restricting their use in peacetime. The report is to address what could be done upon issuing the mobilization order to provide for their support from any base, for their conversion and preparation for use as auxiliary cruisers on the high seas. The Commander in Chief has demanded that in the case of a positive result of the examination the largest possible number of auxiliary cruisers should be available by 1941–1942.

[signed]
Nordron
Government Senior Inspector[5]

SS *Bremen*
At sea
August 26 to 28, 1939

That Saturday, August 26, Radio Officer Gerstung brought the captain the second warning:

QWA 8—All ships don camouflage paint and return to German ports immediately, avoid Strait of Dover.

"This doesn't make sense," Ahrens muttered to Warning as the two officers stood in the chart room with Radio Officer Gerstung again standing close by.

"How the blazes are we going to camouflage the ship by painting while steaming at twenty-seven knots?" Warning asked bitterly.

"I'm sure it could be done," Ahrens replied. "But I'm thinking this order couldn't apply to us." Indeed, the order seemed vague, with empty words. Ahrens turned toward his first officer. "No, of course we're not sure what will happen. This warning could be extended indefinitely; we're not at war yet."

Ahrens lit his pipe thoughtfully and began pacing his cabin. He was quiet for a few moments, inhaling deeply, then blowing the smoke out toward the large mirror over the ornate cabinet where a few photos of his previous ships stood. Also on the cabinet was a model of *Columbus*, his last command before taking over *Bremen*, now Norddeutscher Lloyd's lead ship and Germany's top liner.

Ahrens thought his decisions could soon prove to be of national importance. He liked that idea. "I think, Mister Warning, that we should call a meeting with the six envoys and the key first-class passengers in the Hunting Salon. It's just past five P.M., please call them individually and invite them to meet with the two of us following the dinner for brandy and discussion of an important question. I want to reply to Berlin with the full backing of these key individuals. Begin with the Baron von Schön, who's going to be our ambassador in Chile; he is very senior."

"Aye, Captain," Warning replied. The first officer was more apt than his captain to follow orders blindly. As a naval reserve officer, he had no interest in the views of German diplomats and especially of wealthy Americans. To Warning, things were black or white, no questions asked. But he was loyal and carried out his captain's orders without question.

Warning left the sea cabin and strode to the bridge, picked up the intercom, and, reading from a list of passengers hanging by the phone, started to dial the various first-class passengers. He stopped suddenly and instead dialed Dr. Gertrude Ferber, the director of special passenger services. Let her earn her keep, he thought. Ferber was on excellent terms with the special passengers and had a knack for cajoling them to do whatever the captain or the first officer wanted without a hint of coercion. She was smooth, and the passengers liked being pampered. Warning hated dealing with the stuffy diplomats and loathed the sight of the paunchy American industrialists and their perfumed ladies. He'd rather spend time with Frederich (Fritz) Müller's stinking engineers, Gerstung's sharp communicators, or even Schulwitz's SA Bordsturm thugs. At least they were predictable.

At 9:00 P.M. a group of passengers met with the captain and the first officer in the Hunting Salon as Ahrens requested. A long, heated discussion took place, lasting two and a half hours. At 11:30, Ahrens and Warning returned to the bridge and stood on the open port wing. Ahrens leaned forward, opened a voice tube, and called into the wheelhouse, "Have Mister Gerstung report to me here." As the two officers stared out into the oppressively warm night, the captain turned to the first officer, who stood properly on his left and slightly behind. Ahrens thought, How predictably correct this officer is. He ought to be a regular naval officer instead of in the merchant fleet. He's too stiff for the passengers. "Mister Warning," he said suddenly, "post a notice on the promenade deck tonight announcing that we will continue to New York and arrive on Monday evening instead of that morning. Then adjust the track with the navigator to arrive off Sandy Hook at four P.M. Monday. I'll have Gerstung radio ahead to Captain Drechsel so he can arrange the clearance, pilot, and tugs. Then, of course, I'll draft the answer to Berlin." He paused. "And, Mister Warning," Ahrens looked directly at his second in command. "Then, and only then," he said, moving toward the outboard side of the bridge wing, "will I wire Berlin and tell *them* what we are going to do. That way we'll spare them the necessity to direct us. I'm sure this is the right thing to do."

The first officer responded properly, "Aye, Herr Captain," while thinking, I hope so, for our own good.

When Radio Officer Gerstung arrived on the bridge, the captain was in the chart house finishing the draft response to the QWA warning message. He handed the draft to Gerstung, who read it quickly:

> Considering six German envoys and 1,770 passengers aboard, intend to continue to New York.
> Ahrens

Despite the order to maintain radio silence, the next day Ahrens ordered Gerstung to transmit a second message to Berlin:

> Distance to New York 700 nautical miles. Fuel board for three days. For the Navy High Command: Spain impossible, Havana possible. Intend to disembark passengers in New York then head to Havana.
> Ahrens

When First Officer Warning read the captain's draft, he smiled. The captain certainly knew what he was doing. Gerstung transmitted the message in the clear, knowing that every listening American station would intercept and relay that nugget of intelligence to the British. When *Bremen* left New York, all eyes would follow her south, and then she would simply disappear. Warning was pleased. Ahrens was more clever than he realized. This was going to be fun, he thought. But first they had to get into and out of New York. That same day Britain had signed a mutual assistance treaty with Poland.

The next morning passengers hovered around the bulletin board on the promenade deck, reading the notice that despite rumors to the contrary, the ship would continue to New York to disembark passengers, arriving on Monday evening the twenty-eighth, the scheduled date, only about ten hours late. One irate American passenger, Dr. George Priest, a professor of German language at Princeton University, complained to First Officer Warning that the extremely high temperatures and humidity of the past two days had convinced him that the ship was heading south toward South America instead of west to New York, and he demanded to look at a plot of the ship's track. After Warning calmed the angry passenger with assurances that there were no deviations of track, the passenger promptly stomped into the bar for a morning drink. While sitting at the bar, he complained to a fellow passenger about the termination of the wireless service for passengers. "They won't allow us to send notice of our delay, and I think it's because they don't want to reveal the position of the ship."

The reply to Ahren's message came in from Berlin:

Proceed to New York then comply with measures in QWA 9.

Ahrens was happy; he had *told* Berlin what he was going to do instead of asking. That was an important issue to him. He had always sought independence of operations.

The captain's farewell dinner was held as usual that Sunday evening followed by a short and early dinner the next day before their 6:00 P.M. arrival in New York. The ship steamed in on a swift flood tide, so strong it required ten tugs to go alongside their usual berth at Pier 86.

The White House
Washington, D.C.
August 28, 1939

President Roosevelt issued the following order:

> From FDR for the Acting Secretary of the Treasury:

> The Secretary of Treasury under your direction may issue instructions to all collectors of customs substantially as follows: Immediately upon the President being satisfied that Germany is in armed conflict with another nation with or without formal declaration of war seize all German and Italian vessels in American territorial waters remove officers and crew therefrom and take all precautions against sabotage in engine rooms or otherwise.[6]

The cause of the sudden action may have been a report not yet seen by any German eyes. A radio message sent from U.S. Coast Guard District Headquarters in San Francisco on Monday, August 28, 1939, to Coast Guard Headquarters in Washington, D.C., contained the following information: "An unofficial source stated that the German liner S.S. *Bremen* had a false bottom in her swimming pool and that she is to be met at sea by an undersea craft which will place special equipment aboard her." The report further recommended that New York customs control be informed as quickly as possible to search *Bremen's* swimming pool.[7]

Just prior to *Bremen's* arrival in New York, President Roosevelt made the following demand to Acting Secretary Hanes: "I want to know whether *Bremen* is carrying guns or not."

2

Roosevelt's Neutrality

SS *Bremen*
New York Harbor
Monday, August 28, 1939

The ship entered New York at 6:00 P.M. on Monday, August 28, and tied up at Pier 86 as usual. It was hot and muggy, the air still and putrid. The crew noticed there were considerably more welcomers than usual, many of whom seemed excited and relieved to see friends or family as the passengers disembarked. The ship's company had been told initially that there would be no leave since they expected to turn around immediately after taking on fuel and depart again without passengers.

The French liner *Normandie* was already berthed across from the ship in Pier 88. The *Bremen* crew were good friends with many of the French crew. They had defeated them in the soccer match during their last visit and were due to receive the $2,500 Caroline de Lancey Cowl New York trophy for the display case on the A deck passageway during this visit. But the New York YMCA officials announced that the ship would receive a smaller substitute trophy and individual gold medals for each team member since their future return to New York was uncertain. The large trophy would remain in New York until the situation in Europe improved.

After their arrival in Manhattan the crew heard that their sister ship, *Europa*, had turned around one day out of home port. Instead of stopping in Southampton to unload passengers and pick up German citizens flooding out of Britain, she had steamed at full speed past the Isle of Wight in the direction of Bremerhaven with her lights doused and ports darkened, refusing to answer radio calls. *Columbus*, the third express liner, was due to sail from Curaçao, Netherlands West Indies, in two days bound for New York. The *Bremen* crew wasn't sure they'd see her, since they were due to sail right away. Most figured she might also scurry back to Germany as so many other German ships were rumored to be doing.

There was a noticeable number of blue-clad New York policemen on the pier, more than usual. As soon as the gangway was in place, Captain William Drechsel, the Norddeutscher Lloyd shipping agent, now entitled the chief marine superintendent in New York, was the first to board, along with Passenger Manager John Schroeder. Drechsel did not look his usual jovial self.

Born in 1879 in Koetzschenbroda, near the Polish border, Drechsel first went to sea in 1896. In 1901, he was already with Norddeutscher Lloyd as a fourth officer and by 1906 he became a leading first officer. During World War I, he served as the first officer with the Deutsche Ozean-Reederei, the famed steamship company that had operated the world's first merchant submarines, *Bremen* and *Deutschland*. In 1919, Drechsel worked in the technical bureau of Norddeutscher Lloyd, and in 1920 he took several commands of Norddeutscher Lloyd ships, among them *Bremen*'s predecessor *Bremen* III. In 1924, he became the Norddeutscher Lloyd chief superintendent in New York, where he remained for the duration. After the war he resigned from Norddeutscher Lloyd, became a U.S. citizen, and died in 1963 in California.

He had been a stalwart supporter of the shipping company but soon grew disenchanted when the Nazis spoiled the wonderful relationship that had existed with the New Yorkers. Drechsel had been a pillar of the solid and long-standing relationship the German shipping companies had enjoyed in New York. Following World War I, the relationship had been initially strained, but as the years wore on the close working relationship among those representing Norddeutscher Lloyd and New York had improved so much that there were no feelings of hostility left.

When the partnership between the Hamburg-American and Norddeutscher Lloyd lines had formed into a cooperative union in

Bremen docked at Pier 86 in New York City. (Hanns Tschira—courtesy of Deutsches Schiffahrtsmuseum, Bremerhaven)

1933, called Hapag-Lloyd, the good relations had continued. The German American clubs and restaurants in Yorkville, on the upper East Side of Manhattan around Third Avenue, in which so many small business owners participated, had fully recovered from those war years and the competitive relationships between businessmen of German origin and their Irish, Italian, and Chicano counterparts were healthy and vibrant.

Yet, the last few years since the German intervention in the Spanish civil war had witnessed problems developing in New York. Demonstrations, believed to have been organized by small and active cells of the popular communist groups, often began near the West Side piers when German ships arrived and had, on occasion, grown ugly. The New York Police Department had been responsive and generally rallied its counterdemonstration uniformed police and plainclothesmen in time to avert trouble. Yet there had been rough scenes, especially since the flag issue had erupted two years earlier. Attacks on German sailors ashore had risen in the recent years as popular sentiment against the new German chancellor Adolf Hitler began to grow in the Jewish community, especially after the outrageous response to the German liner *St. Louis* during the incident in the summer of 1939, when the Cuban and U.S. governments had prohibited the landing of passengers from that ship, consisting of European Jews and other refugees, seeking asylum in the West.

There seemed an inordinate number of American officials aboard talking to Captain Adolf Ahrens and First Officer Eric Warning. The group hurrying aboard from the shipping office met Captain Ahrens on the bridge before he had time to prepare for callers in his inport salon. Following the greetings and shaking hands, Drechsel began glumly, "Best tide for sailing is seven A.M. tomorrow. We will have just twelve hours to disembark passengers, luggage, and cargo and to top off with fuel. It's short but our staff can do it." As he spoke, Ahrens escorted the two visitors quickly into the chart house and closed the door.

The bridge was still humming with activity. The watch was putting away phones and scrubbing down the deck, and the watch officer had shifted to the main deck at the forward gangway, where the ship's bosuns and electricians were busily hustling to and fro with the usual mooring chores.

In the quiet of the chart room, Passenger Manager John Schroeder informed Ahrens that President Roosevelt had just signed an executive neutrality order putting new regulations into effect governing all foreign ships. The gist of the order was contained in the August 28 White House memorandum (quoted previously). Schroeder handed a copy to the captain, who read it and said nothing.

Later that evening, a gaggle of American officials marched aboard behind New York customs collector Harry Durning at the forward gangway. First Officer Warning escorted them to the captain's inport salon, where Ahrens waited with Drechsel and Schroeder. Things didn't look good. It was oppressively hot and sticky and the ship was supposed to refuel right away, yet no fuel barge had shown up. They were scheduled to take on provisions, but no trucks waited on the pier like they usually did. The engineers were angry. Chief Engineer Frederich Müller paced the poop deck in his stained refueling coveralls swearing even more than normal. Inside the captain's cabin the conversation was heated. Durning, the senior New York customs officer, represented the Treasury Department and was responsible for giving all foreign ships clearance papers to depart. He had just advised Ahrens that his inspectors would be aboard the next morning to begin a full search of the ship in accordance with the new instructions imposed by the U.S. government. He explained that all foreign ships, regardless of flag, would be required to show they were not armed and, in the case of potential belligerents, were not carrying arms or contraband. Durning had assured all those present that the measures would be applied to all foreign ships present, including the French liner *Normandie* berthed alongside the opposite pier.

"We are being held for no good reason. I believe we are really the only ship being held up," Ahrens said in an unpleasant voice. Captain Drechsel was standing next to Durning, and an officious looking officer from the Department of Immigration and Naturalization Service (INS) stood next to him.

The matter then turned to the fate of thirty men who were on the pier waiting when *Bremen* had arrived, seeking transit home to Germany. It turned out that seventeen of them were seamen from other Hapag-Lloyd ships that had departed New York earlier than scheduled, leaving them in uncertain situations. Many of them had been off with local girlfriends or had not been called back in time. Others were German technicians and businessmen who had been visiting or on vacation, and still others were Germans working in U.S. firms. One was a student from the Fordham University medical school.

"Please sir," said Ahrens to Durning in a respectful tone, "we need to address those thirty folks. If they can't board as passengers, we wish to sign them on as crew." First Officer Warning looked pleased the captain had quickly taken his suggestion to sign them on as additional crew, since taking passengers was out of the question now.

Customs Collector Durning replied, "First of all, you have no permit to embark passengers, and furthermore, to sign them on as additional crew is not legal. We will have to hold you in port until your home office clears the necessary additional crew and until we clear them with our immigration people. Some of these appear to be American citizens, yet I understand a few are German army reservists. This will take another several days to clear up."

Captain Drechsel began to explain the matter, which became more and more confusing. Durning then shrugged and passed the question over to the INS officer, who deferred the question until he could check with his superiors. In the meantime, Captain Ahrens, again obliging his first officer's request, allowed the group of thirty to spend the night aboard ship, since they would certainly not sail until the day following inspections, and assuming Durning would grant them clearance. The flurry of discussion continued in Ahrens's cabin, and then one by one the American officials left.

As soon as they were all gone, Radio Officer Kurt Gerstung returned again to Ahrens's inport salon with the next urgent message from Berlin. Ahrens read it, smiled, and handed back the message to Gerstung. "That's precisely what we're going to do. The question is: When can we leave here?" The message read: "When topped off with fuel return to homeport."

As Gerstung was returning to his radio room, he passed an unhappy looking Captain Drechsel with the group of American customs officials trailed by a stern looking First Officer Warning, who ignored Gerstung as they passed. Warning and the Americans were clearly distressed.

HMS *Berwick*
Bar Harbor, Maine
August 28, 1939

Commander Raymond Portal sat in his inport cabin watching his steward prepare his dress white uniform. He and all off-duty officers were planning to attend a soiree at the Frenchman's Cove yacht club at 6:00 P.M. A signalman knocked on the cabin door. "Enter," the commanding officer called as he fastened his gold cummerbund.

"Sir, urgent signal from Home Fleet." The ram-rod stiff signalman stomped in three paces and saluted. He wore a duty guard belt and his white summer flat hat. Portal took the signal and read in silence:

> From: Commander Home Fleet
> To: Commanding Officer HMS *York*
>   Commanding Officer HMS *Berwick*
>
> Secret: Commanding officers' eyes only
> Subject: High interest German ships
> 1. Berlin has ordered all German merchant ships to return home or seek safety of non-belligerent ports. High speed passenger ships SS *Bremen*, and SS *Europa*, hereby designated high interest, possible candidates for conversion to commerce raiders. *Bremen* arriving New York 28 August, *Europa* west-bound in north Atlantic, further intentions unknown.
> 2. Make all preparations to locate and shadow both ships. Current situation indicates hostilities imminent.
> 3. Set readiness Condition Two, top off fuel earliest, and remain near Halifax operating areas until further instructions.
>
>   Forbes

Portal grunted and finished cinching his cummerbund. "Right, Flags, call Commander Robinson, have him come to my cabin immediately. Tell the officer of the deck to call me on the squawk box."

The signalman stepped back, stomped his boot, saluted, spun around, and disappeared through the door. "Bloody, hell," Portal murmured. "Always happens just before something nice." He unfastened his cummerbund, sat down behind his desk, and began to study a chart.

Heavy-cruiser HMS *Berwick* had entered Bar Harbor for a six-day visit on Wednesday, August 23. She and sister cruiser HMS *York* were assigned patrol duties to guard the northwest anchor of the busy great-circle shipping lanes between major North American and European ports. *York* was in Halifax for the weekend before the two would rendezvous for gunnery exercises off Halifax next week. Both ships were standing normal Condition Three watches, that is, until the signal arrived. Portal studied the chart just as the executive officer, Lieutenant Commander Desmond Robinson, knocked and entered.

"Sir," he stepped into the cabin and stood before the captain's desk.

Portal looked up. "Desmond, we've got new orders. Please summon all officers to the wardroom. The next few days might prove a bit interesting."

New York Customs Collector's Office
Duane Street, Manhattan
August 29, 1939

The order to Harry Durning, New York's senior customs officer, which came personally from the acting secretary of the treasury's office, was a little hard to believe. On Sunday evening, Durning had been called at home and told to delay *Bremen* as long as he could, using any measures to keep her in New York, and that the order had come directly from President Roosevelt. This was a first. From the president no less! Durning suspected that there must have been some hard intelligence that triggered this action. The political situation in Europe had made everyone tense, and ever since Friday the New York papers had been full of the strange activities of the German and Italian merchant ships. Many had asked for early clearances to leave or had failed to show up for scheduled arrivals. This was being reported all over the world and not just in New York.

The week before, other mysterious events had been occurring on the world's maritime passenger scene. The German Navy High Command had taken control of all German ships on Friday and the British Admiralty had taken control of all British shipping two days later. On the same day in Lisbon, Portugal, two German Hamburg-bound steamers, *Erna Olldendorff* and *Rio de Janeiro*, had entered the harbor for coaling despite a thick fog. Their names and ports of registry were painted over in black and they showed no national flag. Their officers stated to local authorities that the ships had been disguised in case of war to avoid internment or arrest. Pernambuco Harbor in Brazil was reported as congested with ships, including three disguised German freighters and the passenger liner *Cap Nord*, their names and ports of registry also painted over. From Melbourne came a report that the German liners *Lahn* and *Strassfurt* and the Italian liner *Romolo* had vanished from the eastern Australian coast and failed to appear at their next declared destinations. The same day in Manila the German liner *Scharnhorst* sailed for an unannounced destination after discharging her cargo and putting ashore her non-German passengers.

The *New York Times* reported on August 28 that the Hamburg American German liner *St. Louis* left her berth on the Hudson River in Manhattan that day just prior to 8:00 P.M. and put to sea without passengers declaring for Hamburg. This was the same ship whose ignominious voyage the summer before had caused such a scandal. She had been prohibited from discharging her passengers, 915 Jewish refugees from Germany, first in Havana and then in Miami. The last-minute cancellation of her regular schedule in August indicated that the liner had been suddenly recalled to Germany. Some of her crewmen had been left in New York and were standing around the Norddeutscher Lloyd office on Canal Street waiting for instructions. Meanwhile, U.S. citizens were streaming home from Europe aboard every available passenger liner. The *New York Times* reported Saturday that Joseph P. Kennedy, the U.S. ambassador in London, stated, "All Americans who are interested in securing shipping accommodations are requested to communicate with the Embassy on Tuesday, August 29."

So now, Durning thought, I have to hold *Bremen* as long as possible. He was well aware of the rumors and reports that the United States was taking strict measures to ensure foreign ships were not being configured as possible commerce raiders, but he never thought it would come to this. He dreaded the next few days when surely the Norddeutscher Lloyd office, and probably even the German consulate would be ringing his phone off the hook. But Durning knew what his orders were and he went about them in an efficient and imaginative manner. While *Bremen* was still disembarking passengers, her first officer had phoned the port collector's duty officer and again asked for clearance to sail as soon as she had bunkered and taken on fresh provisions, as if testing American resolve to hold the ship. Of course, the duty officer had denied the request and stated that a team would be aboard *Bremen* the next day to supervise the search and that the new policy directed by the U.S. government would be enforced: to inspect all foreign ships, regardless of flag, to ensure compliance, that is, that they had no armament or contraband aboard. This order had triggered another terse call by *Bremen*'s leading first officer, who had threatened testily that Captain Ahrens intended to sail with or without clearance. The duty officer had told the first officer in a matter-of-fact tone that they would not be given tugs or a pilot and that he would inform the U.S. Coast Guard District Headquarters of their threat to depart without clearance, and that was that. Based on the action of his duty officer, Customs Collector Durning expected a call from the German consul general Hans Borchers, whom he knew well and considered a polite but arrogant Nazi. The next few days were not going to be fun for Durning and his staff.

At 10:45 the next morning, just after seeing his team of inspectors board *Bremen*, Durning received a call from Herbert Feis, the State Department senior adviser on international economic affairs in Washington, relaying the substance of his conversation with acting Treasury secretary John W. Hanes, who had called in a panic that morning. They were both aware that *Bremen* had again asked for clearance to leave, this time at 8:00 A.M., Wednesday, August 30. Durning advised Feis that he told *Bremen*'s first officer that they would complete the inspection as soon as possible, but that he had only a limited number of inspectors.

SS *Bremen*
Pier 86, New York City
August 29, 1939

Captain Ahrens and First Officer Warning stood on the port bridge wing watching the parade of U.S. customs inspectors cross and recross the gangway. "Mister Warning, tell Chief Purser Rohde to submit a request for additional suntan oil, tropical clothing for the crew, and additional navigation charts for the Caribbean, Bahamas, and coasts of South America and western Africa." The first officer, looking at Ahrens, thought to himself, Has this to do with real future plans or to cover our tracks?

Ahrens continued looking down at the pier activity and thought that no matter how hard he tried he could never keep ahead of his first officer. The idea to take obvious steps to indicate a future track had come to the captain late last night as he tried to sleep in his inport cabin, unable to bar the thoughts and doubts of their next course of action from his troubled mind. Yes, Warning, his brilliant number one, had already gleaned that he was taking measures to deceive the Americans, whom he suspected of being cozy with the British to the point of reporting to them every measure *Bremen* undertook during these tense times. He had read the radio message sent from Berlin the day before ordering all merchant ships to take measures to prepare to scuttle their ships rather than to allow them to fall into the hands of the British. The Americans would not hesitate, despite their proclaimed neutrality, to send the Royal Navy every tidbit of information they could gather about *Bremen's* intentions. He had not yet told his leading first officer to carry out the preparations by bringing mattresses and flammable material to the promenade deck and to disperse flammable liquids in canisters ready to ignite. They would do that after clearing New York Harbor. He didn't want to tempt his efficient officers into getting a head start, one that would show the Americans their intentions.

"You might say, Mister Warning, that I would like them to think we are heading south after clearing territorial waters. It's just a precaution." Ahrens looked directly at Warning. "Carry out those orders quite naturally and openly." Then he smiled, "You and I will have a talk with all the officers once these sham inspections are over and all extra eyes have gone ashore."

"Aye, Herr Captain," Warning replied with an understanding look and quietly left the bridge.

Ahrens felt the pressure, not necessarily because of the inspections by the Americans, but rather of the unknown. What would his orders be? Was he expected to make a dash for it? What were the British cruisers doing off Nova Scotia? What about the obvious British blockade? Ahrens spun around and stepped briskly to the bridge telephone, turned the dial to the radio room, and cranked the ringer.

"Gerstung," came the voice on the other end.

"Captain here," Ahrens replied. "Come to the bridge, please, Mister Gerstung, I wish to speak with you in private." Ahrens replaced the heavy hand piece in the cradle with a click. He returned to the starboard bridge wing and noted the smell of sausage and sauerkraut wafting up from the blower exhaust humming loudly just aft of the bridge. Without the relative wind of her normal 27-knot speed, cooking odors surrounded and clung to the bridge. Even though they made his stomach growl, he wasn't hungry; his stomach was sour after a half-dozen cups of coffee since arising at 5:00 A.M. He was fighting a case of heartburn and indigestion exacerbated by the tensions of the unknown. He longed for the open sea, the wind and clean ocean air. It was hot in New York and the air was foul and misty. He wanted desperately to be underway and out of this state of uncertainty. No ship commander enjoys his ship being controlled by outsiders.

Ahrens returned to the bridge phone, dialed his steward, and asked that a light lunch be brought to his sea cabin behind the bridge. He wished to eat in solitude, away from the clamor of the inspectors, the thumping of engineers' feet, and the stench of the fuel oil. They had finally begun taking on fuel after waiting more than twelve hours for the fuel barge. The usually efficient Americans, it seemed to him, had suddenly taken on a slow-motion attitude, with obstructions to every normally efficient operation. Ahrens hated inefficiency.

Gerstung appeared on the bridge breathing heavily after the run up a level from the radio room. "Aye, Captain," he wheezed. The captain stood staring down on the pier, watching the activity and seemed not to notice the young radio officer's presence. He remained still, giving Gerstung the impression he had not heard him arrive. Gerstung cleared his throat, "It's Gerstung, sir," he repeated softly.

"I know," Ahrens replied calmly. "Have you seen all that activity and the numbers of police roaming the pier? Makes you think something big is going on." Ahrens seemed bemused and in no hurry to speak to or acknowledge the junior officer, who stood still waiting to be recognized.

Captain Ahrens had now been aboard since November 1936, when he had replaced *Bremen's* first master, the tall more senior Commodore Leopold Ziegenbein, who had brought the ship out of the construction yards, through trials, and then through nearly ten years of glorious steaming. Gerstung, too, had been aboard since the trials, and except for his period at communications training, he had made most of the transits. Despite the growing tensions and the increasing shift from routine passenger service communiqués, Gerstung thrived on the increase in classified operational traffic, much of it already coming from the Navy High Command in Berlin, as the fleet communicators poured background references out to the merchant fleet. There were voluminous contingency operation orders, secret antisubmarine procedures, and detailed electronic countermeasure and radio direction finding procedures for the radio officer and his staff to decode, absorb, file, and protect. The thought of the increase in secret traffic and war preparations excited the young officer with visions of future adventures and the possibility of action on the high seas. Gerstung was the product of the new Germany, and he found that his training and exposure to the newly reconstituted German armed forces was exhilarating.

Gerstung had been in the court with Captain Ahrens and First Officer Warning when the four *Bremen* crew had been summoned to the New York Federal Court in May the year before, following the escape of the German spy Dr. Ignatz Griebl. One of those subpoenaed was his second radio officer Wilhelm Boehnke, another two were stewards, and the fourth a pastry cook.

Originally from the Bavarian town of Würtzburg, Griebl served the German army in World War I as an artillery officer on the Italian front. He was wounded and after beginning medical studies in Munich, he came to the United States with the help of his fiancée,

Maria Ganz, an Austrian nurse who had treated his wounds in Italy. He studied first at Long Island Medical College and subsequently at Fordham University. He then began a successful medical practice in Bangor, Maine, but eventually moved to Manhattan's German community of Yorkville, on the Upper East Side around Third Avenue and Eighty-sixth Street, home of wurst, beer, and sauerkraut. By 1928 Griebl was a well established New York physician and became a medical officer in the U.S. Army Reserve. Although he and his wife became U.S. citizens, they had cottoned to the new Nazi ideals and soon were active in the German American society as Nazi propagandists and avid fans of Adolf Hitler. Griebl began, on his own volition, to cultivate German sympathizers influential in key U.S. military-industrial factories and carefully formulated a plan to subvert these sources into a well-oiled German spy ring. He then volunteered to become the coordinator of important U.S. information for the German propaganda minister, Joseph Goebbels, to whom he had been introduced by a friend of Goebbels's brother. Goebbels forwarded Griebl's voluntary offer to the Abwehr and the Gestapo, both of which were already operating fledgling intelligence networks inside the United States. Griebl was eventually introduced to the Gestapo's maritime bureau in Hamburg, which had first organized Nazi intelligence cells in the highly popular German transatlantic passenger ships. The leaders organized an efficient network that, when energized, would set into motion a large number of agent handlers embedded in the largest and most famous German passenger ships *Bremen, Europa,* and *Columbus,* and the lesser-known liners *New York, St. Louis,* and *Reliance.*

Griebl's first success was with an ethnic German employee named Danielson, at Bath Iron Works in Maine, which built top-of-the-line navy destroyers. Danielson purloined copies of the newest destroyer plans and shipped them to Germany aboard *Bremen* using Karl Eitel, a first-class steward, as a courier. Another one of Griebl's agents was Herman Lange, who worked as an inspector in the Manhattan factory that produced the Norden bombsight, reputed to be the most accurate in the world. In various stages, Lange sent copies of the bombsight plans, initially via *Reliance* and then *Bremen*, to ecstatic German Luftwaffe officials.[1] In one spectacular blunder, a New York customs inspector apprehended William Lonkowski near Pier 86. Lonkowski was headed to a German passenger ship carrying a violin case loaded with stolen plans from an aircraft plant. The stash included photos of the new Curtis pursuit airplane, the Vought scout bomber for naval use, and information regarding three Boeing bombers, including the army's new four-engine B-17, the Flying Fortress. The inspector released Lonkowski with an admonition to return to the customs house the next day when the counterintelligence folks returned from vacation. Lonkowski skipped to Canada, with Griebl's assistance, and then home on a German freighter.[2]

Griebl eventually overextended his network and found himself under increasing scrutiny by the FBI. Feeling the heat the night of May 12, 1938, he drove to Hapag-Lloyd Pier 86 while *Bremen* was in the final preparations to sail and walked aboard with no passport or ticket for passage. He was reported missing by his distraught wife, who suspected him of participating in a lover's tryst. After *Bremen* sailed and was two hundred miles from the Verazzano Narrows, the Norddeutscher Lloyd chief port inspector, Captain William Drechsel, responding to the pleas of the FBI, radioed the ship and demanded that Captain Ahrens heave to and await agents being flown to *Bremen*'s position by seaplane to arrest Griebl. After a delay, during which Ahrens requested orders from Berlin, he responded that rough sea conditions ruled out a seaplane recovery and promised to give up the wanted stowaway in their next port of call, Cherbourg, France. When FBI and French agents met *Bremen* in Cherbourg four days later, Captain Ahrens refused to give up the spy, claiming the officials' documents were inadequate, and returned Griebl directly to Germany. All this was splashed in the headlines of the *New York Times* when, on their next visit to New York, a U.S. attorney summoned Ahrens, a Bordsturm radio officer, a second radio officer, a pastry cook, and a steward from *Bremen* as material witnesses to a hearing about Griebl's escape. Ahrens's leading first officer, Eric Warning, also appeared.

Captain Drechsel, now the general marine superintendent in New York for all the German liners, was heavily involved in these deliberations and later stated, after learning through the grapevine that Griebl might try to stow away on Bremen, said, "If I knew Griebl was on board, I would have held up the ship and notified the FBI."[3]

Gerstung smiled as he recalled the excitement of receiving a high-priority radio telephone call for the captain from the New York marine operator and how he had patched himself into the call and listened secretly as Captains Ahrens and Drechsel discussed the FBI demand to stop the ship and await a seaplane to fly out to arrest the agent.[4] Ahrens had directed Gerstung to put a priority call to the Norddeutscher Lloyd office in Bremen, and then to the Transport Ministry in Berlin, informing them of the situation and requesting instructions. Ahrens had allowed Gerstung to make the calls by himself and had trusted him to give the details. He had been thrilled to be in the limelight as he received instructions from the Abwehr on how to fend off the American counterintelligence people. Gerstung could not have enjoyed it more because he had exercised real independence thanks to Ahrens, who had shown complete trust in him. Their appearance in the American court had been especially entertaining as the naive Americans seemed dumbfounded when Gerstung's second radio officer had admitted he was part of the Nazi SA Bordsturm organization. Captain Ahrens had to explain to the judge why such an organization existed and why Nazi Party officials were aboard. The Americans seemed horrified that the party influence, what all Germans accepted now as part of life, could be so widespread in society. Gerstung had actually felt sorry for the American judge and the FBI officials, who seemed totally at a loss at what to do next. The whole episode had ended as a flash in the pan, and the four Bremen crewmen, including the pastry cook, had been released on bond for $15,000. The FBI had misidentified the cook for the steward Karl Eitel, whom they had been hunting earlier. Eitel, an Abwehr agent handler aboard Bremen, had been replaced after he got involved with Lonkowski. The federal court hearing had ended

rather inconclusively with none of the crew accused of any wrong-
doing. In an unexpected gesture, Captain Ahrens had invited all
those involved to his cabin for a drink and snack, including the
cook, which was quite a departure from normal protocol. Officers,
much less the master, never drank with crewmen. But times were
unusual and it had all been very exciting to Gerstung.

"Yes, Gerstung," Ahrens faced the young officer and returned his
salute. "Come with me to the chart house." The captain led the
way into the large bridge, which was vacant except for one quartermaster, who stood watch by the main binnacle and saluted as
the captain passed. The two walked aft through the door to the
chart house just aft of the expansive bridge. In the center was a
large slant-top chart table. Shortly after they entered and closed
the door, there was a sharp knock, the door reopened, and First
Officer Warning stepped over the combing and closed the door
quietly. The captain motioned both men to the chart and began to
speak smoothly, as if he had rehearsed his words in advance.

"Gentlemen, we are in a particularly delicate position. As you
know, we are being held by the Americans, ostensibly because of
their new precautionary policy to search all foreign vessels for contraband and arms. We know this is just a ruse to hold us as long as
possible until British warships can position themselves along our
anticipated track." He glanced first at Warning and then at Gerstung. Both looked fully absorbed. Ahrens particularly liked and
trusted these two key officers. He continued, "All German-flagged
ships have been ordered home. Those more than five days' steaming from German soil can seek neutral ports. We have been told to
make every effort to return to Germany. Except for this New York
visit, all German ships are to avoid American ports, for obvious
reasons."

Warning nodded and then said, "Sir, Customs Collector Durning just called me again before I came up here. He is demanding,
now that we are refueling, that tomorrow they inspect our safety
procedures. They want us to cycle all our lifeboats, lower them,
and demonstrate our passenger safety procedures."

Ahrens listened intently as Warning continued. "The silly bastards want to inspect the bottom of our swimming pool, it's a damn foolish . . ."

Ahrens replied, "Let them do whatever they wish, Mister Warning, we have nothing to hide. The sooner they run out of excuses to hold us, the sooner they'll let us go. I know it's all just a sham. Also, put all of the thirty German American hitchhikers ashore with their baggage. I'm sorry, but their presence will only give the Americans more reasons to keep us here longer as they dither with the decisions whether or not we can take them on as crew. We can't afford to be delayed one more moment. I just spoke with our consul general this morning and Berlin has been notified; our embassy in Washington is submitting a diplomatic protest."

"Sir," First Officer Warning said, "I found out today from talking to them that some of those thirty men are German crewmen from non-German-flagged ships who were ordered quietly to leave their ships and come to us for return transit home." He paused, looking directly at Ahrens. "They were told we would take them home."

"That may be," Ahrens replied, "but nevertheless insisting on taking them aboard despite American formalities will only delay us further." Ahrens looked toward the door. "I'm sorry, it's an uncomfortable decision, but it must be if we are to get out of here as soon as possible."

The captain was interrupted by another rapid knock on the chart house door. The first officer opened it brusquely.

"Yes? We're in conference. What is it?"

A young duty officer stood breathing heavily, obviously having run up all seven levels from the gangway, "Sir, one of our sailors, Seaman Slominski, was arrested on the pier. He was with the purser's party coming from the chandlers and got in a fight with an American policeman. They brought him aboard with a bloody head, possible concussion."

Ahrens listened then put up his hand. "Warning, take care of this. I'll see you in my inport cabin after. I want to go over the communications points with Gerstung, I'll tell you later." Ahrens turned back to the chart table as Warning and the young messenger quickly disappeared into the large empty bridge.

Ahrens continued, "You've seen the alert message from the Naval High Command about the British cruisers?"

"Yes, sir."

"Well, our consul general just sent me a note that there are two of them in and around Halifax: one is the eight-inch-gun cruiser *Berwick,* don't know the name of the other. Their positions and intentions are most important to us. Their location is exactly where the normal great-circle tracks begin for eastbound transits and they know we are expected to steam close to their area. I am still weighing in my mind which track we'll follow when we finally depart this overheated city. But you must fine-tune your people to the communications capabilities, frequencies, and habits of the Royal Navy cruisers we know are in the vicinity of Nova Scotia now. Also," he added as an afterthought, "be ready to monitor American Coast Guard working telegraph frequencies. Put your best English speakers on to watch their conversations, as we can assume anything the Americans learn about our intended track after leaving here will be passed to the British."

Gerstung nodded quickly, loving every minute of the suspense and growing excitement. The captain continued, "You must inform me of every intended move of the British and American ships as far in advance as possible so we can take evasive action. Also, you must monitor all other known merchant shipping communications to determine in advance what ships may be in the vicinity so we can evade all visual sightings. And Gerstung!" the captain grew dramatic, standing up from his leaning position over the chart table. "I intend to have this ship disappear as soon as we are outside visual range of this coast." He smiled, "Understand?"

Gerstung's heart was beating rapidly; he was enthralled with the anticipation of the coming days. Ahrens continued, "You and your men will be our ears. I will supply the eyes, but our safety rests in your ability to ferret out the intentions of the enemy, so we can steam as a ghost ship. I," the captain puffed up proudly, "intend to take this ship home to Germany without being seen. Understand?"

Gerstung stood at attention, his hands trembling with energy. "Yes sir, Herr Captain, right away."

"You may go," Ahrens said quietly. "Make it work, Mister Gerstung."

Gerstung saluted and disappeared through the door. Ahrens remained in the chart house, picked up a pair of dividers and parallel rulers, and began to plot out various tracks, all to the north and northeast of New York—none to the south. He smiled, pushed back his peaked cap, and continued plotting. When he finished, he straightened his cap and looked at the ship's chronometer, its shiny brass works shimmering in the glass case. The captain left the chart house quietly and walked toward his sea cabin, suddenly remembering that he had ordered lunch from his steward. He was now hungry, his nervous stomach much improved after giving orders. He was also excited now and more certain of the future.

3

Obfuscation and Delay

Washington, D.C., and New York
Tuesday, August 29, 1939

At 4:50 P.M. Acting Secretary of the Treasury John W. Hanes spoke by telephone with New York Customs Collector Harry Durning:[1]

HANES: I just spoke with, you know who, and he said, "Tell, Harry that I said that I wanted that boat held 48 hours, and last night at 6 o'clock was when she got here, that would be tomorrow night at 6 o'clock." I am just repeating to you what he said.

DURNING: That is all right. That's the orders. We got to contemplate difficulties.

HANES: You going to have some trouble?

DURNING: I think so. They are waiting for the tide. We'll just tell them there is no clearance. I don't know what the dickens we can do now.

HANES: Maybe some of those doctors and technicians, maybe they should have a going over by the FBI. Has he got passenger clearance? She has no passengers. Here's Huntington Cairns. [Cairns was from the Department of Immigration and Naturalization Service.]

CAIRNS: Did she surrender her passenger certificates?

DURNING: No. We have her official papers. We cleared those last night. The point here would be that she did probably cooperate through the day while we kept going on searching. We picked up a Zeiss camera.

CAIRNS: Now suppose you held that these thirty technicians were passengers and not members of the crew?

DURNING: They took them off. That baggage all came off. They are ahead of us on that.

HANES: They took the thirty men off? Have you given it a shakedown? Well, listen. The idea is to find something with some way to comply with the order and not get us in trouble.

DURNING: We can just say we refuse clearance. You see we have the *Normandie* in here. We went along pretty well. The same to her as to the *Bremen*. Of course the newspapers didn't take that at all. So we followed that out. We have pictures here on the front of the *New York Sun* of lowering the life boats. Now the only thing I can see is just—we find out all these things last night. But you know—the Germans have been very punctilious, and we coming in and out of port. I expected that we would have—we are really on the spot on it. I will have to be on the spot, that is all. Next to Hitler's answer to London, they [the press] think it is the biggest thing we have here [the *Bremen* being held up]. I am going to see what we can try to work out and keep our face clean. But what the dickens reason I can think of there. I can put them [the customs inspectors] back there again tomorrow.

HANES: Harry you stand by and we will put our heads together here and see what we can figure out.

DURNING: The only thing we can do is say it is not complete. In the meantime we have to clear the *Normandie*.

HANES: If you can hold her up the same time, well so much the better.

DURNING: Well, we can hold both of them up and give it to them. It would be the easiest thing to do.

HANES: We will explore that possibility and call you back.

DURNING: I will stay right here.

Washington, DC.
August 29, 1939

At 5:15 P.M., the following conversation took place between Hanes at the Treasury Department and Herbert Feis at the State Department:

HANES: I reported the matter across the street [the White House] just as I reported it to you, and we now have different instructions.

They are not going to let her go. So I have to change my story that I told you.

FEIS: Those are your orders. How were you told to explain it?

HANES: I wasn't.

FEIS: It's going to be a mess isn't it?

HANES: I understand that the President discoursed on the subject for a long time.

FEIS: Did you see the ticker?

HANES: No, I was told about it. He told a long story about it.

FEIS: Where did he get the stuff from?

HANES: From me.

FEIS: Is there any grounds in it for explaining why it isn't to go?

HANES: The only thing we can say is, "Harry Durning, just say that your inspection is not complete."

FEIS: Is there anything in the press conference of the President today that would explain it?

HANES: He was explaining why the American government must protect itself. He said today that the United States has adopted a policy of searching merchant vessels of nations [of any] big belligerents so as to avoid the possibility of this country becoming liable.

FEIS: What I'm afraid of is that by doing this he prejudices something about the Neutrality Act.

HANES: I see what you mean. I am afraid he is unwise, but hell.

FEIS: I don't know. You want to sit down and talk with us?

HANES: I don't believe so. I think this is more serious because they are getting restless. The only news in New York today is the *Bremen* and the English note [probably referring to the note sent by Prime Minister Neville Chamberlain to Adolf Hitler, the British response to the threat of German reprisal actions against Poland].

FEIS: Well, there may be more news tomorrow morning. I will report this downstairs [at the Secretary of State's office].

HANES: If they want me, Herbert, call me back right away.

FEIS: I will report at once, John, and let you know.

At 5:56 P.M., Hanes called Durning:

HANES: We haven't got anything more to offer.

DURNING: I didn't think you would because we had exhausted ourselves on that. We got a hold of the tug boat people; they will not supply a boat pilot tonight. They won't get a pilot from the association. We are all right for tomorrow morning. Now to get through tomorrow morning, I think I have got to hold up for 8 hours the *Normandie* and for 6 hours the *Aquitania* [British]. We are in a ridiculous position. There are boats going out with passengers and cargo, and here we are holding a boat that is just going out with crew alone. We've got ourselves in a ridiculous position. We haven't finished our search and we're going to search all three boats tomorrow morning. I think the French people will see the point.

HANES: I think it is very important that you get some word to them, and I would go ahead and do it on that base. It seems to me to be a reasonable thing and I think it would save an awful lot of embarrassment.

DURNING: We are in a fairly good spot if we have a French boat, an English boat, and a German boat all delayed together. Then I would continue the search on all three boats tomorrow and then give them all clearance at the dock at the same time.

HANES: That makes damn good sense to me, Harry.

DURNING: We have got a break on the weather here tonight. We have got a northeast storm blowing right down the river, and I don't think that one boat could get out in any event. She would muss herself up terrible. Now, we can keep off the tugs and everything else, so that she would have to go out herself. We might be able to hold the lines there. Now you've got the one thing, of course, that we talked to the Coast Guard last night about, that is if she started out. I have a cutter up the River [Hudson] all set—to come down and block her out. You got a big question there. It didn't come up today and I don't think it will come up tonight, but maybe tomorrow.

SS *Bremen*
Pier 86, New York City
August 30, 1939

Captain Ahrens sat in his inport salon waiting for Customs Collector Durning to arrive. It was unbearably hot despite the feeble efforts of the large ceiling fan turning quietly above his head. He was reading the New York papers about the reply by Chancellor Hitler to Britain's latest demand. It had already arrived in London but was being guarded with elaborate secrecy, as all diplomatic communications between Germany and Britain had been over the past several days. There was great tension building and Ahrens could feel it even in New York.

It was early afternoon and the entire day thus far had been spent lowering and test running the ship's lifeboats and counting life jackets. Ahrens and his officers were becoming more and more impatient with the delays as the American inspectors took their time observing and nodding, since all systems seemed to work. The frustration of counting life jackets had finally been completed after several false starts, with the inspectors purposely miscounting and delaying. It was all Ahrens could do to keep First Officer Warning from throwing the leading inspector into the river. "I've had it with these idiots," Warning complained to Ahrens as they waited for Durning to arrive.

While they were talking, First-Class Steward Ernst Henningsen entered the salon carrying a tray of cups, a pot of steaming coffee, and a plate heaped with Chef Hans Künlen's warm apple strudel. He stepped quietly to the table and swiftly set out the refreshments. Walking to the door, he glanced down on the chart displayed on the captain's desk and took in the two tracks laid out, one to the south, and another to the north. Puzzled by the two tracks, he left the salon and returned to the galley to report to the leading chef the momentous discussions underway and that *Bremen* might be heading to Cuba or maybe to Greenland. Rumors soon began swirling throughout the ship.

"I have a feeling we will be released soon," the captain said, as Warning paced by the door. "There's not a whole lot more they can look for. What did our thirty guests do when they disembarked? I heard the police took them off to Ellis Island."

"Yes, sir, they loaded them in wagons and drove them off with their luggage. I hated to see it, but you were right; insisting on signing them aboard as crew would have given the Americans more ammunition to hold us. I feel sorry for them, in any case."

"Are all the purser's men back from the chandler supply run?"

"Yes, sir, and we're ready to execute the scuttling preparations as soon as we're out to sea."

There was the sound of a large crowd approaching outside in the passageway. Warning opened the door just as a group of ten men emerged from the ladder and came toward the salon. Warning stood aside as Harry Durning and Captain Drechsel entered the cabin with several others from the customs office. It was 4:30 P.M.

"Well, Captain Ahrens," Durning stepped forward and stretched out his hand holding an envelope "Our inspections are complete; there are no violations, your clearance to depart is here," he handed Ahrens the envelope. "We wish you a good voyage, and, well, I'm sorry it had to come to this, but, like you, we are just following orders."

Ahrens took the envelope and handed it casually to First Officer Warning. "Yes, thank you, I trust all is in order for us to depart immediately, tugs and pilot—"

Captain Drechsel interrupted, "Pilot Miller's already on the bridge and tugs are on the way. You are cleared to leave as soon as the visitors are ashore."

Durning smiled, "We won't delay you any more. Oh, yes, there is one other thing." He glanced at the others standing in the cabin, "As you know, the new neutrality procedures just put into force call for all foreign ships to indicate their intended track upon departing U.S. waters. We assume you are returning directly to Bremerhaven, where you have declared, and that you will be taking the normal great-circle track."

Ahrens did not bat an eye. "Our track will be along the normal shipping lanes. We are planning to return to Germany, but, and

I'm sure you agree, I can adjust our track as our company and I deem necessary. I reserve the right of all masters, that is, to put the safety of my ship and my men first. We will proceed in accordance with our safest track and speed. Thank you, gentlemen."

First Officer Warning smiled, proud of his skipper for not telling them anything, yet remaining correct to the letter.

Durning smiled, stepped forward, and shook hands warmly with Captain Ahrens. "In any case Captain, Godspeed, and good luck." He turned abruptly and left the cabin, his assistants trailing silently behind.

Captain Drechsel turned and looked at Ahrens. "Well, that was easy. I thought they would put up more of a fuss to get a copy of your track with that new rule."

"Nonsense, we can declare where we want and change plans due to weather or other safety considerations. They are in no position to enforce any of that garbage. Mister Warning, I'll be up on the bridge in five minutes. Make all preparations for getting underway. I'll escort Captain Drechsel to the gangway." Ahrens picked up his cap from the hook by the door. "After you, Willy," he motioned to Drechsel, and the two made their way aft to the ladder. Their relationship was cordial and warm. Drechsel was always efficient and helpful, but there was a little strain between them mainly because Ahrens knew of the deep friendship that had existed between his predecessor, Commodore Leopold Ziegenbein, and Drechsel over many years. Ahrens dismissed any ideas of creating a closer bond, since he considered Drechsel more American now than German, especially since the Griebl spy episode, when Drechsel had appeared to side the entire time with the FBI against the Germans. In any case, there were more important things to worry about now, for example, how he was going to take Germany's prize luxury liner and crew of 950 home, full of fuel and no passengers, with British warships lurking God knows where and with war just around the corner.

"Good-bye, Willy," Ahrens stood erect at the edge of the gangway and extended both hands to the departing Drechsel.

The longtime Norddeutscher Lloyd New York superintendent paused, then responded, "Farewell Adolf, I know you'll bring her through safely." He smiled, shook Ahrens's hands warmly, saluted, and walked off the ship, across the long gangway, and into the passenger hall. Ahrens watched his colleague disappear into the large building and wondered if he would ever see him again.

4

Into Oblivion

SS *Bremen*
Pier 86, New York City
Wednesday, August 30, 1939

Captain Adolf Ahrens stood on the port wing of the bridge and looked down at the Eighty-sixth Street Hapag-Lloyd pier. It was strangely empty. Each time he had sailed since taking command in November three years ago, the pier and the two-story passenger terminal building had always been crowded with well-wishers bidding farewell to the passengers, with ribbons, sparklers, champagne, confetti, and flowers. For Ahrens, this day was bittersweet, empty in a way, despite the lingering uncertainty of the coming days. A line of blue-clad New York policemen stood along the edge where normally well-wishers had thronged. The air smelled of the Hudson River, fish, and oil. It was still extremely hot and humid, but a slight northeasterly breeze had begun to usher in a promising front of heavy black clouds.

Ah, New York! Ahrens had loved his long affair with the city, with its noise, smells, music, and lights. The dark alleys where for many years his sailors drank, caroused, and, more recently, had been attacked by demonstrators. A whirling mass of humanity, a city he had grown to love. His relation with the city had begun years ago while he was a young officer. Then aboard *Columbus* as master, he had enjoyed a spectacular social life and had become acquainted with New York's celebrities, including many in the city government such as the mayor. Ahrens wondered when he would next return. He had no idea that six years from this day Germany would lie in ruins, while New York would revel on, visibly undisturbed by six years of catastrophic strife, the city that never weeps.

"Single all lines," Captain Ahrens ordered to the third mate standing next to him to relay commands to the pilothouse. "Mister Warning, muster all hands not on watch to the afterdeck. This is a proud moment; we are not to appear like a dog skulking home!"

"Aye, Herr Captain." The first officer was busily supervising the line handlers and directing the tugs using a signalman with semaphore flags who stood high on a platform located on the wing of the bridge.

Six tugs stood by, while the captain watched the line handlers poised by the bollards. It was clear to see that he always enjoyed this moment. He desperately wanted his pipe, but he never smoked on the bridge. He did not allow it for others either, of course. He inhaled, then began. "Take in numbers one, two, four, and six. Rudder left five degrees, port engines back slow. Sound one long blast, followed by three short." It was exactly 6:00 P.M., August 30, 1939.

"Aye, Captain." The quartermaster pulled the bright, brass-handled whistle lever, opening the valve on the 150-pound reduced steam line leading to the whistle mounted high on the trailing edge of the forward gleaming yellow stack. After several seconds of hissing, as water was purged from the steam line, the air was suddenly shattered by the deep resonant voice of *Bremen*'s whistle, signaling a change in status, and followed by, "my engines are backing." The cheeks and heels of the sailors on the bridge shook with the vibration of the deep whistle. The stifling, late summer air of New York City was rent by the whistle as it blasted its farewell song, heard no doubt all the way over on the East Side and the foot of the Battery, in the back alleys, in the restaurants along the West Side, the bars, cafes, and diners, New York's dens of comfort, meccas of gluttony, waterholes for sailors and elegant first-class passengers, beckoning with available wine and women. These haunts, sprouted in the heyday of ocean travel, and Manhattan's West Side would never be the same. From this day on, as the world lurched into the dark abyss of war, the songs, tears, and joys of the

Bremen departing Pier 86 on August 30, 1939. (Hanns Tschira—Courtesy of Deutsches Schiffahrtsmuseum, Bremerhaven)

passenger piers would never again resonate with quite the same delight and zest of life.

The ship backed smoothly into the Hudson River. As Ahrens turned the towering bow toward the south, he suddenly noticed the stern of the elegant French liner *Normandie* towering across the pier. To his amazement, he saw its stern was crowded with French crewmen, arrayed in a mix of dress: white smocks, checkered trousers, black-and-white-clad waiters and stewards, and blue-uniformed engineers. These were *Bremen*'s counterparts, comrades, sport competitors, and perhaps a few lovers. Ahrens watched, transfixed by the scene. Although he was briefly stunned, as he watched the events unfold, he realized he was not surprised at the show of camaraderie by the two crews. These were the same men his crew had known off and on in New York and other ports for years now, and although hailing from different lands, with different customs and now, with widely diverging political beliefs, they still acted like schoolmates.

The crew cheered when the French tricolor slowly dipped three times in succession as *Bremen* slid back, turned, and rumbled ahead, the 130,000 horsepower engines thrusting four screws and churning mud from the river bottom. First-Class Apprentice Waiter Wilhelm Bohling recalled the moment, "Our bosuns dipped the colors in response. It was a sight I shall always remember. Those fellows aboard *Normandie* were our friends; we had played them in soccer, we had gone ashore carousing in Manhattan with them, and now suddenly, as we departed, we looked at them as disappearing friends. We would all soon be in different uniforms, fighting each other, but at the time we didn't really know that. It was a sight I will always see in my mind, especially after I ended up fighting on the western front in France. Ah, that moment still lives in our hearts."

The new flag, embarrassing to many, was now the Nazi swastika on a red-and-white background, its very existence credited to Adolf Hitler's angry response to the incident aboard *Bremen* in this very port four years ago—the scandalous disorder that had spilled aboard the ship a half hour before sailing on that day in May 1935. Seaman Heinz Slominski recalled the time that fight became history, "My shipmate Deck Seaman Rehling had his front teeth knocked out in the brawl with the demonstrators. By the time the new flag ceremony occurred two months later, Rehling had a new set of front teeth, all bright gold. The joke among us crewmen was that Rehling's new teeth had been supplied by a grateful Adolf Hitler in reward for his pugilistic services to the party."

The ceremony hoisting the new flag had been held by the three German liners *Stuttgart*, *Albert Ballin*, and *Bremen* in New York Harbor on September 17, 1935. Captain Ahrens, who had temporarily relieved Leopold Ziegenbein while on vacation, had addressed nine hundred crewmen and crewwomen from all the German ships assembled on *Bremen*'s foredeck:

> Comrades on board ship, the Reichstag party, the party of freedom, has laid a heavy duty on us sailors. Through the new flag regulation formulated by the Reichstag on Sunday, the battle flag of Der Führer has become our commercial flag. Let us proudly face the duties this flag places upon us. It not only "was" a battle flag, it "is" a battle flag in so far as the rest of the

world of opposition is concerned. I urge you to forget all controversies and to clasp hands in a united effort, that the flag might have honor and respect, even from those who deny respect for it today.

Ahrens had paused and called for the three victory cheers, then continued:

With unprecedented pride, we look at this flag as being representative of a people who have found themselves again, and have attained honor and strength. Let us transfer the love we bore for the old flag to this new banner of our leader, Hail Hitler, the reconstructor of German honor, unity and freedom.[1]

The ceremonies had closed with the singing of "Deutschland Über Alles" and the Nazi "Horst Wessel" song on all three ships. Ahrens had wondered how he had sounded. He wasn't sure about the words of that ceremony, which had actually been sent in a message from the Ministry of Propaganda, drafted personally by Joseph Goebbels, for all German ships abroad. Most assumed they were Captain Ahrens's own words, that is, all but Radio Officer Kurt Gerstung, who had copied the speech over the wireless from Berlin, and, of course, First Officer Eric Warning, who was so enthralled during the national anthem that tears were seen running down his cheeks as they sang. Ahrens thought later that he should have let Warning read those words; at least he believed in all the chest thumping. Somehow the ceremony had made Ahrens a little sad. He remembered too well his friend's return from the Verdun trenches twenty-three years earlier, and how he had become gaunt and distant, gradually losing his mind to alcohol. Adolf Ahrens was not a party man nor would he ever be. Despite his position of leadership, he was first and foremost a sailor, then a German. He celebrated his fifty-sixth birthday four days later.

Later that same year things had not gone well for the German sailors in New York. In December a threat had been received by the New York Norddeutscher Lloyd office that Bremen would be attacked. A Coast Guard ship met them at Ambrose Light and escorted them to quarantine, where they sat all night while the Coast Guard cutters Icarus and Calumet and several police boats

Captain Adolf Ahrens
at the 1935 flag raising
in New York. (Courtesy of
Deutsches Schiffahrtsmuseum,
Bremerhaven)

patrolled around the ship in the lower bay. A New York police
bomb squad searched the ship and found nothing. Captain William Drechsel, the marine superintendent, claimed that it was all
part of a plot by American communists to damage the ship. So the
Bremen crew were growing accustomed to becoming somewhat
less popular in New York than they had been before, yet most kept
a warm spot in their hearts for the city; they had just too many
friends there to let these things bother them.

After leaving the pier that day in August, Ahrens watched intently
as the ship slowly headed south through the harbor. He never let
the pilot maneuver the ship; it was merely protocol to have him
aboard, and he was even more precise with his commands with
the American pilot, Captain Herbert Miller, standing next to him
observing. Miller, a member of the Sandy Hook Pilots Association,
had become the company pilot some years before. Ahrens knew
him well.

At that moment Hanns Tschira, the ship's photographer, appeared on the wing of the bridge with his camera and vest filled with film and other photo paraphernalia. Tschira was recognized aboard Norddeutscher Lloyd ships for the excellent quality of his photography. He traveled from ship to ship and had published many articles in popular German photo and travel journals. His round visage and slightly plump figure were well known to the sailors aboard *Bremen*, and he seemed especially busy during this voyage.

According to rumor, when earlier this month the merchant ships reverted to control of the German Navy High Command, Tschira and his assistant came immediately under the control of the Abwehr collection directorate. With hostilities anticipated any day, it was a natural requirement for the Abwehr to demand current photo coverage of key installations in Britain, France, and even the United States for their naval intelligence database. As a result, the crew noted that Tschira had been busy on the commander's flying bridge shooting away with his large lens when the ship had been in Southampton. The officers guessed he was covering the latest positions of the Southampton antisubmarine nets there. While they lay at anchor for two hours in Southampton shuttling passengers, Tschira took panoramic pictures of the area from the flying bridge, being extra careful to be discreet and out of sight of the passengers. In Cherbourg, Tschira had taken full panoramic coverage of the harbor and had commented several times to observing crewmen that the harbor was unexpectedly empty of French naval ships, most probably having been gathered in the Mediterranean.

The value of intelligence photography of New York was more vague, but Tschira had been seen again taking full panoramic photos of the entire harbor, including the military installations on Governor's Island, Fort Hamilton, and the old coastal artillery batteries on Fort Wadsworth in the Narrows as they sailed in. Now, he was again on the port wing of the bridge all loaded for bear, and on seeing Pilot Miller, had slipped further aft, behind a large stanchion, with his large two-hundred-millimeter lens fixed to his camera.

The Staten Island Ferry was ahead slipping swiftly by into the Battery; another had just passed heading into the slip at Saint George, Staten Island. The weather was overcast and getting dark quickly. Heavy clouds were visible through the Narrows. A small black-hulled New York police patrol launch followed close astern, giving the impression *Bremen* was being escorted out for some misdeed. And still worse, about three-quarters of a mile astern was a U.S. Coast Guard ship reinforcing the sense that the German ship was less than welcome. What had happened to the days, wondered Ahrens, when *Bremen* had been the metaphor for German-American friendship and close relations? The pall of the current situation seemed to hang over the entire crew, despite the fact they were eager to get out and on their way home.

Ahrens interrupted his musings. "Mister Warning," he said, motioning the first officer away to the corner of the bridge wing, out of earshot from Pilot Miller. "I want full passenger lights showing topside. We will extinguish them on my command after clearing Sandy Hook. Then I want a fully darkened ship, understand?"

"Aye, Captain."

Bohling recalled watching the events from the after end of the sun deck, "We were passing the Statue of Liberty when someone in the crew, mustered on the raised afterdeck, began to sing the national anthem, that fine music composed by Joseph Haydn but whose words would be altered subtly by the Nazis. The sound of the voices swelled as we passed the statue, and then burst into the party theme song 'Horst Wessel.' It was a moving moment and I can still hear the music today and see the outline of the New York skyline and the Statue of Liberty." Tschira recorded the departure on film, many scenes of which became famous.

Ahrens was not so deeply moved by the spontaneous singing. He wondered gloomily, as they passed the New York points, when he would ever return. He was not optimistic.

Press airplanes flew over the ship as it plowed through the steaming heat out past Fort Wadsworth into the mist and overcast of the late summer evening. In the dwindling light, the crew on deck could make out the blinking headlights of a single car on the side of Leif Erickson Drive near Fort Hamilton on the Brooklyn

Bremen passing the Statue of Liberty in New York Harbor during its departure on August 30, 1939. (Hanns Tschira—courtesy of Deutsches Schiffahrtsmuseum, Bremerhaven)

side of the Narrows. That was Captain Drechsel, the Norddeutscher Lloyd's marine superintendent, who always paid *Bremen* a farewell gesture from that position by flashing his headlights. None of the crew knew then that it would be his final farewell.

It was just past 8:00 P.M. when *Bremen* slowed to disembark the pilot. That done, they continued steaming to reach the outer limits of the three-mile U.S. territorial waters. Then, as the final daylight faded and the bright lights shone through the foggy mist, Captain Ahrens commanded, "All full ahead, right full rudder, turns for twenty-seven knots, steady on course one-six-zero," a course that would confirm to all nosey observers that *Bremen* was indeed headed to the Caribbean and Havana.

As the ship steamed southeast from New York, the winds increased from the northeast; the sky was overcast and it began to rain. Ahrens waited another ten minutes to ensure that any observers could see clearly that they were heading southeast. Then, with a voice full of eagerness, he barked, "Now, extinguish all topside lighting, including navigational running lights. Maintain total darkness throughout the ship. Mister Warning, increase the lookout watch according to plan." That plan called for a total of twenty-six lookouts.

First Officer Warning stepped out on the wing of the bridge just moments before with his raincoat and peaked cap dripping from the rain. "Mister Warning, please enforce the darken ship order meticulously. I want all violations reported to me. Any crewman who shines a light topside will be placed on restriction." He was deadly serious.

"Aye, Herr Captain," Warning replied and stepped back into the protection of the pilothouse.

Ahrens was astounded at the total darkens that engulfed the ship. Then, waiting a few more moments, he leaned into the voice tube, "Left full rudder, come to new course zero-four-zero degrees."

HMS *York* and HMS *Berwick*
Halifax, Nova Scotia
August 30, 1939

As *Bremen* headed northeast at 27 knots on the night of August 30, the ship's company didn't know that the British cruisers *Berwick* and *York* were heading into Halifax after conducting joint eight-inch gunnery exercises in the Halifax operating area with the Canadian ocean tug HMCS *Fundy* providing target towing services. That location was dead ahead on *Bremen*'s track, whichever lane they chose to return to Germany. The British had chosen well where to place their intercepting force.

The two cruisers anchored that night in Halifax alongside the host ship *Fundy*. Both British cruisers were now standing port and starboard watches, six on six off. They intended to remain the night in port, with *Berwick* returning to sea in the morning and *York* staying behind to take on fuel and provisions. The focus of the world press remained on the worsening situation in Europe and the mystery of where *Bremen* was headed.

The home of Undersecretary of State Adolf A. Berle
Washington, D.C.
August 30, 1939

At 7:00 P.M., German chargé d'affairs Dr. Hans Thomsen called the State Department requesting an appointment to discuss the holding of *Bremen*. He was invited to call at the home of Undersecretary of State Adolf A. Berle. Thomsen arrived at Berle's home at 8:45 P.M. carrying a teletype account of President Roosevelt's press conference about the holding of and search of potential belligerent ships. At the time of the meeting, neither the chargé d'affairs nor the undersecretary was aware that *Bremen* had been granted clearance to sail and had in fact departed New York Harbor.

Thomsen asked Berle for a clarification because he was unable to find reference to such actions in the U.S. Neutrality Act of 1937. Berle carefully explained that the president was referring to neutrality acts throughout U.S. history. The question of the conversion of merchant ships into commerce raiders had been a part of U.S. history since the nation's founding. The concern about commerce raiders had come up during the French Revolution, the Napoleonic Wars, and the U.S. Civil War, when the United States was heavily damaged by raiders outfitted by foreign powers. The U.S. government was referring to the many statutes on the books concerning these matters. Thomsen stated that the president inferred that *Bremen* might not have any armament aboard but that it was possible she might be fitted out with guns at sea after leaving port. He asked if the president had any intelligence to indicate that *Bremen* was so configured and did the Americans know that such an act might indeed take a long time to accomplish. Berle replied that clearance to sail would be withheld only if there were reason to believe that such a threat existed. The meeting ended on a cordial note.

The next day, Thomsen called the State Department and in an apparent act of conciliation announced that the German express liner *Columbus* had sailed from Curaçao and anticipated that it would proceed to New York as scheduled. Was that subterfuge, and did he not know that all German liners had been ordered home?

SS *Bremen*
Off Long Island
August 30, 1939

As *Bremen* steamed northeast through the patchy rain and mist toward Nantucket, the crew learned from Gerstung's intercepted news broadcasts that the U.S. Coast Guard cutter *George W. Campbell* had just departed the Norwegian port of Bergen after embarking Secretary of State Henry Morgenthau Jr. and financial expert Professor James Viner and a small staff. The cutter headed west toward Botwood, near Saint John's, Newfoundland, where a Coast Guard aircraft was scheduled to pick up the secretary and his party for a flight back to Washington. The gist of the news was ominous. Although Chancellor Adolf Hitler sent Prime Minister Neville Chamberlain an encouraging note the day before *Bremen* sailed from New York, the war of nerves caused by Germany's continued mobilization was beginning to tell on the entire crew. As soon as they left New York, they had noticed that the SA Bordsturm men began to take on new and more obvious functions in each section, including standing lookout, the wheelhouse, and even engineering watches. SS *Sturmbahnnführer* Ernst Sauer, the assistant to senior Bordsturmleiter (Bordstorm leader) Erwin Schulwitz, was seen often consulting with First Officer Warning, much to the latter's obvious distaste for their presence. It was clear that they had assumed a new elevated importance in the running of the ship, and it made most of the crew uneasy.

5

Running North

SS *Bremen*
At sea south of Nantucket
Wednesday August 30, 1939

"Mister Warning, summon all the off-watch officers in the ballroom. I wish to describe our intentions and plans in case we pick up a warship shadow," Captain Adolf Ahrens said, staring out into the dark night. He was expecting to pick up the Nantucket Lightship in a few hours. He sensed danger, for steaming at 27 knots in poor visibility with no running lights was not exactly the safest thing to do in these waters, which served as a graveyard for so many notable passenger ships.

Waiter Ernst Henningsen recalled, "Those of us in the crew felt the tension all around and were aware of the importance of maintaining a completely darkened ship. But when we were told to bring mattresses from the tourist-class levels up to the promenade deck, and saw the bosuns placing cans of petrol every twenty meters along the same deck with the mattresses and other flammable materials, we got the sense of exactly how serious the captain was. We were filled with a fear of the unexpected; none of us had ever made a crossing without passengers. It was eerie."

Even though Radio Officer Kurt Gerstung had placed extra radio monitor watches sweeping the various frequencies he had looked up for British and American warships and Coast Guard patrols, as well as the normal maritime distress and coordination circuits, he was still not sure if all were covered. He paced behind his men, who sat hunched wearing headsets in front of their Telefunken E-381-H receivers, the newest in the field, which had come out in the mid-1930s, replacing the older E-362-S models. *Bremen* had been first on the list of passenger ships to receive this new equipment, also in use aboard first-line German warships.

Gerstung had banned smoking on watch because he considered the habit distracting. He allowed a relief rotation so that the men stayed fresh and could stretch cramped muscles every two hours, walk to the adjoining cabin, have tea or coffee, and smoke a cigarette. He had enough men available now with the recent augmentation for this trip. He was proud of his men and felt he had one of the best and most effective teams on board. They all had been through the DEBEG training and had enjoyed their time at the Abwehr school in Wilhelmshaven for their SA Bordsturm indoctrination. Gerstung was not particularly fond of the political haranguing there, but the fact that he and his men were being trained using Kriegsmarine manuals had intensified their interest and sharpened their senses. Gerstung insisted on complete silence in the radio room to prevent his monitors from being distracted from their work.

"Sir, we're picking up some sporadic chatter on the Canadian HF net. I believe it's Halifax." Wilhelm Bauer turned from his station and looked quickly for his supervisor. Gerstung came immediately to his side.

"What language?"

"English, sir, but with a British accent. There it is again." The young man leaned forward concentrating. Gerstung turned up the volume on the receiver and stood closer. He could hear the intermittent sound of voices through the static. Radioman Bauer was from Hamburg and had come to Gerstung's radio division from a Hapag Hamburg ship, with already a one-round-trip transit aboard the liner *St. Louis* under his belt. He was one of the best English speakers in the division.

"There we are, sir, much clearer." The sound of a clipped British accent came through the speaker. "Sir, I can't quite make out the name of the call he's using; sounds something like Urrick.

"Quick, get a bearing." Gerstung was excited.

"Roughly zero-five-five, sir." Bauer turned the dial on his receiver. "Looks like somewhere between zero-five-zero and zero-five-seven. Here it is again clearer."

Gerstung stepped quickly to a chart tacked down on a plotting board. *Bremen*'s track was displayed on a northeast heading. He glanced at a clock, marked off the current position with a pair of dividers, then took up parallel rulers and ran a line out at a bearing of 055. It cut along a line well to the southeast of Halifax, Nova Scotia. Gerstung was thrilled. Then he paused, "What did you say the voice was using as a call?

Radioman Bauer twisted around and lifted one of his ear pieces, "Sorry, sir, what did you say?"

"What call is the voice using?" Gerstung had the feeling he was hitting pay dirt.

Bauer looked at his notes, "Something like Urrick or Burrick, sir."

Gerstung thought for a moment. He had learned his English mostly in the United States, but he had visited Southampton often and had cruised the bars in New York and in Bremerhaven with British seamen. He thought hard, then remembered suddenly: Urrick, Burrick, that's Scottish pronunciation for Berwick, the port city in Scotland—Berwick-upon-Tweed. Gerstung sprang for the door, then quickly returned to his desk and scooped up his cap bearing the DEBEG insignia of radio officers who had qualified after completing the course in Hamburg. He was proud of that insignia; it was unique among the other merchant officer cap insignia aboard the ship—an embroidered golden *T* with lightning bolts shooting forth, the symbol for DEBEG-qualified radio officers. He had worked hard to earn it: three years of practical work aboard ship followed by the final exam. He raced forward to the ladder, took it four steps at a time, and ran to the bridge. He was caught off guard by the sudden darkness and collided with a figure standing just inside the after door to the bridge.

"Shit. Get your night vision before you come onto the bridge," an angry voice swore.

"Silence," another voice rasped. "Silence on the bridge."

Gerstung paused, waiting for his eyes to grow accustomed to the pitch black. The only thing he could make out was the glow from the binnacle where the quartermaster stood silently gazing into the compass. The only sound was that of the rain against the bridge windows and the hum of the forced draft blowers sucking the hot exhaust from the boiler rooms and out the forward stack just behind the bridge. "Where's the captain?" Gerstung whispered to the unknown figure he had just smashed into.

"The hell you think he is, asshole?" The angry voice stank of tobacco. "On the starboard bridge wing, stupid. Don't ever come up here until you can see—"

Gerstung cut him off. "Listen, you! I am Radio Officer Gerstung, and you watch your mouth. I've got to speak to Captain Ahrens; take me to him now or I'll have your ass in detention." Gerstung was bursting to tell Ahrens his news.

"What is it Gerstung?" the captain asked against the wind as the radio officer found him with the help of the unknown cigarette voice.

"Sir, we've picked up the British cruiser *Berwick*," he spat out between gulps of air. He was still out of breath from running up the ladder.

"Where?" the captain asked immediately, all ears.

"Sir, she's out of Halifax." Gerstung gradually controlled his voice. "We got her chattering with a Canadian ship called *Fundy*."

"Are you sure she's at sea out of Halifax?" Ahrens asked calmly. "Our current track takes us by Halifax tomorrow with a closest point of approach of about fifty miles. If she's out at sea we may have to alter course."

"Our first cut put her out, sir, but I'll watch carefully and tell you if there's any change of bearing."

"Very good, Mister Gerstung, well done." Ahrens stood still, watching the large swells that were growing by the hour. The wind was still moderate from the northeast but the barometer was falling. He knew the foul weather was going to intensify, and he was relieved. The rain was still coming down and the visibility was about two miles. It was imperative the weather remain foul. Yet in the morning he hoped to begin painting the ship in camouflage colors. Gerstung hurried back to his radio room.

Ahrens reached for the sound-powered telephone and dialed the first officer. "Mister Warning," he spoke over the sound of the wind, "please come up to the bridge and relieve me. I will go below to the ballroom now and speak to the officers. Gerstung's got a bearing on the cruiser *Berwick*. She's left Halifax. We've got to get by her undetected."

Ahrens placed the phone back into the holder with a click.

The next forty-eight hours would be critical. He knew there were two British warships in the area off Nova Scotia; he had *Berwick*, but where was the other, and who was she? He also knew he had to take all measures to remain undetected by any ship, which would be difficult in the daylight. In this pitch dark it was easy, but tomorrow it would be crucial. He intended to camouflage the ship with the required haze-gray paint they had aboard just for that purpose and in accordance with those QWA warnings, but he was going to have to do it without slowing. He smiled as he recalled Warning asking before entering New York how they could paint the ship while making 25 knots? Well, now they would have to do it at 27.5 knots and in these seas. We won't win any painting competition for looks, he thought, but we can change our appearance significantly by modifying the signature yellow stacks to gray and by turning the hull from the distinctive black into nondescript gray. The painting would challenge the seamanship of his first officer, but he knew he could do it. After all, he was a reserve naval officer.

Ahrens passed the watch on to Warning, who had just stepped out on the bridge wing. After a curt exchange of information, Ahrens returned Warning's salute and stepped through the door to the bridge, shutting it with a clang.

First Officer Warning turned his collar up, glanced down at the compass repeater, and noted the heading was still 047 degrees, churning a wake with 27.5 knots northeast into the blackness. He felt a chill run down his back. Warning preferred order and precise planning, and despised uncertainty and doubt. He did not like the thought that there were two, maybe more, British warships ahead, lurking, and a state of war waiting to erupt at any moment.

Warning had seen war at sea as a young officer twenty-three years earlier. It was exhilarating, provided you were not one of those who had been too close. He had seen the fighting only in the distance. He recalled his classmate who had been aboard the battle cruiser *Lützow* and survived her sinking in the Battle of Jutland in 1916. His friend had described the carnage and told how his shipmates had been blown to pieces when they had first been hit in her forward turret. He had spoken of the unbearable stench of burning human flesh, stepping over headless bodies, and seeing chunks of jagged steel sticking out of unrecognizable bodies of shipmates. Although the loss of his right arm had not been a serious handicap in later life, Warning's classmate had never recovered from his mental wounds. Any ship going down in the dark sea was a frightening thought and Warning chose not to dwell on the idea that night with so much uncertainty lying ahead for *Bremen* and her crew.

On the way down to the ballroom, the captain stopped at the radio room, opened the door slowly, and stepped in. He noticed immediately that the space was unusually full of watch standers, yet was surprisingly quiet. The air was close and smelled of tobacco and perspiration. Gerstung ran a taut organization, and Ahrens liked that. He saw the radio officer standing behind the operators, gazing at their dials and listening in on their circuits with his own set of earphones plugged in to spare jacks on each receiver. Captain Ahrens observed as one of the watch standers typed out the text of a news broadcast. He moved closer and began to read over the sailor's shoulder. He was copying the daily news broadcast from Berlin to all Norddeutscher Lloyd and Hapag ships.

Ahrens picked up the first sheet that lay next to the typewriter. He read it slowly: Germany and the Soviet Union had signed a nonaggression pact a week ago on August 23. It was the first time it had appeared in the news sheet. That was odd, Ahrens thought. He wondered why. The two leaders, Adolf Hitler and Joseph Stalin, had always seemed ideologically at odds, especially by the looks of the fighting in Spain. The German thinking was that the communists were the real culprits. It seemed the Red threat had always been the Nazi's bête noire. Puzzled, he put the news sheet down and walked over to where Gerstung stood monitoring his radio watch standers.

Gerstung was startled by the captain's sudden appearance in the radio room. It is unusual for Ahrens to come in here, Gerstung thought. It must mean he is more intent on another important intercept. Before Gerstung could acknowledge the captain's presence, Ahrens put his hand on the young man's shoulder, "Let them work in silence, I was just checking to see if there was anything else we could do to enhance your men. It is vital that they pick up every tiny bit of intelligence."

"Yes, sir, I know. They're doing fine, sir. If it's out there we'll hear it."

"Sir," one radio monitor raised his hand, "here's a message coming in from Berlin, another QWA warning message, and a long text broadcast in code. It will take some time to decode this by hand."

The QWA came in the clear. Ahrens and Gerstung read it scrawled in the radioman's handwriting:

QWA 10—Proceed at best speed to Murmansk.
Avoid Strait of Dover.

Ahrens recalled the news release he had just read of the German-Soviet Nonaggression Pact. So, this is a direct result of that, he thought. Makes good sense even if it seems an unnatural alliance.

The longer encoded message was a bare bones operation order from the German Navy High Command code-named "Basis North." It called for all German-flagged merchant ships in the north Atlantic unable to enter German waters without transiting British-controlled waters to head directly to Murmansk.

Gerstung had brought Ahrens the decoded operation order to his sea cabin just after Ahrens had spoken to the ship's officers in the ballroom. There, he had outlined the plan to paint the ship in twelve hours to enhance their invisibility, and to do it while steaming at just over 27 knots. The crew would use the lifeboats, lowered on their davits to paint the hull at various levels without slowing. Those men painting the stacks topside would do so rigged in bosun's chairs. They would begin at first light, which was 6:00 A.M. The seas were still building into sizeable swells, but not so large as to preclude this emergency painting. Ahrens had implored the officers to strictly enforce the darken ship rules and said that violators would be dealt with harshly.

Now that Ahrens held the "Basis North" order in his hand, he was able to lay out their full track. He called First Mate Warning, Leading Engineer Frederich Müller, Radio Officer Gerstung, Purser Julius Rohde, and Leading Steward Hans Junghans to the chart house behind the bridge. There he explained to these key officers that their revised track would take *Bremen* through the Denmark Strait between Iceland and Greenland, past Jan Mayen Island, directly over North Cape into the Barents Sea, and then into the Kola fjord and the safety of, now allied, Soviet waters. Ice conditions were at this point unknown, but the normal presence of summer icebergs was a real danger. During the spring of 1939, the international ice patrols reported seeing more than ninety-five icebergs, a number that was higher than normal. There was still a strong chance, even in late August, of an encounter with a lingering berg, which was a daunting thought. To avoid collision with icebergs and to spot any other ship early to keep from being sighted, the topside lookout watches were to be doubled, and, as if reading his first officer's mind, Ahrens added that the ship's SA Bordsturm would also provide men to augment the topside watch. Warning had recommended this earlier, as it added to the military spirit of the ship's current situation.

Ahrens then explained to the officers that after sighting a warship all preparations must be in place to scuttle the ship. He outlined the procedures. All hands except for designated firefighting parties would abandon ship quickly and in orderly fashion via the normally assigned crew lifeboats, then the fire parties would set the promenade deck alight and then proceed to their boats. The designated engineering party would then open sea cocks in all four engine rooms and proceed smartly to the boat deck and join the captain, the chief engineer, and the first officer in the last boat. That, of course, would be exercised only if a state of war had been declared. If the warships were in sight or in surveillance, the entire crew was to be ready to execute the ship's destruction only on Captain Ahrens's command.

The words describing the actions to destroy their beautiful and beloved ship fell harshly on the crews' ears. Deep inside each of them they dreaded what might be around the corner.

Ahrens also ordered that all crew berthing in the forward-most compartments in the bow be evacuated and moved aft. Steaming at this high speed through poor visibility was normally unheard of. It was considered highly dangerous and unseamanlike, but they all understood that in this case, to escape possible capture as a prize, continuous high speed in all conditions was necessary. The captain was concerned that should they collide, at least they could minimize casualties by steaming with the bow compartments empty of all personnel. That order was indicative of how Ahrens thought constantly about the well-being and safety of his men.

Not many of the crew slept well that night. The next day was the last day of August, and unknown to them at the time aboard *Bremen*, it was the last day of peace.

Captain Ahrens's first concern was to get by Halifax swiftly and unseen. He was tempted to increase speed to 29 knots, but Chief Müller's idea of saving fuel in case they needed a burst of speed to outdistance a warship, if sighted, convinced the captain that 27.5 knots would have to do in case of a pinch. The whole matter depended on Gerstung's radiomen's ability to detect the British cruisers before they could be sighted. Ahrens returned to his sea cabin and tried to relax by reading his favorite Hermann Hesse book.

That night three entries were made in *Bremen's* deck log: Electrician Wilhelm Krause was placed on restriction for being tipsy on duty at his post and shining a flashlight irresponsibly in the passageway between the ballroom and third-class writing lounge. Dishwasher Wolfram Büttner was placed on restriction for unauthorized smoking on deck while the ship was darkened. Florist Anna Eckert was placed on restriction for shining an unauthorized light on the main deck.

The next morning at 4:42 A.M. they sighted the Nantucket Lightship bearing 355 degrees and passed her at seven miles. The continuing wet weather caused the captain to postpone painting the ship.

Then, shortly after noon they had a scare. As Walter Renneberg described:

> Most of the off watch crew were having dinner in the crew's dining hall, when we felt the ship suddenly increase speed. We could feel the unmistakable accelerating high pitch whine of the turbines and the rumbling vibrations of the four propeller shafts. We felt the ship heel slightly as we turned hard to port. It was rare with passengers aboard to feel turns this sharp. It was Norddeutscher Lloyd policy that the comfort and safety of the passengers came above all, and violent maneuvers, such as this, were rarely felt. Something was happening! It was all we could do to carry on eating as if nothing was going on, but we tried to show our nonchalance. Then one of the bosuns finally rose and went to the window, which was larger than a port, and looked out. There in the distance was a small ship on the horizon. Within a few seconds the small shadow of the ship disappeared and after a few tense moments steaming on this more northerly course, the ship turned slowly and returned to the previous northeasterly course and slowed again to 27 knots. Fortunately, the lookouts located in the crow's nest on the foremast had sufficient height-of-eye to spot the other ship thought by the bridge watch to have been a freighter, while it was hull-down, that was long before she could have sighted us, thus avoiding a radio report of our presence.

New York City
August 31, 1939

On the day following *Bremen*'s departure, the New York press was already printing stories speculating on their destination, track, and future. Reports came in from all over the world: BREMEN LEAVES NEW YORK BOUND FOR HAVANA; BREMEN DEPARTS NEW YORK HEADING FOR BREMERHAVEN TO OUT-RACE THE WAR; and BREMEN DISAPPEARS, EVADING BRITISH BATTLESHIPS.

The whole world was wondering where *Bremen* had gone, and the press was already reporting sightings of them in the Caribbean, off the coast of the southern United States. Another had them being held in a French port. *Bremen* had simply vanished into thin air. The crew had a wonderful time reading the headlines Radio Officer Gerstung posted on the bulletin board as they were received. The whole world was looking for them, and it was a comfortable feeling to be totally hidden in rain and foul weather.

The White House
Washington, D.C.
September 1, 1939

The following memorandum from the acting secretary of the treasury was received by President Roosevelt. The report had been slow in arriving and had come from a British intelligence officer in New York who was monitoring the *Bremen* situation:

August 30, 1939

The *Bremen* took aboard in New York 5,531 tons or 35,953 barrels of fuel oil. She had asked and had been granted permission to take 50,000 barrels. I am informed that the amount is a comfortably adequate supply for a high speed run to Bremerhaven. On her former trip to Hamburg she used 880 tons per day to develop 28.5 knots. A normal fuel supply for an eastward crossing is 4,700 to 4,900 tons. She has a bunker capacity for 6,616 tons or between 42,000 and 43,000 barrels. So far as we can judge from the bunker data, therefore, the Master of the Bremen planned merely a high speed run to a home port.[1]

[signed]

John W. Hanes

New York Harbor
Friday, September 1, 1939

A few days after *Bremen* left her Eighty-sixth Street pier, the Esso tanker *Panamanian* sailed from New York with the same Pilot Herbert Miller aboard. He described *Bremen*'s departure to the tanker's mate by saying that Captain Ahrens had shaken his hand with both of his and then turned away. Miller then said that German junior officers had escorted him to the lift and to the boarding ladder to the pilot launch. When Miller entered the cabin of the pilot launch, he turned to look for *Bremen*, but she was nowhere to be seen. She had completely disappeared, course and speed unknown.[2]

6

Close Encounters

SS *Bremen*
At sea, 180 nautical miles southwest of Halifax
4:00 A.M.
Friday, September 1, 1939

The news from Germany was that mobilization of all resources was continuing to prepare the population for the eventuality of a blockade by Britain. The wireless daily report contained fragmentary information about the imposition of a rationing system for all of Germany. That news was especially disheartening for the crew, since they were used to living rather comfortably during the transits with international passengers. They had access to luxury goods on a daily basis and were usually able to sneak some scarce items home. The thought of losing these privileges was a serious blow to their morale.

Radio Officer Kurt Gerstung retired to his small bunk room just off the radio room to rest a few minutes. He had been in that cramped space for the past three watches supervising his monitors and he felt his eyes begging to shut. He had drunk a great deal of tea and was now a little off his mark. He lay down thinking of what loomed ahead, the images of British warships, radio call letters, the stutter of the telegraph. As he lay still, gradually sinking into slumber, the buzzer by the side of his bunk suddenly rang, yanking him awake. Gerstung leapt to his feet, pushed open the curtain separating his bunk room, and rushed into the radio room, which glowed with dim blue lights. His operator, Wilhelm Bauer, was watching the curtain to his alcove and quickly motioned to Gerstung to come nearer.

"Sir, I've got the *Berwick* again." Bauer was excited and lifted one ear piece for Gerstung to hear. "She's still outside Halifax, calling the Canadian tug the *Fundy*. Something about towing for an event for later today."

"Get a bearing." Gerstung was wide awake now.

"I did, sir; it's southeast, about one-two-zero degrees."

"My God!" exclaimed Gerstung. "She's well to the east of our track."

"Sir," Bauer was right on top of the situation, "the two British ships are keeping better radio discipline, unlike a couple days ago. There is hardly any chatter. Only the odd call and request for information. They are still talking in the clear."

Gerstung patted the operator on the back, "Well done. Stay on it." He grabbed his cap from the hook and then paused. "Did you ever recover the name of the second British warship?" he asked, reaching for the door.

"Oh, yes, sir." Bauer scanned his note pad. "I think, yes, it's the *York*, still in port at Halifax. Oh, and one more thing," the radioman studied his notes, "both ships apparently have aircraft aboard, probably seaplanes." That meant both ships were carrying Walrus floatplanes for extending their eyes well beyond the horizon. Furthermore, it meant *York* was also a cruiser.

Gerstung swung the door open and bolted into the passageway. He ran to the ladder and, taking three rungs at a time, raced to the captain's sea cabin. He knocked briskly and heard the captain's voice. "Yes, what is it? That you Gerstung?"

Gerstung opened the door and stepped in quickly. "Yes, sir, Captain, we've got a another cut on the *Berwick*, well east of our track, already to the southeast. The second cruiser is the *York*, and she's apparently still in Halifax." He then told the captain about the seaplanes.

"Good, Mister Gerstung, call the first officer and have him meet us in the chart house." Gerstung started to leave the cabin. "Wait, call the chief engineer and have him come up too. We may need to run at full power shortly."

Gerstung left the cabin and raced for the bridge intercom, while Ahrens quickly dressed and prepared to go forward to the chart house. Glancing at the chart on his desk, he suddenly stopped and thought, My God, a cruiser to the southeast and another in Halifax, both with search aircraft, and an American Coast Guard ship to the north. That means we're nearly surrounded. Our only hope is the weather. It must remain foul!

Ahrens strode forward to the bridge. The low blue lights in the passageway helped accustom his eyes to the dark so that when he reached the chart house he could clearly see the two figures already waiting there.

"That was fast, Mister Warning," the captain said. "You must have been up here already. What's the matter, can't sleep?" He was goading the first officer, while he himself had found it hard to sleep, given the events hanging in the balance.

The three officers studied the chart. Gerstung took the parallel rulers and laid out a bearing 120 degrees from the ship's present position and ran a light line; then he measured the distance from Halifax.

"Turns out we're an even one hundred eighty miles from Halifax. The cruiser Berwick's somewhere along this bearing." He pointed to the chart. "Her signal strength was medium, indicating she is not more than sixty or maybe eighty miles away."

Ahrens studied the chart intently. "Thank God the visibility's so poor; their seaplane won't be much good for reconnaissance even if they managed to safely launch it in this scud. Mister Warning, have a continuous sweep made of the topside spaces to ensure no lights are visible." He turned to the radio officer. "Mister Gerstung, go back to radio and keep a sharp ear tuned in. I'll be on the starboard wing of the bridge, and—" Chief Engineer Frederich Müller stepped into the room smelling of oil and sweat. "Chief, be ready for max power. We've got two British cruisers nearby and an armed American cutter ahead. We may have to give them a good run for it. Stand by for full power on short notice. How are we on feed water?"

The one element Ahrens understood well about the ship's engineering was the absolute necessity to have ample feed water

The main engine control area was the heart of *Bremen*'s systems. (Courtesy of Wilhelm Bohling)

for high-speed running. The normal procedure while carrying passengers was to distill more fresh water for the passengers than for boiler feed water, since the ship normally ran at a steady economic speed of 27 knots on each crossing. The total distilling capacity was two hundred tons a day. But at higher speeds, the propulsion plant needed considerably more feed water to replace the inefficiency of the condensers to recover all of the steam back into feed water for the twenty boilers operating at a pressure of 350 pounds per square inch.

"We can put all the distillers on to feed water now, because we have ample fresh water without passengers," Müller responded.

Müller was a solid engineer who knew the quirks of the propulsion plant like no one else. He had served aboard as an assistant under *Bremen*'s original leading engineer Julius Hundt, who had brought the ship through construction, trials, and the nine years of Atlantic operations. Under Chief Hundt, Müller had acquired the unique ability to sense by the sound and smell of the engine and boiler rooms when something was amiss. The engineering spaces, now the sole domain of Chief Müller, were immaculate and glistened with brightly shined brass and stainless steel, and smelled of hot lubricating oil and fresh coffee.

He boasted that his engine room coffee was better than that served in the first-class dining room, a boast resented by Leading Steward Hans Junghans. The crusty engineer scoffed at the rotund head of all the ship's stewards, which far outnumbered his engineers. But the antagonism was generally good-natured, that is, unless the stewards caught the engineers stealing pastries from the cavernous bakery on F deck. The week before, the cooks had interrupted a major theft of delicacies by the engineers just before entering New York, which had resulted in Leading Chef Hans Künlen hauling three engineers up before the first mate for punishment. After having vigorously denied any knowledge of the theft, the engineers were forced to confess when they failed to explain the presence of whipped cream and custard stains on their oil-stained coveralls. The incident seemed almost irrelevant now, given the new seriousness of the situation.

Bremen and her sister ship, *Europa*, were not only among the fastest ships at sea at the time, but the broadest. The beam's relationship to the length must be exact to make the ship faster, and the ships were made even more stable and faster by the incorporation of the bulbous bow, also called the bulbous forefoot. It consisted of a pear-shaped bubble in the steel hull located at the foot of the stem. This protrusion makes a hole in the water as the ship plows ahead, forcing seawater away to both sides and downward, thereby reducing drag on the skin of the ship, increasing the mass of the water at the stern, and strengthening the bite against which the propellers can thrust. The two ships also possessed Frahm antirolling tanks. These two tanks, located on the extreme beams on either side of the hull, were filled with seawater and connected with a single pipe. When the seas were calm, the connecting line was closed by a valve. When the seas became rougher, the valve was opened, allowing the water to slowly drain from the high tank to the lower at a much slower speed than the roll of the ship, thus damping the amount and speed of roll. Another speed-enhancing factor that the experienced Leading Engineer Müller incorporated was adjusting the trim of his fuel and water tanks to counter the act of pitching into bow seas. For example, as *Bremen* encountered higher head seas while running north, he shifted ballast aft to raise the bow, thus decreasing the pounding effect of the bow rising and falling in the swell, and in turn gaining additional speed.

Müller loved to challenge his engineering plant. He had been involved in the design, construction, and operation of *Bremen*'s propulsion plant since her construction, and if anyone knew how to coax out an additional few knots, he did. He loved his glistening engine and boiler rooms. His engineers drifted throughout the holds nine decks below the bridge like elves with a purpose. They grew into legends to the other crewmen, who knew only a little of what they did and how they lived, for topside sailors never ventured into Müller's black holds. The reputation of the engineers grew to legendary status. Their representatives were seldom seen, but when present were carefully scrubbed and washed and sent topside to negotiate with Apprentice Chef Walter Renneberg for special favors from the galley. These negotiations were conducted mostly in sign language to avoid detection and generally produced fantastic results for the engineers, who ensured whatever services the galley needed, such as fresh water for cooking, auxiliary steam for heating the gigantic kettles, or uninterrupted electric power for their massive baking ovens. It was a quiet, symbiotic alliance that worked and was never challenged by officers, who although aware of the barter, turned a blind eye.

"Aye, Herr Captain," Müller disappeared from the room like a shot. All *Bremen*'s officers knew that Müller felt uncomfortable on the bridge. Some chided him for his reluctance to come that far above the bowels of the ship, saying he suffered nose bleeds at that height; others said it was because his uniforms were always so stained and foul smelling he couldn't associate with normal humans. In fact, Müller preferred to remain belowdecks in his beloved world of steam pipes, boilers, lube oil, fuel, hot coffee, and his similarly soiled engineers. *Bremen*'s engineering plant was

The boiler room. (Hanns Tschira—courtesy of Deutsches Schiffahrtsmuseum, Bremerhaven)

reputed to be the best in Bremerhaven's Norddeutscher Lloyd and certainly far superior to any other ship of the Hamburg Hapag fleet.

Müller left the bridge and made directly for the officers' elevator behind the wheelhouse on the sun deck level, which took him silently down the nine deck levels, seventy-five feet to the warm bosom of his engine rooms. There was new purpose in his gait; he had the utmost confidence in his propulsion plant. He walked into the engine room across the metal grillwork, grasping the shining handrails, and arrived at a small desk where a third engineer was filling in a log. The engineer sprang to his feet. Müller greeted him briskly.

"Stand by for increased speed, Mister Schmidt. Also take double the number of readings on all main thrust bearings each hour. We're in for some delicate running." He then smiled, and added, "And I know your watch is ready, Schmidt."

HMS *Berwick*
At sea, ninety nautical miles south of Halifax
4:00 A.M.
September 1, 1939

Lieutenant Commander J. P. Hunt, *Berwick*'s navigator, stepped out onto the signal bridge. "Morning, sir," he said as the two signalmen on watch rose from their protected booth behind the bridge and greeted the navigator. "Not too good for stars, sir."

"Morning chaps." Hunt looked up and saw it was still overcast; visibility was poor, probably less than three miles. He had risen as normal before dusk to take his morning star sightings for the 8:00 A.M. position report and stopped by the wardroom for a cup of tea, then climbed the ladder slowly to the bridge, greeted the officer of the deck, and then walked aft toward the signal bridge. It was humid and sticky, but cooling somewhat after the southwesterly winds of the past two days had virtually stopped, leaving the heavy overcast and mist in place.

Hunt had been disappointed that the ship's stay in Bar Harbor had been cut short. He and three of the Port Section officers had found several cozy watering holes in Frenchman's Bay that served Canadian beer, their choice over the watery American beer, and they had reveled in the sumptuous steamed clams, lobster, and corn on the cob. It was absurdly inexpensive and they enjoyed the afternoons away from the ship. Fresh shellfish was unheard of in Britain at these prices. Ever since their increased alert status, two days before, they were required to be back aboard ship by dark. Suddenly their relaxing routine had changed. They were now conducting gunnery exercises daily off Halifax and standing watch six hours on, six off, which had soon grown tiresome. They were due to join up with the cruiser *York* later in the day for a continuation of exercises. Like *Berwick*, *York* had a Walrus floatplane and catapult aft. Their aircraft would be used to tow a sleeve for antiaircraft gunnery shoots, but had most recently been made ready for ocean reconnaissance. They were alerted that the famous German liner *Bremen* may be headed toward their vicinity, and they were to locate and shadow her, but the weather was not cooperating and their seaplane had been grounded due to continuing poor visibility. Hunt was a close friend of Lieutenant David Tibbits, the *York* navigator. They had been in naval school at Dartmouth together and cruised as midshipmen. Hunt's commanding officer in *Berwick* was the highly respected Commander Raymond Portal, also a former navigator aboard destroyers and cruisers. The two ships had operated together now for several weeks as part of the North Atlantic patrol force under Admiral Charles Forbes, the Home Fleet commander in chief.

USCG *George W. Campbell*
At sea, five hundred miles northeast
of St. John's, Newfoundland
4:00 A.M.
September 1, 1939

Commander Joseph Greenspun was steaming his cutter west at 20 knots with the VIP group aboard. This was probably the most highly visible, if not the most important mission he had undertaken since taking command a year ago. With Secretary of the Treasury Henry Morgenthau Jr. and party aboard, Greenspun's goal was to make St. John's, Newfoundland, as quickly as possible. Coast Guard ships in those years were subordinate to the Treasury Department, and having the secretary aboard was much like a U.S. Navy ship with the navy commander in chief embarked.

"Captain, the wind is dying, and the fog's thickening. I recommend we sound fog signals." The officer of the deck was Chief Fire Controlman Rick Moore.

"Very well. Sound fog signals as necessary and post additional lookouts," the captain responded. "I'll be in the wardroom." He left the bridge and descended the ladder to the wardroom.

Greenspun found Lieutenant Henry Meyer, the navigator, drinking coffee at the mess table. "What, no morning stars to shoot?" he asked Meyer while taking a cup and pouring himself some hot coffee.

Meyer started to rise. "Relax, sit," the captain said. "Doubt you'll get any sightings today; it's thick as soup out there." As if to punctuate his words, their fog signal shuttered throughout the ship. "That ought to wake our guests."

The young navigator resumed his seat. "I don't think Secretary Morgenthau slept at all last night. I heard them talking in your cabin until the midwatch was relieved."

It was customary in a Hamilton-class cutter like *Campbell* that the commanding officer surrender his in-port cabin to seniors or VIPs aboard. Greenspun had relocated into his sea cabin on the 01 level while the ship was in Norway before the entourage came aboard. Morgenthau's companions were berthed in the operation officer's and navigator's cabins. Navigator Meyer had to move aft to the three-man officers' bunk room, but he didn't seem bothered.

"I'm like you, sir, I never can sleep when the weather's this soupy. Too many navigators' balls have been hung out to dry when they go aground in this kind of weather."

"Don't talk that way, Gator. Can you imagine the stink if some-thing happened with the big boss aboard? Can't stand to think about it. By the way, when you first see the comm officer, tell him to prepare a marine telephone link to Saint John's at noon. The secretary wants to talk to Washington, and they'll patch him from the Canadian switchboard. Also, get a good weather report for today. This stuff may stay around and it's going to slow us down considerably. The secretary and his party are determined to get home as soon as possible. Things don't look good, and he doesn't want to be away when hostilities begin. It may be any day now."

The navigator finished his coffee and excused himself. He was a few steps into heading for the bridge when he remembered the captain's words, so he went instead to the radio room. He opened the door and walked in. "Sparks, when does your boss show his face at work in the mornings?"

The first-class leading radioman was listening to baseball scores on the short-wave radio. He pulled off his headset as soon as the lieutenant walked in. "Sir, he was up until after midnight listening to the BBC. Things are falling apart over in Europe."

"Yeah. Who's going to win the pennant? Brooklyn?" Meyer was from Brooklyn.

"Too early to tell, sir, but my money's on the Yankees." He was from the Bronx. "If I were allowed, sir, I'd put twenty on the Yankees for the pennant and the series."

Just then the communications officer, Lieutenant Junior Grade William Collins, stepped into the room.

"What the hell's this, the ladies aid meeting?" He showed circles under his eyes and his hair was mussed. "Couldn't sleep in this crap, fog horn going every few seconds. Here read this." He handed a board of messages to the navigator.

Meyer took the board and began to read. "Hey, we may see something big. The CO seen this yet?"

"Yup, just showed it to him in the wardroom. He wants to set additional lookouts, but we already did for the fog."

"Is that about that kraut liner?" the signalman asked.

"Yeah, we're supposed to keep a sharp lookout and if we think we see her we're supposed to send a message to this list of addresses." The comm officer took the board back from Meyer. "Listen to this: If we see what we think is the German liner SS *Bremen*, we are to immediately send a message in the clear to the following addressees: commandant of the Coast Guard, commander in chief of the U.S. Navy, and get this, the president of the United States and the bloody commander in chief of the British Home Fleet. Now, I didn't know we were choosing sides on this matter. Sounds to me like we're already supporting the Brits. But then shouldn't we be." The discussion ended abruptly when the executive officer walked into the room.

"My, it's crowded in here. What's the matter—can't you all sleep?" He took the board from the comm officer and began reading. He looked up and asked Meyer, "What are those two British cruisers doing in Halifax? Maybe the Brits know something we don't." He continued reading.

"Oh my God, look at this!" the leading radioman handed a message to the exec that he had just copied from the telegraph key.

The exec took the message. "Oh boy, type this up and run it to the captain. No." He changed his mind. "Hell, take it like this." He changed his mind again. "No, I'll take it," and he left the radio room abruptly.

"What the hell was that?" the navigator asked.

"Sir, that was a news flash from the AP. The German army just marched into Poland." The radioman suddenly put his earphones on and began copying another signal. "Treasury in Washington wants a direct marine operator phone link with Secretary Morgenthau." He was still copying out a long note. He finished, tore it off the pad of yellow paper, and handed it to the comm officer, who read it quickly.

"I'll have to take this to the captain right now, and then to the secretary. Hold on to your britches." He paused, "Clean up this space, Sparks. We're going to have a lot of VIPs in here talking on the radio. Get the port section here and start trying the Newfoundland marine operator on the HF transmitter, all in the clear, of course." He left the room, followed by the navigator. It would take the next four hours for *Campbell* to raise the marine operator in St. John's.

The weather continued to deteriorate with the seas increasing from the northwest and the thick fog persisting. During the four-to-eight evening watch, the ship was forced to turn into the heavy seas and slow to 10 knots to ease the motion, further delaying their arrival in St. John's. It was virtually impossible to see another ship in the foul weather.

SS *Bremen*
At sea, eighty miles south of Cape Breton
Noon
September 1, 1939

Again, Gerstung stood on the bridge with Captain Ahrens and First Officer Eric Warning. "Sir, we have the American Coast Guard cutter *Campbell* in HF communications with the Newfoundland marine operator. The bearing is almost dead ahead, signal strength weak but increasing. She is closing us, but is no doubt bound for Saint John's. There is apparently an aircraft waiting in there for the Morgenthau party. He's reporting heavy seas and poor visibility, causing them to slow." Gerstung was almost out of breath after spewing all that. But he took the dividers and parallel rulers and extended their track, then looked up. "Captain, based on a projection of their assumed track and ours, we should cross within several miles of each other about noon tomorrow."

"They're talking in the clear?" the captain asked.

"Totally." Gerstung was getting weary. He had been up and down to the bridge at least a dozen times over the past twenty-four hours.

Without hesitating, the captain responded, "Mister Warning, tell the watch officer to come to starboard and take new course one-one-zero for the next two hours to open that projected meeting, then come back to base course zero-six-nine degrees. That should take care of avoiding an unwelcome sighting, even in this poor visibility."

Over the next two watches, Captain Ahrens spent a great deal of time in the chart house with the first officer. The noon position was merely an estimated position based on dead reckoning, since the navigator could not get a sun line. It showed that *Bremen* was sandwiched between the cruiser *Berwick*, somewhere to the south, and the cruiser *York*, which was still in Halifax to the north but due to get underway momentarily to join *Berwick*. Ahrens thought, Darkness can't come soon enough. But visibility was still poor and looked as if it would continue that way into the next day.

"Our best option is to keep steaming on this heading. Absolutely no transmissions of any type," Ahrens emphasized to Gerstung. The captain looked out onto the bridge and shook his head, "I wish I had taken on more fuel in New York, but then we didn't know we were heading to mother Russian, did we? In any case, I'm going to increase speed a little. If we can shoot past Halifax before the second cruiser comes out, we've got them. I don't think the cruisers can launch their aircraft in this." The captain turned to his mate, "Mister Warning, tell the third mate to increase rpm

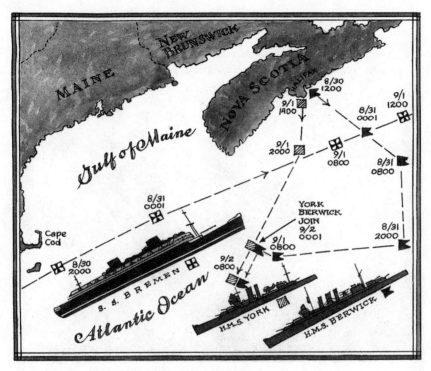

Evading the cruisers HMS *Berwick* and HMS *York*.

to twenty-nine knots. Müller can moan about the fuel expenditure, but we've got to get out of this exposed position."

The ship shuddered as the four huge propellers churned faster, spewing white foam as the bow dipped in the swell and their speed increased from the economical 27.5 to 29 knots. Ahrens thought, At least Leading Steward Junghans won't bellyache about discomfort to the passengers, nor will Dr. Ferber complain about the ship's excessive motion for the aged passengers, for there weren't any aboard.

As the three officers stood in the chart house, a red-faced and winded young radioman arrived with another message in his hand for Gerstung, who immediately passed it to the captain. Ahrens read it, then looked at the others with a long face. "This is it; our troops have just marched into Poland." He handed the message to Warning and walked out on the bridge wing. The others stood by silently.

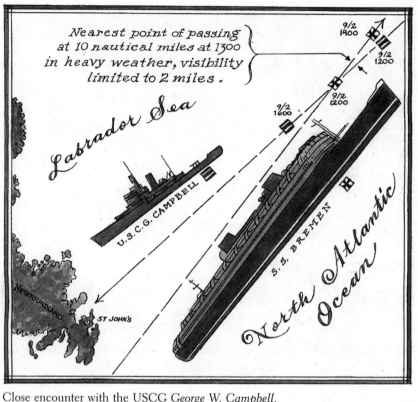

Close encounter with the USCG *George W. Campbell*.

Captain Ahrens felt deeply saddened by the news. He recalled the anguish of the last war and what it had brought to Germany. He did not feel this was in the best interests of his homeland. Yet, he clearly had his duty to do and he fully intended to bring his fine ship and crew home safely. The rest of the future, well, that would just have to come.

Early the same afternoon, the cruiser HMS *York* weighed anchor and departed Halifax bound due south at 25 knots for a scheduled rendezvous with the senior cruiser HMS *Berwick* eighty miles southwest of Halifax. By the time the two cruisers joined company slightly past 7:00 P.M., *Bremen* had slipped between Halifax and *Berwick*, coming within forty miles of one another and before *York* had cleared the harbor. Ironically, the position of the cruisers' rendezvous lay right on *Bremen*'s track, but in her wake a good twelve hours after she had slipped past. The two British cruisers met shortly after 7:00 P.M., and *York* fell in astern *Berwick* at five thousand yards. For the next two watches they steamed southwest, challenging all merchant ships they detected. It was far too foul for launching either of their seaplanes. The wind was still mild but the seas were heavy and building, with visibility remaining well below six miles. They spotted only one merchant ship, who identified herself as the SS *City of Lyons* declared for St. John, New Brunswick.

Bremen's track was now converging on the planned track of the U.S. Coast Guard cutter *George W. Campbell*. Had the latter not slowed and turned into the seas during the 4:00 to 8:00 P.M. watch, and had Ahrens not come to the southeast for two hours and slowed back to the fuel-saving speed of 27.5 knots, the two ships would have come within visual range of each another sometime after noon on September 2, the second day of fighting in Poland.

7

Running for Refuge

North Atlantic, off Halifax
Saturday, September 2, 1939

Throughout Saturday, September 2, 1939, the cruisers *Berwick* and *York* operated together, challenging all merchant ships passing in the western end of the normally traveled great-circle transit route between north European and North American ports. There were many contacts that, when challenged, were cooperative and gave their names, nationalities, and destinations. Yet the restricted visibility, still mostly under six miles, and high seas precluded the combatants from identifying more ships and from launching their aircraft.

At 8:00 A.M. the following morning, both cruisers recorded the following entry in their logs: "State of war declared to exist between Great Britain and Germany." By curious coincidence, shortly into the next watch, at 12:15 local time, the two cruisers detected a large contact on the horizon. We have finally hit pay dirt, *Berwick's* captain thought. It was an exciting moment. "Number One, sound action stations. This may be the *Bremen*."

The two cruisers computed an intercept course, rang up flank speed, and ran toward the contact, their crews at action stations, guns manned, and eight-inch projectiles hoisted and ready on the loading trays. Powder bags were stacked and ready for lifting. For any sailor who drilled unceasingly during the many long hours of the day and long weeks underway, the realization that his country was at war and the excitement that a high-value enemy ship was nearby naturally set the heart pounding. For those who witnessed sea action in the past, the anticipation was also probably edged with dread.

As the two cruisers grew near—now steaming in a loose column formation, their white Royal Navy ensigns fluttering menacingly from their foremasts—they could make out in the heavy seas that the contact was a large liner. Every man topside strained his eyes to make out the image. Those below in the black engineering holds stood tensely at their stations poised for news. The bridge officers watched through their binoculars, while the gunnery spotters aloft in the directors peered through the scud with powerful optical rangefinders, and would be the first to identify the nationality of the approaching black-hulled liner.

Only something didn't match. As the form of the large ship came into full view, it became clear she had three funnels, not two. Then, as the crews of both cruisers watched, the contact grew into a splendid form that must have stirred their hearts; she was indeed a large passenger ship, not *Bremen*, but the British liner RMS *Queen Mary*, the pride of the merchant fleet and current holder of the transatlantic speed record, bound for New York. One might imagine the emotions of those sailors observing that elegant ship, just a few hours after learning they were at war.

For the U.S. Coast Guard cutter *Campbell*, which had passed less than ten miles to the west of *Bremen* that same Saturday, in the teeth of a gale, the day would be a busy one. The seas had finally subsided enough for the cutter to resume her southwesterly course and increase speed gradually back to 20 knots. At 11:55 A.M., Sunday, they sighted the Newfoundland coast off the starboard bow.

They stopped to pick up the pilot, Mr. John Button, entered St. John's Harbor, and anchored shortly after 1:00 P.M. Ten minutes later, a launch brought the American consul general, Newfoundland's commissioner of finance, and a government aide to greet Secretary Henry Morgenthau Jr. and his retinue. The entire party immediately departed with the secretary, escorted by Commander Joseph Greenspun in *Campbell's* boat, to find the Coast Guard seaplane V-167, a twenty-ton Martin PBM-1 Mariner, waiting in nearby Big Bull Pond for the secretary and his party's flight to Washington.

SS *Bremen*
At sea, northeast of Newfoundland
September 3, 1939

That same morning, *Bremen* was well northeast of Newfoundland, clear of the busy shipping lanes and heading for the Denmark Strait between Iceland and Greenland. The heavy cloud cover and driving rain had blanketed the racing liner through the night into the early morning. Even though the weather had improved somewhat and the rain had stopped, it was still heavily overcast with gigantic swells. Captain Adolf Ahrens decided to issue orders for the crew to commence painting the ship.

It was difficult, but not impossible, to paint the entire ship while making 27.5 knots through heavy seas. The men attacked their work with renewed spirit, the hard physical activity finally giving vent to the emotions built up over the past several days. Most of the crew had merely been passive receivers of the earth-shattering news of their homeland's plunge into war. Except for the engineers, radio operators, and the galley staff, who were immersed in their normal work, most in the passenger service divisions had been idle since departing New York, at least compared to their usual crossings. The challenge to paint the ship while at high speed in marginal weather called for precise concentration and eased some of the tension.

As they went about their work, some began to sing, which pleased Captain Ahrens and First Officer Eric Warning to no end. "See how they bend to the task," Warning had said proudly to Ahrens, as they watched the crew clamor over the superstructure, splashing gray paint over the once brilliant white, yellow, and black steel. The spectacle of scores of men hanging precariously on boson's chairs, perching on ledges high above the sun deck level, and swinging over the side with paint applicators rigged on long poles was impressive indeed.

Wilhelm Bohling recalled:

> The scene looked a little comic. For us to completely repaint the ship under these conditions was a matter of great urgency and eventually pride. Until this point, most of us in the passenger service divisions had been unable to contribute to the situation,

Painting *Bremen* at sea on
September 3, 1939 (Hanns
Tschira—courtesy of Deutsches
Schiffahrtsmuseum, Bremerhaven)

Female crew serving coffee
on deck to crew painting
Bremen gray. (Hanns Tschira—
courtesy of Deutsches Schiffahrtsmuseum, Bremerhaven)

but without passengers many of us were idle. We tackled the painting as if our very lives depended on finishing in time to fool any approaching warship. I shall never forget the way the ship was transformed over a matter of mere hours into a hulk of gray steaming through the high swells. We learned later from those who observed us that we were barely visible with the new disguise, especially in the gray background of the dismal weather which seemed to be following us along.

As *Bremen* continued to run northeast, the crew painted until they gradually ran out of daylight. Many of the men hung in bosun's chairs on the sides of the huge stacks, while others rode down the sides in lifeboats painting the hull. Since the seas were from the northwest, the port bow rode up the swells neatly with minimum rolling and only the occasional crash of white foam over the bow. The painting went on despite the swells; although it would not win any award for neatness, it was effective. They splattered paint everywhere, but got most of it on the ship despite spilling large amounts into the sea. By the end of the day, the men had converted the ship into a hulk of haze gray, resembling an oversized destroyer. They learned that, since the declaration of war, their ship was now subordinate to the navy instead of Norddeutscher Lloyd and the Ministry of Transport.

Unknown to any aboard *Bremen* at the time, while they were players in the drama unfolding in the western Atlantic, an action took place that same day on the European end of the shipping transit lanes that would change the scope of the sea war over the coming years.

North Atlantic, in the waters west of Ireland
September 3, 1939

On Sunday, September 3, the German submarine *U-30*, commanded by Senior Lieutenant Fritz-Julius Lemp, was patrolling the waters west of Ireland. Lemp was born in Tsingtau, China, to a German businessman, and was a member of the Flensburg Naval Academy class of 1931. He had taken command of *U-30* in November 1938.

Early that morning, Lemp received a report from the German Naval High Command that a state of war existed between Germany and Britain and that he was authorized to commence covert offensive operations at sea. At 7:30 that evening, when the submarine was about three hundred miles northwest of Malin Head, Ireland, a ship approached that they could not identify in the dark.

It was the British-flagged Atlantic Donaldson liner *Athenia*, approaching from the east. Having left Liverpool the day before with a total of 1,410 passengers and crew, it was bound for Montreal. The ship had gained a reputation as a cozy family ship and had been fully booked with passengers because a number of the largest liners had already been pulled from service for conversion to troop ships. Among the passengers were six socialites from Houston, Texas; the mayor's wife of Saratoga Springs, New York; and more than 150 refugees from central Europe who had fled the Nazis and gained visas for entry to the United States. Captain James Cook, the master of the 14,000-ton ship, was steering a zigzag course with all topside lights extinguished and navigation lights dimmed. Because of the situation, the cautious master had ordered an abandon-ship drill soon after departing port. *Athenia* steamed westward at 16 knots, just two hundred miles west of the Hebrides.

The lookout in the submarine's conning tower sighted the approaching ship and reported to the captain. In the darkness, Lemp observed her form and determined, by her appearance, absence of lights and steering of a zigzag course, that she must have been a British Hilfskreuzer (a commerce raider or naval auxiliary). In the first action of the sea war, less than twenty hours after Britain and Germany commenced hostilities, Lemp intended to fire a spread of two G7 torpedoes, weighing 617 pounds each. Although the first fired smoothly, the second failed to clear the tube and began running—a jammed hot torpedo. The initial torpedo ran true and struck the passenger ship's port beam, causing a large explosion and rapid flooding of several holds. Meanwhile, Lemp immediately took U-30 deep to try to clear the jammed torpedo. After several attempts the torpedo cleared the tube and ran an erratic course before exploding in two bursts. These two explosions were later described by witnesses aboard *Athenia* as Lemp's deck gun firing at the listing passenger ship.[1]

Athenia swung heavily to port but remained afloat with a thirty-degree list for fourteen hours, plenty of time to wire for help. *U-30*'s radioman George Högel intercepted the stricken vessel's distress call, allowing Lemp to positively identify the ship for the first time as *Athenia*. They surfaced and lingered until first light, watching passengers, including women and children, leave the ship in lifeboats. The scene of the sinking and rescue took on a tinge of comedy when an unusually large pod of whales appeared and in the lights of emergency flares plunged and frolicked amid the survivors struggling in the icy waters. *U-30* finally departed the scene when the British destroyers *Electro* and *Escort* arrived to render assistance, together with the Norwegian motor vessel *Knute Nelson*, the American merchantman *City of Flint*,[2] and the Swedish yacht *Southern Cross*. In total, 1,305 people were rescued. Of the 118 lives lost were sixteen children and twenty-two Americans. With this being the first attack without warning on a merchant ship in World War II, it was initially interpreted by the Allies as the beginning of a German policy of unrestricted war at sea.

SS *Bremen*
North Atlantic
September 3, 1939

One of Radio Officer Kurt Gerstung's telegraphers had intercepted *Athenia*'s SOS and reported it to Captain Ahrens. At first, the *Bremen* radiomen had interpreted the signal as emanating from a ship close by, which caused a great deal of commotion in the wheelhouse. Gerstung had run to the bridge with the report that an unidentified passenger ship had been torpedoed. The radio operator had misread the position sent by *Athenia*'s clear request for assistance. Instead of copying the correct longitude, he had erred by placing the position roughly fifty miles east of *Bremen*'s position. The confusion was compounded when it was believed to be a German ship sending an English-based report. When it had all been sorted out by First Officer Warning, it was obvious that *Athenia*, a British ship, was sinking more than seven hundred miles to the east of *Bremen*'s track. Making a note in their log, Ahrens continued steaming ahead, but the alarm had an ominous ring to it and caused all aboard *Bremen* to begin thinking earnestly about the threat of British submarines this side of the Atlantic.

Berlin and London
September 3, 1939

The criticism of the Germans commenced immediately in the world press. By signing the Anglo-German Naval Treaty of 1935, Germany tacitly accepted provisions in the prior Naval Treaty of 1930, which forbade signatory powers from attacking merchant ships without warning and first providing for the evacuation of the passengers and crew to safety.[3]

The sinking was reported quickly in the press, but was not clearly attributed to a German submarine attack until an investigation was completed fifteen weeks later. The accounts by survivors proved too confused and contradictory to confirm a submarine attack, although a dozen eyewitnesses swore they saw a submarine of undetermined nationality on the surface in the light of the fires following the explosion. The master, Captain James Cook, had stated following his rescue and arrival in Galway, "There's no doubt about it. My ship was torpedoed. The torpedo went right through the ship to the engine room and completely wrecked the galley. Passengers were at dinner when the torpedo struck the ship and the explosion killed several."

The German navy denied responsibility, initially in good faith as they couldn't believe Lemp would have defied standing orders to spare passenger ships. Lemp was clearly aware of the constraints on sinking unarmed ships in the Hague Convention and in the various naval treaties and had received the most recent instructions to refrain from attacking passenger ships and French ships of all types. His senior, the commander of the Second U-boat Flotilla, Senior Lieutenant Werner Hartman, had made these instructions clear to all of his skippers. However, German propaganda minister Joseph Goebbels heatedly denied the sinking was a result of a U-boat attack and claimed initially that the ship had probably hit a drifting mine and then later that it was a British conspiracy to pull the United States into the war against Germany. An irate Adolf Hitler immediately ordered that no further attacks be made against unarmed passenger ships or troop transports.

Although Lemp purposely failed to report the sinking by radio, he reported personally to the submarine force commander in chief, Admiral Karl Dönitz, when he returned to Wilhelmshaven on September 28, thus informing the German leadership for the first time what had actually happened. Lemp was flown to Berlin and made to report personally to the commander in chief of the Germany navy, Admiral Erich Raeder, that he in fact had violated orders. By this time, however, the propaganda machinery was in full motion and Lemp was returned to his boat with the instructions to change the page in his log. He deleted all references to *Athenia* and changed the position of the encounter to match that of a fictitious merchant ship. These changes were made even though the logs were routinely marked as secret. They were, however, used as training aids at the submarine training school in Wilhelmshaven. By falsifying the logs, the true act was officially relegated to oblivion and the Germans successfully hid the truth until after the war. This had been the act of one man, and the sinking had dashed the British hopes that Germany would only gradually return to the former habit of unrestricted U-boat warfare as they had in World War I. Thus, it precipitated the British return to the use of the convoy as the only sure method of defending against unrestricted warfare at sea.

The following chronology of the German "Sink on Sight" policy is repeated here to enable the reader to understand the *Bremen's* position in the incidents to take place in the near future.[4]

September 4, 1939—The orders issued immediately following the *Athenia* sinking read: "By order of the Führer, and until further orders no hostile action will be taken against passenger liners even when sailing under escort."

September 23, 1939—"The Führer agrees to action without warning to be taken against any merchant ship definitely established as enemy (excluding passenger ships)."

September 24, 1939—The Führer authorized all submarines to use "armed force" against any allied merchant ship broadcasting the submarine alarm, "SSS"; such ships were subject to "seizure and sinking, . . . rescue of crews to be attempted."

September 24, 1939—"Allied passenger ships carrying 120 people or less (and thus presumed to be mainly cargo ships) could be sunk." A request by the submarine commander in chief Dönitz to sink on sight all armed ships and all blackened-out ships sailing close to the British Isles had been denied.

October 16, 1939—Hitler revised the rules again to allow attack of any enemy merchant ship, British or French, except large passenger liners. He agreed to the torpedoing of passenger ships showing no lights and in convoy after warning. The protocol remained in force for all neutral ships not in convoy and not blacked out. If they were deemed to be carrying contraband they could be sunk albeit assuring rescue of crew. Ships of Italy, Japan, Spain, Ireland, Russia, and the United States could not be molested.[5]

February 3, 1940—"The Führer declares it permissible to sink passenger ships sailing without lights even if showing only navigational lights." This is believed to have been precipitated by the encounter by the German battleship *Scharnhorst* and the British commerce raider HMS *Rawalpindi*, a converted passenger ship mounting eight 6-inch guns.[6]

On September 12, 1942, *U-156* torpedoed the old 19,965-ton British Cunard White Star Line passenger liner SS *Laconia* in mid-Atlantic, 550 miles southwest of Cape Palma (Northwest Africa). The liner was steaming a zigzag northwesterly course at 16 knots, with lights doused, and was armed with two 4.7-inch naval guns, six 3-inch antiaircraft guns, six 1½-inch antiaircraft guns, and four rapid-fire Bofors. The ship sank, leaving nearly 811 British military and civilian passengers, including women and children, plus 1,800

Italian army prisoners of war foundering in shark-infested waters. Before sinking, the liner sent off an SSS report signaling that she has been attacked by a German submarine. Upon observing the casualties scrambling for safety and learning of the POWs, *U-156's* commander, Werner Hartenstein, reported to Admiral Dönitz and gained permission to remain and render all assistance possible. Dönitz then ordered other U-boats to the area to help. *U-507* arrived with the Italian submarine *Cappellini*, and while the three submarines were busily pulling survivors from the water an Allied B-24 Liberator bomber, never positively identified as American or British, attacked the rescue submarines, then marked with red cross emblems, scoring near misses and killing some surviving *Laconia* passengers in lifeboats. Hartenstein reported the incident, and Dönitz flew into a rage and issued the infamous order prohibiting his submarines from taking any surviving crew of ships they had attacked. The order was subsequently used against Dönitz during his trial in Nuremburg for war crimes. Eventually two Vichy French warships from North Africa, the destroyers *Dumont-d'Urville* and *Annamite*, joined the submarines at the rescue scene. The damage had been done, however, and the no-rescue order was enforced, although many U-boat commanders ignored the order.

The *Athenia* sinking, on the first day of the declared war, however, proved to be just the first of many attacks on passengers ships and transports to take place over the next five and one-half years by both sides. The most infamous was the sinking of the SS *Laconia*. Indeed, the loss of life in such sinkings would soar from the 118 lost on *Athenia* to the heavy losses to follow, including the most lives ever lost in a single sinking, when the German passenger ship *Wilhelm Gustloff* was torpedoed in the Baltic in January 1945 by the Soviet submarine *S-13*. The commander of that submarine, Captain Second Rank A. I. Marinesko, was later awarded a high decoration for causing the loss of more than seven thousand lives, mostly refugees: women, children, and seriously wounded soldiers being evacuated from the marauding Red Army. The next month another Soviet submarine torpedoed the German ship *Steuben* in the Baltic, killing thirty-five hundred wounded

Wehrmacht soldiers. In the final month of the war another five thousand refugees were lost when the freighter *Goya*, part of the fleet attempting to rescue citizens from the approaching Soviet Army, was sunk by yet a third Russian submarine in the Baltic.

The *U-30* commander's action against *Athenia* in September 1939, among other things, contributed to the severe limitation of operational autonomy of German submarine commanders throughout the Atlantic war. This clearly led to the eventual defeat of the German submarine fleet, when the Allies began to exploit the intricate German communications command and control system. This incident would also relate to the fate of *Bremen* less than three months later. Lemp, *U-30's* commanding officer, later received the Knight's Cross for his subsequent action in other submarines and was lost aboard *U-112* in September 1944.

SS *Bremen*
West of Nova Scotia
September 3, 1939

Captain Ahrens ordered the crew to move most of the three thousand passenger mattresses topside from the empty cabins and spread them around as shrapnel protection in case of air attack. They certainly weren't needed belowdecks in the empty cabins. The presence on the promenade deck and all upper decks of the inflammable material ready to ignite, the mattresses, and the newly reprovisioned lifeboats reminded all of the seriousness of the ship's situation. The crew were now ready, within an instant of sighting a British warship, to scuttle their beloved ship and home, and to make for the lifeboats, a sobering thought!

Headquarters, British Home Fleet
North Atlantic
September 4, 1939

The British Home Fleet commander in chief, Admiral Charles Forbes, had thrown up a blockade of combatants between Iceland and the Faeroe Islands to intercept returning German merchant

Inflammable material ready to ignite was placed on the promenade and all upper decks. (Hanns Tschira—courtesy of Deutsches Schiffahrtsmuseum, Bremerhaven)

ships. Under his command were two battleship squadrons (*Nelson*, *Ramillies*, *Rodney*, *Royal Oak*, and *Royal Sovereign*), one battle cruiser squadron (*Hood* and *Repulse*), the aircraft carrier *Ark Royal*, the Eighteenth Cruiser Squadron (*Effingham*, *Emerald*, *Cardiff*, and *Dundee*), the Seventh Cruiser Squadron (*Diomede*, *Dragon*, *Calypso*, and *Caledonia*), and the Eighth Destroyer Flotilla (eight Tribal-class and nine F-class destroyers) searching between Scotland, Iceland, and Norway, with the mission to scoop up all homeward-bound German merchant ships, especially *Bremen*.

On September 4, the German freighter *Hannah Böge*, loaded with a cargo of wood pulp, was sunk by the British destroyer HMS *Somali*, part of Admiral Forbes's blocking force, while patrolling forty miles southeast of Iceland. Another British combatant group, called the "Humber Force" (cruisers *Southampton* and *Glasgow* with eight destroyers), was crossing the Atlantic west of the Hebrides searching for *Bremen*, the flagship of the German merchant fleet, on the anticipated normal return track from New York.

All the lifeboats had been reprovisioned to prepare for what might come.
(Hanns Tschira—courtesy of Deutsches Schiffahrtsmuseum, Bremerhaven)

SS *Bremen*
Denmark Strait
September 4, 1939

To the great pleasure of the *Bremen* crew, they heard that same day that a radio broadcast from Paris announced they had already been captured by the British and were being brought to Portsmouth for internment. Captain Ahrens also learned that *Bremen* was included as one of many German merchantmen in Operation "Basis North," which called for all ships in the North Atlantic unable to reach German or other neutral ports, with the exception of the United States, to enter Murmansk. Eighteen merchant ships eventually did so before the end of September.

After the camouflage paint job was completed, the main concern aboard *Bremen* centered on avoiding possible icebergs, even though it was not the season for such encounters. The seawater temperature was dropping alarmingly; by the time the ship reached the Denmark Strait between Iceland and Greenland, the water was only a few degrees above freezing. Again, Captain Ahrens increased the lookouts and implored them to be more watchful, particularly during the lengthening hours of darkness. The long nights passed without seeing a single ship. As the heavy overcast continued, there were several false alarms when lookouts shouted reports of contacts, which turned out to be imagined images of icebergs, other ships, and airplanes, which usually turned out to be brief star sightings.

During the midwatch on the morning of September 4, they had a terrible scare. They were steaming along at 27.5 knots in the pitch dark, with overcast skies and diminishing seas, when suddenly the watch in the radio room called in a panic stating an unidentified ship had just broadcast an iceberg sighting at a position that plotted only twenty miles from *Bremen*'s current position. The first officer on watch called Captain Ahrens, who immediately appeared on the bridge.

"Where away?" Ahrens asked, trying to accustom his eyes to the darkness on the bridge. The watch officer began explaining the radio intercept. Ahrens calmly listened, then said, "Stop engines."

The watch ordered all engines stopped. It was an unsettling experience to stop suddenly after steaming at high speed for several days. They listened to the engines slow and then stop. The quiet was uncanny. First Officer Warning appeared on the wing of the bridge, and all hands on watch strained their eyes. Minutes passed and then half an hour. The ship rolled in the swell now in the deathly quiet and still they could see nothing.

Radio Officer Gerstung queried the ship that called in the sighting but received no response. Then suddenly the port lookout reported a light off the port bow, fairly close. All eyes on the bridge and the lookout stations strained to make out the contact. They saw a small, dim light fairly low in the water, appearing to be within about four miles. The ship remained still in the swell, the only sound the purring of the forced draft blowers. No lights shone on the ship. Nevertheless, Ahrens ordered the leading first officer to tour the topside decks to ensure no lights were showing. He left the bridge with a quartermaster and after twenty minutes returned.

"No lights visible aboard, sir," Warning reported.

The bridge team watched as the dim light drifted across their bow, still unable to discern its size or source. At first they thought it might have been a merchant ship, but then it grew more obvious and must have been a small fishing craft, as it seemed to dance on the swells, which by now had diminished to about nine to twelve feet high. The *Bremen* lookouts watched in silence as the contact drifted away to starboard, then disappeared. Nevertheless, they wallowed for more than an hour before Ahrens gave the order again to get under way, slowly at first, then gradually increasing speed to 27 knots. It was still several hours before the horizon would brighten sufficiently to see a contact within two miles. Captain Ahrens had decided it was better to make time while they were still within reach of the British cruisers. He had no idea if the iceberg sighting had been bogus nor the source of the light.

"We will have to take our chances," Ahrens said, then returned to his sea cabin. Nothing more was ever heard about that sighting, yet the lookouts continued to scan the dim seas before them and held their breath each time the bow lifted and fell back into the seas with a cushioning shower of spray. It was growing bitterly cold.

Bremen passed Jan Mayen Island on September 5 and sighted not a single other ship. As the captain took the ship north of North Cape and entered the Barents Sea, the air temperature grew bitterly cold. Late the next morning they had another scare. Seaman Heinz Slominski recalled, "The mast lookout reported a ship on the starboard beam approaching fast. Then as its form began to take shape out of the thick mist, it transformed into a warship with a large bow wave. We thought this was finally the end. The captain ordered all hands to action stations. We'd have to activate our scuttling plan. I had feared this moment for days, and now it was going to happen. I could not imagine setting fire to the piles of mattresses and then abandoning ship into the frigid sea."

After arriving at his assigned post for scuttling, Slominski noticed the figure of a young sailor standing in the corner of the promenade deck near the Hunting Salon, a first-class lounge and ornate dining room used only for special parties or for men as a smoking lounge. The salon was not a large room but was low-ceilinged and full of dark wood furniture. Two of its walls displayed arrays of stuffed wild animal heads such as deer, elk, boar, and mountain goats, while a huge Gobelin tapestry covered the remaining two walls. The decor was plush, the color scheme dark maroon, and the overstuffed leather chairs gave off a conservative clublike aura. It was a place where few passengers gathered, mostly older men who sat after dinner for brandy and cigars.

Slominski immediately recognized the young seaman as Gustav Schmidt, also from the bosun's deck force. Slominski thought the young man was a little strange, and had observed him several times near the inflammables, seeming to study them. He had seen him rearrange some of the piles. Schmidt had been among the working party that had originally gathered the mattresses and inflammables after leaving New York, and he often hovered around that area, looking strangely intent on ensuring the material was still in good order, ready to ignite, and had not shifted in the motions of the heavy seas. The starboard-most forward part of that section of the A deck was his cleaning post, so he had good reason for being there, yet Slominski sensed there was something peculiar about this young man's fascination with that area. He watched the seaman for some time, then left as he was called away to help prepare the ship's motor launch for entering port.

"If she's British, we're going to dash into territorial waters," Captain Ahrens said, as he lowered his glasses after studying the approaching contact. Then suddenly, he transformed into a bundle of energy. "All engines full ahead, rpm for twenty-nine knots." Ahrens picked up the pilothouse telephone and dialed main engineering control. "Mister Müller, stand by for full power; we have an enemy warship approaching. I want all you can give." He returned the handset into its cradle with a click. "Mister Warning, how far to the nearest Russian waters?"

"Fifty miles, to Soviet waters, sir," the first officer replied after glancing at the chart. "We can make it." The ship began to shudder as she turned directly toward the coast to outrun the approaching ship.

"If we can just make Soviet waters, we'll be home free. Can't be that far. By this morning's eight o'clock position we were less than sixty miles from the Kola Peninsula." Ahrens spoke calmly, as if there was nothing amiss.

The tension rose as vibrations increased and the two ships began a race to the south; the separation was five miles and closing. Most of the crew had not noticed the contact, yet they gathered by the sudden acceleration that something was up. Then the word spread and the crewmen found ways to glance out toward the contact. It was a frightening moment. After coming all that way they had finally been discovered! What a pity, and how would it all turn out? Would they have to execute the drill they had planned? Would they actually muster at their abandon ship stations, prepare the lifeboats, and then board them as the party of designated bosunmates ran down both sides of the promenade deck, pouring gasoline on the mattresses and combustible furniture piled in clumps along the deck, before returning to the others in their lifeboats? The last man, the leading bosun, would run by each pile and ignite it with his torch before descending to the lifeboat deck. Engineers belowdecks would scurry up the long escape trunks as designated men opened the sea cocks on the lower engine room levels, then scramble up the ladders to the lifeboat deck.

These were terrible moments. They feared the worst. Was it a British combatant? Would the warship fire first? Would shells explode on deck, sending giant shards of shrapnel in all directions? Could Leading Doctor Anton Fischer deal with combat wounds? Where would they treat the injured if there were many? When would the officers leave the bridge? The anxiety and tension grew as the contact neared. The decks vibrated as the propellers surged ahead. Black smoke poured out of both stacks. The ship must have been nearing 30 knots. White spray flew from the stem as the bow cut the waves, sending a fine salt spray as high as the bridge window. It was cold, yet the spray was not frozen.

Given the black smoke pouring from her stacks, the approaching contact was also making high speed. She must be a warship to be making speeds close to *Bremen*'s, Ahrens thought.

"Four and a half miles, steady bearing, range closing, sir! She's trying to cut us off." The first mate stood, feet planted apart as if bracing for impact. Every man on the bridge watched in silence as the destroyer, belching more black smoke, began drifting toward *Bremen's* bow, then seemed to turn inward toward her. "The leading bosun reports ready to carry out emergency destruction and ignite the promenade deck." The words spilled off Warning's tongue before he realized the gravity of his statement. Would this be the last of the proud ship? Were they really going to do themselves in and head for the boats? The first officer glanced at Captain Ahrens.

The captain seemed almost amused. "Well, if we collide we'll hardly feel it, fifty-two thousand tons versus probably two thousand at most; they will be destroyed in one smashing moment, as long as they don't launch something at us first." The range was now closing at a rate of fifty miles an hour as the ships bore down on each other.

Warning stood motionless studying the warship with his glasses, then suddenly spoke calmly but loud enough for the whole bridge watch to hear. "It's an old style minelaying destroyer, Novik type, pre-1914 vintage . . ." then, "it's Russian all right, a very old Russian," he said firmly, holding his ten-power Zeiss glasses to his eyes. He turned to Ahrens, who was also staring through binoculars at the rapidly growing contact.

"I agree," Ahrens said. "But let's make sure." He turned to the pilothouse and barked, "Bosun have the signalmen hoist the Soviet national ensign from the main truck. It will signal them that we intend to enter their waters." Within a few minutes a Soviet national flag appeared on a halyard sliding up *Bremen's* starboard yardarm of the mast.

It was a tense few minutes as all hands topside watched the menacing destroyer draw closer to the ship. Some of the crew looked at the piles of combustible materials on the promenade deck imagining them bursting into flame while they ran for the lifeboats. The water temperature was hovering about six degrees centigrade above zero, and no one envied the thought of having to

The Soviet destroyer *Bremen* encountered in the Kola Bay on September 6, 1939. (Hanns Tschira—courtesy of Deutsches Schiffahrtsmuseum, Bremerhaven)

be immersed in the chilling foam. Finally, a lookout on the bridge called out, "Soviet naval ensign flying aloft!"

The relief on the bridge was immediately apparent. Then everyone noticed a rapidly blinking light on the destroyer. "Have Seaman Ostersen report to the bridge," Warning called to the bosun on watch. Ingo Ostersen was one of the ship's Russian speakers. "They're signaling us by flashing light."

The destroyer swept by the starboard side, turned abruptly, spewing foam and spray and heeling way over as if ready to capsize, then slowed and fell in at *Bremen*'s speed broad on the bow. The ship was clocking nearly 30 knots. The Russian ship was obviously pouring all she had to keep up with *Bremen*, as black smoke poured from her two ancient stacks.

"Quartermaster, slow to twenty knots; don't want her to stress herself trying to keep up," the captain said, smiling triumphantly. Immediately, *Bremen*'s four screws slowed and she settled in with her new escort. First Officer Warning walked aft briskly toward the signal bridge and returned with Seaman Ostersen in tow.

Ostersen said, "Sir, they're sending, 'You are approaching Soviet waters, what are your intentions?'" Everyone on the bridge was greatly relieved.

The captain replied immediately, "Answer, 'German passenger ship *Bremen*. We desire to enter Murmansk. Send a pilot.'"

There was a brief pause and then the destroyer answered curtly, "Follow me."

"Good. Send back that we are prepared to follow into port." Ahrens was relieved. The Russians were obviously expecting them; no doubt there had been some communications between Berlin and Moscow. Ahrens thought, How important we have become, a real pawn in the relations between two major powers!

As *Bremen* followed the destroyer, the crew soon sighted the ragged gray coastline of the Rybachi Peninsula, all different shades of gray flecked with white. The sky was also a heavy gray and the whole scene looked frigid and unwelcome. The Germans soon found that to be synonymous with the way the Russians would act toward them the entire time they were in Russian waters.

8

Soviet Support

SS *Bremen*
The Kola Bay
Wednesday, September 6, 1939

Marquis de Custine, the famed French writer, visited Russia in 1839, one hundred years before *Bremen* pulled safely into the northern Russian waters off Murmansk. In ironic retrospection, he described the arrival formalities that seemed identical to those the *Bremen* crew observed in September 1939:

> [His passenger ship] was at once boarded by an army of customs officials—and there ensued, throughout the hours of the morning, an interminable ordeal of inspection in the grand salon of the cabins. [This caused Custine to observe blandly, as his first impression of Russia, that in the administration of that country a concern for the minutiae did not exclude disorder.][1]

Bremen gradually came to a halt with the Russian destroyer keeping station on the beam at 550 yards. The crew watched her lower a launch from her port side as both ships drifted in the swells. Captain Adolf Ahrens was astounded to see that the destroyer had a pulling whaleboat and not a motor launch. Ahrens smiled, "I haven't seen one of those on the high seas since my sailing years." The scene was suddenly interrupted by a loud pop and hissing. The boiler safety valves suddenly lifted on the forward stack with a roar.

"Poor Mister Müller's precious steam is venting to the atmosphere. Mister Warning," Ahrens said, his good humor showing that he was relieved. "Please pass my congratulations to the chief engineer, and apologize for stopping so abruptly. Tell him we clocked nearly thirty knots. Well done to all those belowdecks." The captain smiled broadly. It was obvious that he was greatly pleased with events.

Erwin Schulwitz, the ship's SA Bordsturmführer group leader, suddenly materialized on the wing of the bridge. He seldom ventured that high above deck. All the officers were aware that the captain had as little to do with the SA men as possible, and it was felt generally that he resented their presence aboard. He did not need their help gaining the absolute loyalty of the crew, and he paid little heed to their obnoxious political ranting.

"Well, Mister Schulwitz, good to see you topside. Ever been in these waters before?" the captain asked in a good natured voice, still watching the whaleboat approach.

"Yes, Herr Captain, once starting in 1915 as a prisoner of war. I and about 50,000 other German prisoners helped lay the track for the Murmansk-Leningrad railroad for two years. Didn't think I'd ever be back in this hell hole." He glowered over the rail as the gray and white landmass heaved into view. "Always hated this place and these people."

"Please, Mister Schulwitz," Ahrens scolded mildly, "they're our allies now. We must speak respectfully. Indeed, they hold our very safety in their hands." The short, stocky Schulwitz remained silent while gazing out at the bleak terrain. The two men watched as the Russian whaleboat crossed the short distance between the ships. It seemed ironic in that day and age to see a warship using a whaleboat with a dozen oarsmen rather than a motor launch. But they looked smart pulling away together on their oars and were obviously well trained. There were four officers in the whaleboat.

Schulwitz and the captain stood together watching as the Russians scrambled up the accommodation ladder and disappeared through *Bremen*'s yawning gangway. The first officer automatically met them and escorted the officers to the bridge. Seaman Ostersen stood ready for interpreting.

Captain Ahrens shook hands with the visitors, who seemed mightily impressed with the grandeur of the ship, their eyes darting around the bridge and topside spaces. The senior, who wore the three stripes of a captain second rank, spoke first. He introduced himself as a liaison officer from the Soviet Northern Fleet Staff and a second officer as a representative of the Fleet Political Directorate. Seaman Ostersen came forward and began to interpret, when suddenly it became apparent the political officer spoke decent English. The visitors asked to see a chart so they could point out the assigned anchorage. They also reported that there were already a number of German ships anchored in the outer harbor of Murmansk and more were expected.

After some time discussing the channel depth and width, Captain Ahrens gave the order to follow the destroyer into the deep Kola Bay with the Russians still aboard. The crew could see that the terrain was incredibly rocky and covered with the stunted growth of the taiga. There was little color, merely different shades of gray and white. They steamed past what the chart showed as Severomorsk, an inlet and deep bay to the east, which the Russian officers indicated was for Russian military ships only. Then, as they drew near to Murmansk, they were assigned an anchorage about three miles out from the city. But when they looked for signs of it, they saw only a group of wooden buildings that looked more like a village than a city of 150,000 inhabitants. Murmansk is Russia's sole northern port that remains ice-free year round as the last gasps of the warm Gulf Stream sweep around North Cape and heat the coast until diffusing its higher temperature into the Barents Sea. During World War I, Murmansk was nothing but a few hovels and a fishing port, but had grown when the railroad was constructed, thanks to the exertion of German prisoners and the labor of the seemingly endless supply of political convicts.

There were at least a dozen other foreign ships in the spacious outer harbor, some of which they were told were German, but the mist and poor visibility kept them from being identified that first day. As soon as *Bremen* was anchored, three cutters approached and made the starboard side, where the bosuns had rigged an accommodation ladder. Then an unusually large number of officials poured aboard. There were naval officers in blue, police in gray, and customs and passport control officers in brown uniforms.

First Officer Eric Warning sat with the group of naval officers at a table in the first-class passenger lounge. The Russian officials' initial request was that all radio transmitting antennas had to be removed. There would be no communicating by foreign ships while in Soviet waters. Soviet regulations, they said several times, as if repeating the fact would make it more acceptable. Poor Kurt Gerstung and his radiomen would be restricted to receiving incoming messages only. The Russians explained that the area was a military zone and no foreign ships were permitted to communicate.

Next, the Russian officials explained that all personal and ship's cameras had to be collected and locked up and sealed in a central compartment. There was no photography allowed anywhere in the area. The ship's photographer, Hanns Tschira, who was normally busy with the passengers' personal photography, as well as with his newly assigned tasks for the Abwehr, had been meticulously recording the crossing ever since the dramatic departure from New York. At first, he was crestfallen to learn of the ban, but later recovered when he discovered that one of the Russian customs officials was a photo enthusiast. When away from the other Russian officers, the official produced his own Leica camera from beneath layers of his parka and proudly showed it to Tschira. When Tschira in turn showed the Russian his photo laboratory, which was well stocked with all the latest processing equipment, enlargers, and a chemical drying room, the Russian fairly gasped in delight. He quietly asked if during their stay, which he understood might prove to be extended, he might bring some of his work aboard to process in Tschira's palace. Tschira gladly obliged and was told that he, too, could continue to use his lab while in port, but of course, only with old exposures. No new photos could be taken.

There followed an endless series of elaborate sessions lasting well into the night, during which the Soviet passport and customs control officials sat at tables set up in the passenger lounge. One by one, the Russian officials positively identified each of the 950 *Bremen* crewmen and crewwomen. As they were brought in to be identified, each was required to bring his or her personal record books to verify the photos with those of the personal passports.

After completing that process, which took nearly ten hours, the customs officers insisted on inspecting the ship from stem to stern. This inspection, compared to the going-over they had by the U.S. customs inspectors in New York, was more comical than thorough.

The Russian inspectors seemed enthralled by the fine accommodations aboard, the elaborate dining facilities, and especially the modern galley equipment. They stroked the sides of the gleaming silver boilers and admired the banks of electric ovens and large, free-standing food mixers. Their eyes widened when they beheld the gymnasium where the very latest exercise equipment gleamed in splendor obviously never before seen by these Russian officials. One sheepishly asked the passenger trainer, Wolfram Rieter, if he might briefly mount the vaulting horse. And there, in the brightly lit space amid the modern gym equipment perched the brown-uniformed Russian customs official with a wide, gold tooth–bearing grin, until he was ushered quickly away by one of his colleagues. It seemed to the *Bremen* crew that these men had never laid eyes on such luxuries.

The arrival procedures finally ended and the captain ordered that the crew be allowed to celebrate with extra beer rations that evening. They all felt greatly relieved, having entered a secure anchorage after six days and thirteen hours of uncertainty in the newly declared war. The future lay like an unopened book before them, but they had learned to take life one day at a time.

The morning following their arrival, Radio Officer Gerstung received a message for the captain from the director of Norddeutscher Lloyd in Bremen. He quickly read it and knew he had something special in his hands. He grabbed his cap, but before leaving the radio room he paused, then went to the telephone and dialed First Officer Warning's cabin.

"Warning."

"Good morning Mister Warning." Gerstung found it difficult to contain his excitement. "I just received a personal message from the head of Norddeutscher Lloyd in Bremen, and it's very good news for the captain. I think perhaps you might wish to be there when I deliver it."

The celebratory dinner for *Bremen*'s crew the day after arriving in Murmansk on September 6, 1939. (Hanns Tschira—courtesy of Deutsches Schiffahrtsmuseum, Bremerhaven)

"Very well, Mister Gerstung, I trust your judgment." Warning, like Captain Ahrens, fully relied on the radio officer, who seemed never to miss the right solution to events. "The captain is having breakfast in his inport salon. I'll meet you there."

Gerstung was waiting outside the captain's salon when Warning approached. He showed him the message, which Gerstung had attached neatly to a clipboard with a cover showing the Norddeutscher Lloyd crest emblazoned in blue with the anchor crossed with the key to the city of Bremen; that same emblem was welded to the gracefully rounded prow atop the ship's slender stem. The stumpy SA Bordsturmführer Schulwitz had given a stack of new correspondence covers to the radio officer to use for routing his important signals, a design with the Nazi eagle gripping a wreath with the swastika centered on a red, white, and black background. Gerstung had conveniently misplaced those covers and continued to use the old Norddeutscher Lloyd crest.

Warning read the message. "Good call, Gerstung," he grinned. "This will be pleasant."

The two officers entered the salon. Captain Ahrens sat at a table next to his desk. Before him lay a silver tray with his breakfast neatly laid out: one boiled egg, a piece of bacon, a few slices of sausage, cheese, toast, and coffee. The china was white with the Norddeutscher Lloyd crest in blue, the identical china used in the first-class dining room. Ahrens beckoned the two officers to sit on the red leather-covered sofa next to his desk. "Coffee, gentlemen?" He patted his mouth with the corner of a white linen napkin.

Gerstung thought how elegant it must be to be a master of such a ship and to live in those graceful settings, despite having just evaded the Royal Navy and now hunkered in uncertainty in a foreign port, little more than prisoners of the Soviets.

The first officer handed Ahrens the message board, "Congratulations, Captain," he said with a smile.

The captain took the board, flipped up the blue-and-white cover, and read:

September 7, 1939

For Captain Adolf Ahrens:

You have, through extraordinary leadership and fellowship, brought the lead ship of the German merchant fleet to safety through the threat of the enemy. Lloyds is proud of you and the crew of its flagship. In grateful recognition we name you Commodore of our fleet.

Norddeutscher Lloyd

Rudolf Firle[2]

"Well, ah, hmmm." Ahrens was taken aback and blushed deeply in front of his two subordinates. "Well, now, we must get to work finding out how long we stay in this relative secure environment." Ahrens was not one to dwell on his personal accolades. "We had better get together with the purser to determine exactly how long our rations will hold out and what we need to order locally, if there is anything here to purchase. Oh, yes, and ask Mister Müller to join us at nine A.M. in the chart house with the purser to discuss provisions and fuel." The captain drained his coffee cup and carefully poured another. "By our seniority, we have become not only commodore of all the German ships here, but also of their source of supplies."

"Captain, if I may, I would like to post this message of your promotion on the crew's bulletin board. Oh, and one other thing." The first officer rarely let a detail slip by him. "Our good Bordsturmführer Comrade Schulwitz has requested that his Bortsturm people stand extra security watches topside since there are two British freighters anchored here as well. He feels they may be a threat to the German ships."

The captain thought for a moment. "Of course, let them stand extra watches, but also assure Mister Schulwitz that I'm sure the two British ships will pose no serious threat in this port of our Soviet allies." His smile disappeared, "I would, however, like to know when they get up steam to depart." He paused, then added, "And Mister Gerstung, please have your operators keep a sharp eye to ensure that we intercept anything the British ships might transmit in violation of the Russian ban on sending. They may try to squeeze in a report about us despite the Russian regulations.

"Aye, Herr Captain." Warning and the radio officer stood and departed the salon.

Later that day, Gerstung received a copy of a sad wireless message sent to all Norddeutscher Lloyd ships that normally ran to New York. It had been written by Norddeutscher Lloyd managing director C. J. Beck and sent to Captain William Drechsel, the New York chief inspector, stating:

> Due to the present uncertainty caused by the European War, we must very reluctantly and to our deepest regret ask you to inform all your staff that their services will have to be terminated as of September 30, 1939.

By mid-October, the Hapag-Lloyd piers on Manhattan's West Side would be returned to the New York Dock Department.[3]

After a few days in the Kola Bay, it became clear to all the visiting Germans that as long as they stayed they would be prisoners aboard their ships. At first thought, that didn't seem so bad given the amount of room the *Bremen* crew enjoyed, as well as their having access to the well-equipped galley, library, theater, gymnasium, and swimming pool. As the days dragged on and the weather grew colder and still grayer, however, they began to long for home.

European Press
September 1939

News of *Bremen*'s successful arrival in Murmansk despite the British navy search was late getting out to the world press. In Berlin, when the American *New York Herald* journalist William Shirer learned of the liner's arrival via undisclosed sources in Berlin and began his radio broadcast, the German military censor rushed in and compelled him to delete it from the text.[4] The Berlin officials were still sensitive about disclosing the news of the ship's whereabouts. It was not until a former *Bremen* assistant baker, Seaman Elbert Post, one of Chef Hans Künlen's crew, who would leave the ship in Murmansk with the group later in September, returned to his native Amsterdam spilling the story of the extraordinary escape and evasion from the Royal Navy that it was finally confirmed in the press that they had arrived safely in the Russian port of Murmansk.[5] Then to the *Bremen* crew's delight they heard on the German news broadcast that on September 20 the London *Daily Express* reported that *Bremen* had been captured by the Royal Navy. The next day the Admiralty called the report absurd.

SS *Bremen*
Murmansk
September 1939

The effort to gather as many German ships into the safety of the Soviet northern waters managed to pull in eighteen German-flagged merchant ships. Each of the arrivals proved a major event, for even though the German ships were prohibited from going ashore, they were allowed limited use of their launches to visit other German ships. The Soviet Maritime Border Patrol kept a launch patrolling the anchorage day and night, and it would have been difficult to violate the rules undetected. The motor vessel *Iller* was in the harbor when *Bremen* arrived on September 6, and the Hapag-Lloyd liner *New York* arrived the next day. *Hans Leonhardt* and *Palime* arrived September 9. *Cordillera* came in the next day, and *St. Louis* arrived from New York on September 11. The *Bremen* crew later heard the details of her historic voyage loaded with Jewish refugees.

During the celebrated *St. Louis* odyssey in seeking to disembark its hapless refugee passengers, she had been turned away by a number of countries including, surprisingly, the United States. *St. Louis* had departed Hamburg on May 13, 1939, with 937 Europeans, many of whom were Jews seeking to flee anticipated Nazi persecution. Some had already been rounded up in camps but through some means had gained release and had paid outlandish prices for the passage tickets. The passengers included many children, entire families, and even some children traveling unaccompanied. Two weeks later at their original destination of Havana, Cuban government officials denied them landing permission. The ship then sailed to Miami and was ordered to hold while customs officials urgently sought permission to land the refugees. Two personal appeals sent to President Roosevelt were ignored and Coast Guard ships were rapidly deployed to prevent passengers fleeing the ship as it hovered within sight of Miami. The ship eventually was forced by dwindling supplies and fuel to return to Europe, where the passengers were split up by agreement among Britain, Holland, Belgium, and France. The U.S. government never clearly explained why these passengers were turned away, and, of course, the crew aboard *Bremen* never knew about these details until later, when they met with some of their comrades from the *St. Louis* crew. Many had been severely disappointed and even shocked by the situation during that voyage, and even though they were German they did not think that either the Cuban or American officials had acted responsibly. It was later disclosed that many of the *St. Louis* refugees eventually perished in German concentration camps.[6]

But at that time the Germans in Murmansk were not aware of those events, as their only news came via Berlin broadcasts from the Ministry of Propaganda, and, of course, they were officially banned from listening to foreign broadcasts. Nevertheless, it was nearly impossible to keep Gerstung's radio operators from turning a dial to listen to the BBC, even with the Bordsturm security keeping watch in the radio room.

Additional ships drifted in throughout the next week until there was a total of eighteen, including the large freighter *Helene* that arrived on September 16 from Yarmouth, Nova Scotia. *Helene's* name and presence in Murmansk would take on a vital importance to *Bremen's* survival in the near future. After that, no more ships came in and the days grew shorter and the nights longer as the crew waited for news.

The ship's engineers began to fret about the availability of fuel. Since Ahrens was asked several times on short notice to change anchorage, and in a rising wind, he was forced to keep main propulsion steam up around the clock. Worried, Chief Frederich Müller repeatedly asked that the ship apply to the Russians for fuel. After several requests, the Russians finally agreed to ask a higher authority; no answer came, however. Ahrens and his engineers were finally relieved when on September 12 the German tanker *Wilhelm A. Riedemann* arrived in Murmansk Harbor. The 10,326-ton tanker had broken through the British Iceland Faeroes exclusion area and evaded being sighted by hugging the Norwegian coast until rounding North Cape. She immediately topped *Bremen* off with as much fuel oil as she had. The next day a second tanker, the 10,397-ton *Friedrich Breme*, arrived to complete the refueling. She, too, had been sent out to run the blockade specifically to refuel *Bremen*. After these two tankers had made the run successfully, Ahrens and his crew began to feel more confident that they, too, could make the return run with impunity, and their spirits soared.

After riding at anchor in the cold confines of the Kola fjord for a week, the ship finally got some news. A cutter came out from the town center with Consular Dr. von Walter, a diplomat from the German embassy in Moscow. Looking haggard, Walter explained he had just survived a grueling seventy-two-hour train ride to Murmansk from Leningrad on the Polar Arrow, and the night before that, a twelve-hour overnight ride on the Red Arrow from Moscow. When he came aboard and joined Captain Ahrens and First Officer Warning, the disheveled diplomat was nearly overcome as he explained his trying trip. He calmed down when the captain offered him a glass of German schnapps to settle his frayed nerves.

"I am quite sure, Captain Ahrens," the diplomat complained, "that Russian train had one square wheel just under my cabin. Why, I didn't sleep a wink the whole trip!"

After von Walter settled down, he provided the marvelous news that Berlin was arranging for 870 of the *Bremen* crew to return to Germany by rail to Leningrad and then by German ship to Bremerhaven. The news shot through the ship like lightning. It was eventually decided that First Officer Warning and Leading Radio Officer Gerstung would go with the returning crewmen and would then report to the Navy High Command in Berlin to discuss further plans for getting the ship home. One hundred thirty-seven crew members—engineers, a full bridge watch, and a sufficient number of deck hands and support personnel to ensure the ship's safety—would remain aboard. The party remaining aboard included Able Seamen Heinz Slominski and Gustav Schmidt. The Russians insisted, despite Ahrens's vehement protestations, that all radiomen be included in the homeward-bound group.

Galley Assistant Walter Renneberg was enlisted by Chief Cook Hans Künlen to supervise the preparation of food for the long journey to Germany. The Russians said the train ride from Murmansk to Leningrad would take forty-eight hours, but, since food was scarce, it would be best if the crew brought what rations they could. Each crewman was allowed to carry only one bag of personal belongings.

Tschira worried about how he could carry all the photographs he had taken since the departure from Bremerhaven last August. There were entirely too many photos, so he set about sorting out the most valuable shots from the trip and locked the rest in his photo lab for the return voyage home, whenever that might be. He insisted that Berlin was waiting for his photo work, a statement that further convinced the crew that he had done some special work for the Abwehr.

Those departing on the train were told to be ready to depart the ship early the next day, which was September 18. But they waited for hours and nothing happened. In the meantime, Renneberg and his colleagues in the galley, supervised by the chief cook, went about preparing five thousand sandwiches for the trip and stowed them in the large ship's reefers. As the delay continued for another twenty-four hours, several of the departing crew wondered how the sandwiches would taste. The crew sat around the A deck lounge with their gear ready to depart. Finally, late the following day, a large ferry came alongside just as darkness settled in the harbor. With the aid of a spotlight, the anxious crew disembarked down the steep accommodation ladder and boarded the ferry. Captain Ahrens watched the boarding from the starboard bridge wing. Warning, looking anxious and wearing his long winter greatcoat, stood by Ahrens. The temperature was below freezing and great clouds of vapor swirled around the water, which was quite a bit warmer than the frigid air. The two officers watched as the majority of their crew began descending the towering side of the ship and packed quietly into the ferry.

It took three runs to the Murmansk landing before Warning turned and saluted Ahrens, "Well, Herr Kommodore, I wish you the best here in the cold. I'm sure Berlin will broadcast news of our arrival in the blind, so you'll know when we get home."

Ahrens was moved. "Look after the men. I'm sure you will, but who knows what the Russians will produce? They seem to know what they're up to, but sometimes one wonders about their abilities." He watched Warning leave the bridge, then shortly later descend the ladder and climb into the ferry. The first officer waved from the deck of the ferry while it noisily chugged away into the darkness. Ahrens wondered when he would see his leading first officer again.

The German crewmen and crewwomen were amused by the reports they heard had appeared in the American press about their ship's whereabouts. According to several reports they copied from the Berlin broadcasts, *Bremen* had been captured again by the British, and in another that they had disappeared, presumed sunk. A lifeboat bearing the marking SS *Bremen* had been found off the coast of Nova Scotia the day after war was declared. Instead of survivors, a radio transmitter was found that allegedly had been sending bogus wireless messages to indicate it was the missing liner that had sped away to the north. British and American authorities claimed the ruse had been used in a well-known past incident to cover the tracks of German naval combatants and commerce raiders and that, if true, would indicate the German superliner may be operating secretly at sea as an armed raider. Radio technicians in New York, however, claimed that the report was probably untrue since it was doubtful that a motorized lifeboat equipped with a radio transmitter could have shaken two British cruisers. Such a portable transmitter would be configured to send only distress messages on a single frequency and if repeated over a long period would arouse suspicion.

The newspaper had cited the precedent of a World War I ruse used by a German cruiser transferred to ally Turkey. When dogged by two British warships, the Turkish cruiser entered Messina, Sicily, for safety. The cruiser's resourceful commander paraded his band topside, and during a heavy fog set several musicians adrift in the harbor in a lifeboat. While the musicians in the boat gradually replaced the band music, the cruiser fled quietly to sea, and the British remained guarding the port still bemused by the musical decoy. It made a good story for the *Bremen* crew who remained behind in the safety of the frigid Russian north relieved to be immune to surprise by the British. But it was merely a temporary boon to the German spirits.

9

Plotting Escape

Murmansk, Leningrad, and Bremerhaven
Tuesday, September 19, to Thursday, September 21, 1939

Those *Bremen* crew who made the journey down the side of their ship that dark, cold night will never forget the ride across the black harbor with the steam and mist swirling over the water, obscuring all the ships as soon as they pulled away. First-Class Waiter Ernst Henningsen recalled the moment vividly: "We saw nothing looking like a major city as we chugged in that cold ferry toward Murmansk."

Walter Renneberg, from the main galley, also remembered that dark journey:

> Finally, as the engines slowed, we could make out some dim lights in the distance. But as we neared the lights, the ferry turned and made its way slowly toward a pitch black space between two dim lights. The boat gradually approached a high sea wall and we could make out long warehouses in the mist. After a long delay the ferry made the side of a floating pier and tied up to two wooden dolphins. Half a dozen Russians in a mix of uniforms and long overcoats with fur hats stood stomping their boots in the damp cold. After waiting for another hour in the drafty ferry, we were gradually led onto the float and then up a steep ramp toward a warehouse. Upon reaching the top of the ramp we could make out the form of a number of train wagons partially hidden between two long warehouses. We were told to climb aboard, but only after filing through a makeshift customs inspection point set up in the cold warehouse. We trooped off the ferry and through the dimly lit warehouse, each passing between two long tables surrounded by

147

green-tabbed border guards in their high boots and fur *shapkas*. The red-tabbed customs inspectors began by searching the bags of the first fifty or so of us, then after that proved slow and cumbersome, they began pushing us through the line without searching our bags. The temperature in the warehouse was certainly below freezing and our breath vaporized in the icy atmosphere.

Finally, after about a hundred *Bremen* crew had filed past, the Russian guards, having abandoned the searches altogether, merely grunted as the Germans approached and pushed them through, giving each merely a cursory glance. The ship's photographer Hanns Tschira was greatly relieved. He had departed the ship with three large suitcases full of photo coverage of the voyage, the sole exception to the Russian's single-bag rule. He had left all his negatives and most of his materials locked in the photo laboratory on the ship, but had taken the chance and brought his most prized prints with him. Several seamen had to assist him carrying the bags. He was lucky going through the inspection line since his Russian photographer friend the custom official was among the gaggle of uniforms standing around smoking their paper cigarettes, which gave off a horrible stench, while the *Bremen* crew shuffled by. By the time Tschira had arrived at the inspectors' bench with his heavy bags, the inspectors were already depleted of energy, bored, and seemed indifferent to Tschira's luggage. Suddenly a very large-girthed Russian in a long greatcoat with a much fancier fur cap and red shoulder boards, presumably an officer, grabbed Tschira by the arm and pulled him out of the line. The Russian jabbered on unintelligibly until another man stepped forward. It was the Russian amateur photographer who had befriended Tschira on board the first day in Murmansk Harbor. Following a loud shouting exchange with the officer, his friend waved Tschira through, stating that he had already seen Tschira's material and it had been preinspected and approved. Elated, Tschira gripped his friend's hand and embraced him in Russian fashion. The two photographers parted amicably and several other Germans helped Tschira drag his bags toward the train.

That was fine, except that there was no platform, so they were forced to heave their baggage up to the lower step, which was over six feet high, and then scramble after the baggage into the large wagons. The train was hissing steam and smelled of urine and coal dust, yet the interior, which was lighted in dim blue night lamps, appeared quite clean and smelled of sweet disinfectant. The crew were assigned to cabins, with each one containing four bunks and a small folding table. Every wagon had a large steam-powered samovar at one end, nursed by a stout female conductor called a *prevozhnitza*. According to Wilhelm Bohling, "these dedicated ladies ruled their wagons with an iron will, yet politely provided us frequently with hot tea in glasses inserted in metal holders stamped with the Soviet railroad crest and ubiquitous hammer and sickle."

As the men waited in their cabins, the train sat still for two more hours before anything happened. It was warm aboard, almost too warm, as the steam heat was going full blast, so they just lay on their bunks and tried to sleep. Finally, sometime after midnight, the train jerked into motion and, after endless backing and filling, eased slowly out of the pier area and began the long journey southward. It was impossible during the darkness to see anything out of the windows, and when the dawn finally cracked into a glorious pink, it was still nearly impossible to see out through the filthy windows, which appeared to have been washed with an oily substance onto which adhered every imaginable type of airborne grit. Nevertheless, the *Bremen* crew were warm and had plenty of tea and dried-out sandwiches, thanks to Chef Künlen and his galley staff.

The train trip continued for a full seventy-two hours. After finishing their rations the first evening, the prevozhnitza brought them steaming bowls of a beet soup called *borscht* that was loaded with numerous unidentified floating bits: possibly cabbage, potatoes, beets, and chunks of some gristly meat from an unidentified animal. The German crew were hot but did not complain, they were heading home.

After hours of passing nothing but forest, the train stopped at a siding for some time. Then a train passed going slowly the opposite direction packed full of Soviet soldiers. It was a sight to behold, recorded Renneberg:

> Never had we seen so many men packed in such small space. They were bunched into the wagons, noses pressed to the glass. There were men on the outside of the cars, crowded onto the platforms, draped in blankets and wrapped in scarves. Many wore fur *shapkas*, but some merely had rags around their heads, wearing their famous gray fabric boots called *valenki*. Flatcars with tanks and artillery passed with scores of men huddled in the cold looking curiously at our train. The train must have held thousands of troops. That sight made an impression on us who were accustomed to luxury and fine accommodations. Little did we know that in less than two years many of us would be locked in combat with those wretched souls.

Even though it was only September, it was terribly cold, and endless snow-blanked forests full of dark evergreens interspersed with shimmering silver birch trees swept by, creating a landscape few of the Germans had ever beheld before. The train reached the outskirts of what appeared to be a large city. They swept past numerous commuter platforms onto which huddled scores of dark human forms clad in heavy overcoats and shawls. Most of the people they observed from the train appeared to be older women and occasionally an elderly man. There were few young to be seen. The darkness seemed to encompass every aspect of Soviet life. Not only were the streets unlighted, but the station platforms were also shrouded in darkness with only an occasional dim light bulb struggling in vain to illuminate the dreary scenes of the elderly populace trudging, heads bowed, to some undefined destination along the endless darkened streets. The train finally bumped through what appeared to be the industrial section of Leningrad, where the German passengers observed piles of twisted rusting steel and stacks of scrap iron lying in unimaginable chaos surrounding large shipbuilding halls. The men in the train could smell the nearness of the sea as the train jounced haltingly through the darkened freight yards. The distant lights of the city center loomed as an orange glow in the distance, yet no clear forms of habitable buildings were evident. All appeared to the Germans to be remarkably primitive and run down, yet throbbing with life. Everywhere it seemed people were walking like ants in a determined direction, albeit with no visible goal in sight.

In Leningrad, the train was shunted down to a dock area again, where the passengers could make out the masts of a number of ships protruding above endless lines of warehouses. After waiting for several hours they were ushered off the trains, again climbing the steep sides from the high steps down to the ground, now covered with an oily brown slush. Snow gusted in their faces as they trudged around the warehouses, dragging their bags and finally coming to a pier where two ships emerged in the dim light. On their sterns fluttered the German national flag. A small party of dock workers and sailors assembled on the pier stared quietly as the Germans filed aboard the ships. They could read the names *Sierra Cordoba* and *Oceana* on their transoms. There was no need to coax the *Bremen* crew up the steep gangways, because they were eager to be standing on a bit of their homeland. Aboard each ship they were treated very well and served with home-cooked German food and beer.

The *Bremen* crew felt greatly relieved after finally departing Leningrad through the long channel and past Kronstadt island, which was cluttered with Soviet naval ships including the dark and foreboding-looking submarines. After steaming out of the channel and into the open sea, several of the passengers began lolling about on deck or in the well-appointed salons and lounges, trying to act as though they had finally attained the status of first-class passengers, although these were budget liners compared to *Bremen*. Suddenly, three unidentified aircraft came screaming out of the direction of the sun. The German crew were terrified as bullets ripped across the deck and splinters flew; there were sparks and the smell of burning paint everywhere. It was absolutely frightening to be aboard a ship that had only two antiaircraft gun mounts firing without effect at the attackers. The three airplanes, which were painted blue and could have been either British or Finnish, came in at about 550 yards strafing and dropping several bombs.

But the bombs fell short or overshot the ships. Then, after two passes, the attackers disappeared as suddenly as they had emerged, leaving the crew badly shaken. The *Bremen* crew were unhurt; only their enthusiasm had been slightly dampened.

Finally, on September 21 *Sierra Cordoba* and *Oceana* entered the Nord-Ostsee Kanal, then turned south into the Elbe estuary, sailed around past Cuxhaven into the Weser River, and arrived in Bremerhaven. There they were met by the Norddeutscher Lloyd band standing in the pouring rain, loyally oompahing them back. Needless to say, their arrival in Bremerhaven was warm, but their thoughts lingered with their shipmates still aboard *Bremen* in Murmansk. Before disembarking, the crew had been cautioned by First Officer Warning not to talk about Murmansk and which ships they knew were there, or to speculate on the possible return of their beloved *Bremen*; those subjects were taboo. Nevertheless, they were glad to be home, though their enjoyment proved to be short lived. Most were required to report within a few days for induction into the military. Wilhelm Bohling, the apprentice waiter, was inducted into the airborne forces, and Ernst Henningsen, the waiter, served on navy minesweepers.

First Officer Warning was unable to go home. Instead, he traveled immediately to Bremen to brief the Norddeutscher Lloyd management on the conditions aboard *Bremen* and when completed, he boarded a train for Berlin and the Navy High Command. He would spend more than eight weeks there planning the future of *Bremen*.

SS *Bremen*
Murmansk
September–November 1939

In the meantime in Murmansk, the weather and Captain Adolf Ahrens's disposition were rapidly deteriorating. It snowed and wind blew and the days grew still shorter. The captain was concerned about a number of items that augured well for trying to break out and run the British gauntlet. He asked the Russians repeatedly for permission to let the remaining crew members go ashore, relax, and look around, but to no avail. He was ignored or told that they would forward the request up the chain. The Russians were not impolite; quite to the contrary, they were warm and friendly. A fear seemed to permeate all uniformed Russians, however, to the extent that none seemed willing to make a decision, no matter how insignificant, but always sought approval from a higher echelon.

The short days and long winter nights stretched on in the dark northern climes. From mid-November through the middle of February, the sun stopped rising in Murmansk, with the short daylight periods reduced to merely a depressing gray glow. As the days passed, the crew received bits of news via the daily Berlin maritime broadcast. Their presence in Russia had first been confirmed accurately in the press on October 3 by a Norwegian sailor who arrived in Oslo aboard a ship having sailed from Murmansk the week before. The keen-eyed sailor claimed he had observed the liner *Bremen* in an anchorage near that port in the midst of a gaggle of other German merchant ships, and that the liner was wearing camouflage paint. Having been seen in Murmansk, Ahrens assumed the rumors of their worldwide adventures would cease, but that was not the case. *Bremen* was again reported in the news as having been sighted at sea by an Italian ship off the coast of Argentina, and again by fishermen off the coast of Norway. Then on October 10, the Dutch pastry cook Elbert Post, one of those lucky ones who had left in mid-September and arrived home in Amsterdam, spilled the full story of *Bremen*'s presence in Murmansk.

Post, who was interviewed by the Amsterdam newspaper *Het Volk*, told the entire story from the arrival and detention in New York, to the departure and painting of the ship, to the run from the two British cruisers off Halifax.[1] "None of us much cared for the Dutchman," recalled Walter Renneberg, who had worked with Post in the galley. "Post had boasted in the his press interview that he alone had not given the Nazi salute upon leaving New York and had even provided the newspaper with a photo of himself not saluting while standing in the midst of crewmen who were singing and hoisting their right arms in the Nazi hail. His details of our story, as we heard them repeated over the wireless news, were pretty accurate. He described in great detail the train journey from Murmansk to Leningrad and the voyage home aboard the two KdF [Kraft durch Freud; strength through joy] transports."

For the remaining *Bremen* crew, it was the first open confirmation that their shipmates had reached home safely, but they were less than thrilled at the voluntary compromise by their former Dutch colleague. Finally, the Germans learned that the first lord of the British Admiralty, Winston Churchill, had announced to the press that "the German liner *Bremen* is believed to be in a northern Russian port." That cinched it as far as they were concerned. Their whereabouts were certainly no longer a secret, and for those still on board, it was just a matter of time before there would surely be a British plan to capture them.

Commodore Ahrens then heard via wireless receiver about the victory of *U-47*, commanded by Günter Prien, who on October 12 had slipped into the northern Royal Navy anchorage of Scapa Flow, torpedoed the battleship *Royal Oak*, and then escaped. The news that *Royal Oak* had been sunk with the loss of 786 crewmen had given German morale a big boost, especially those who remembered the scuttling of the imperial German battle fleet in those very waters. At the end of World War I the ships interned in Scapa Flow were still undefeated, the gallant combatants that had fought so gloriously at Jutland—*Friedrich der Grosse*, *König*, *Kaiser*, *Derfflinger*, *Moltke*, *Seydlitz*, and *Von der Tann*—yet unbeaten ships of a conquered nation. When the news of the German surrender came and with it the details of the Versailles Treaty provisions, it had proved too much for the officers and men who promptly opened the sea cocks and scuttled those grand ships at 11:15 A.M. June 21, 1919. It seemed that the war was coming closer to *Bremen*, as she lay totally unaware of where her future in the bleak northern Russian waters would take her.

The days and long nights stretched on with little change in the situation. On November 2, Captain Ahrens wrote a letter to the German Navy High Command, now his operational senior, outlining his concerns for the ship.[2] He explained that after the local authorities had told him he would be required to move the ship to an anchorage in Sayda Bay, just twelve miles west of Murmansk, he had protested. The proposed anchorage had a stone bottom and would not be a good holding ground for their anchors, and the wind was even stronger there; often building to a force seven to eight. They would be required to constantly use at least two engines to keep from running onto the rocks. That meant the ship's engineers, already reduced in number to barely enough by the shipment home last September of so many crewmen, would have to stand twelve hours on and twelve off just to maintain a steam blanket on the engines for getting up a quick head of steam in order to keep from blowing ashore. It was no picnic for them. There were also no stores available. In view of the uncertain conditions, the commodore wrote, it would be worth considering bringing the ship home during the long polar nights. "I personally endorse such an action," he wrote, "although I do not know the current conditions in the North Sea." To make matters worse, he didn't have a radio communicator aboard, since his radio staff was sent home with the 870 crew members in September. Only one German ship in Murmansk, *Cordillera* with two radiomen aboard, still had a communications capability.

Ahrens then penned a separate report to Norddeutscher Lloyd appended to the letter to the German Navy High Command:

> The personnel situation is such that if we are forced to depart the harbor here for any reason we could not do it without reinforcements. After extensive discussions with my leading engineer it is fully possible with the fuel now on board to leave with all four engines and be able to make 27 knots to a German port in two and one half to three days. Our deck force is weak, only two officers. In that case, regardless of the emergency, I would not like to depart with this manning level. It would take merely two and a half days to get reinforcements from Leningrad here. I request the following:
>
> 4 navigating officers
> 3 engineers
> 3 radiomen

1 doctor (not fully necessary, a qualified nurse would suffice)

3 firefighters

1 tailor

1 boatswain

3 quartermasters (qualified also as signalmen)

10 seamen

3 service personnel (telephone switch operators)

3 auxiliary machinists

Total 35 persons

Ahrens then outlined his view of the homeward dash:

> The entire trip home is about 1500 nautical miles. If we were
> to depart at 2 PM on December 5, it will already be turning
> dark. Barring poor weather we could be at the Andesnaes after
> one day. Daylight lasts from 10 AM to 2 PM and we would have
> to remain clear of the fishing banks to avoid being reported by
> fishermen. After dark we could come in closer to the coast, and
> could by 9 PM on December 7 be by Skudesnaes.

At this point, Captain Ahrens used a tactic in his letter that he
knew would trigger an immediate response from Berlin. He proposed departing on a given date, getting out to sea, and then awaiting further orders when he could communicate. He used the age-
old mariner trick of telling the boss, "Unless you say otherwise, I
am going to do this and such" (in naval terminology such a phrase
has the acronym UNODIR, meaning "unless otherwise directed, I
intend to. . ."). His letter continued:

> The question remains should the Bremen depart on that date
> and await orders or wait here until there are still one and one
> half hours of darkness to use that extra time running inside the
> three mile Norwegian coastal waters, then decide the next night
> whether to enter the Baltic via the Great Belt or head directly
> for the German coast at Cuxhaven.
>
> My draft on arrival would be 32 feet, a little deep for the
> Belt but not impossible, we could not do that without being
> detected in the daylight however. I transited the Belt twice in
> the Columbus six years ago with a 32 foot draft. In any case, it

is easier to make for the German coast unless there are other reasons for not doing so. The most important issue is to keep our departure from here secret. The Russians have in the past given ships a one to two day head start before allowing any other ship to depart, thereby controlling the reporting of any observing ships [transmitting communications of wireless was prohibited by the Soviet authorities and controlled by enforcing the dismantling in the harbor of all transmitting antennae]. In our case that must be done.

On the voyage here we were steaming completely blind with all running lights off assuming all navigation aides [lighthouses] have been extinguished. I would again do so on the run home for added security. [And here Captain Ahrens gets into naval operations.] Now, with things the way they are to the south, would German armed escort be available? It would be dangerous for a U-boat, but for this I need the following information from you:

Have the English established a barrier from the Orkneys to the Norwegian coast?

What route are the Narvik to England freighters steaming?

Where is the best German security there, where and how? Certainly you can provide me more information, which would be very valuable.

As far as the appearance of the ship, the entire superstructure, hull and stacks have been painted dark gray and our name painted out on the hull and lifeboats.

Codes: The H-key we have been using for the *Iller*, is expired, so Bremen needs [a] new code key. [All German ships in Operation Basis North were assigned radio code material using names of other German ships to confuse monitoring intelligence, *Bremen* had been assigned the call for a vessel named *Iller*.]

Finally, Ahrens pleaded for the decision to let him run for it, writing:

The long nights and our great speed advantage are not the only advantages, I'm sure there are other measures to insure this last run succeeds. I can assure you that all measures have been taken so we can destroy and sink the ship to prevent it from falling into the hands of the enemy.

The letter got a swift response from Berlin. On November 22 the German naval attaché in the German embassy in Moscow, Frigattenkapitän (lieutenant commander) Norbert von Baumbach, was launched aboard the Polar Arrow train to Murmansk to confer with Commodore Ahrens about his views for the dash home. In Berlin, First Officer Warning and several officers from the Navy High Command were putting together a plan to spirit *Bremen* home from Murmansk through the enemy-infested Norwegian Sea, across the North Sea, and safely into German home waters.

The first element of that plan was launched on November 14, when *U-38* departed Wilhelmshaven, passed through the minefields off the Weser estuary, and turned north, heading through the British blockade with the mission of proceeding to Murmansk. *U-38*'s initial assignment was to reconnoiter the Russian submarine base at Polyarny as a possible base for future German submarine operations per the German-Soviet Nonaggression Pact. Her presence in the northern waters, however, would soon thrust the submarine into chance participation in the plan to spring *Bremen* from Russian waters and make her dash home. *U-38* was commanded by thirty-one-year-old Heinrich Liebe, who had formed his crew in 1933 and, since the start of the war in early September, had already sunk 16,698 tons of British shipping, not an insignificant total for the early war months. Although his assignment to proceed north to Kola Bay should have been considered an important diplomatic task, Liebe was naturally more eager to go where he could add rapidly to his total record of ships sunk. Thus, the trip north seemed to him and his crew to be removing them from the main field of battle, although running through Admiral Charles Forbes's Home Fleet might provide for chance encounters with fat Royal Navy combatant targets. German attaché Baumbach would carry the news of *U-38*'s visit to the Murmansk region with him to Murmansk. It was part of his mission to see that Liebe and his Type XI boat were properly looked after and obtained a fair and unbiased look at the problems of German northern basing.

British Home Fleet
North Atlantic and North Sea
November–December 1939

In the meantime, the Royal Navy was reinforcing Admiral Charles Forbes's Home Fleet and casting a greater net to intercept all German ships in the North Sea and the Shetland-Faeroe gap. On November 17, the British Third Submarine Flotilla was established at Harwich, northeast of London on the East Anglian coast. That command commenced active war patrols in the southern part of the North Sea.

An important event occurred that involved the HMS *Rawalpindi*, a British-converted passenger liner armed with four old six-inch guns as an armed cruiser and commerce raider. On November 23, in a surface engagement located between Iceland and the Faeroe Islands, the German battleship *Scharnhorst* sank *Rawalpindi* in an action lasting only fourteen minutes. The British-armed cruiser went down gallantly after scoring only one major hit on the powerful *Scharnhorst*. Also on patrol in the same area, yet out of visual range of *Rawalpindi*, were the cruiser *Newcastle*, two C-class, and one D-class cruisers. At the same time, the eight-inch cruisers *Norfolk*, *Suffolk*, and three additional armored cruisers were patrolling the Denmark Strait between Iceland and Greenland.

That same day, Admiral Forbes left the Clyde to go after *Scharnhorst* with the battleships *Nelson* and *Rodney*, the cruiser *Devonshire*, and seven destroyers. Forbes immediately set up a five-submarine patrol on a line of bearing running southwest, at 250 degrees from Lister Light at fifteen-mile intervals. These operations, designed to intercept *Scharnhorst*, were inconclusive and discontinued on December 1. Stung by the loss of *Rawalpindi*, however, Admiral Forbes wanted badly to intercept the prestigious liner *Bremen*, which he knew had been languishing in Murmansk and was expected to make a dash for home waters soon. Thus, in the last week of November, the perceptive admiral sent the cruiser *Glasgow* and two destroyers to the northeast of the Shetland Islands to await *Bremen* should she attempt to make a run home in the lengthening December nights.

German Navy High Command
Berlin
Friday, December 1, 1939

The most time-sensitive mission and most cumbersome to achieve was providing Commodore Ahrens with the crew reinforcements he had request for the run home. The additional personnel were obtained easily enough from Norddeutscher Lloyd volunteers, of whom they received more than the thirty-five requested. Getting these men to Murmansk, however, caused the German official-dom, not an insignificant bureaucracy during Nazi time, a greater challenge than the tactical problem of running the British naval blockade. The bureaucratic obfuscation of Soviet administrators was awe inspiring. It has been said that one of the lesser known reasons resulting in the invasion of the Soviet Union in 1941 was that the German army officers concluded it was simpler to fight the Russians than to be their allies.

As Naval Attaché Norbert von Baumbach was preparing to deliver the final escape plans to *Bremen* in Murmansk, First Offi-cer Warning was setting the wheels in motion at the Berlin Navy High Command and the Ministry of Transportation for obtaining Soviet entry visas for fifty-seven replacement crewmen for *Bremen*, while simultaneously formulating the basic outline of a plan for her dash to Bremerhaven.

10

Salmon *Bags a U-Boat*

SS *Bremen*
Murmansk
Friday, December 1 to Monday, December 4, 1939

Since *Bremen*'s best defense was her speed, her escape plan called
for her to dash at top speed across the North Sea. An antisubmarine defense would consist of the provision of air escort and, in the
case of detection in close proximity, the use of maximum speed
and steering zigzag maneuvers to either side of the base course.
The real danger remained the possibility that a British submarine
could lie in wait for the high-speed liner following entry into the
North Sea. Weather, visibility, and the crafty use of the cover of
darkness would play the determining factor, and with any luck
they might find the area enshrouded in haze and mist as was often
the case in December.

   The operation to mask the return run was based on disguising
Bremen electronically as the merchant ship *Helene,* an 8,000-ton
freighter, one of the eighteen German merchant ships using Murmansk as a safe haven. By taking *Helene*'s international radio call
sign, *Bremen* would slip out of Murmansk under the cover of darkness, proceed west through the Barents Sea rounding North Cape,
then steam south just out of visual range of the Norwegian coast.
The German Navy High Command correctly suspected that
Bremen's prominent silhouette would be reported to the British
by sympathetic Norwegian coast watchers. By remaining outside
visual range of the coast, Commodore Adolf Ahrens would be
deprived of the precise use of visual navigation aids and would
have to chart his way south relying on his own dead reckoning.

The German staff prepared an elaborate deception plan that included stationing radio relay pickets at prescribed times along *Bremen*'s track, giving her navigator brief radio direction finding assistance. The picket units would consist of submarines, destroyers, and mine warfare craft. The plan called for precise timing, as the relay navigation beacons would radiate only for short periods to avoid detection, which required that *Bremen*'s radio direction finders had to be absolutely alert and precise. The burden of intercepting these signals would fall on the shoulders of Radio Officer Kurt Gerstung, who would be returning to the ship with the crew replacements.

Ahrens would steam at the economical speed of 27.5 knots south to 64 degrees north latitude, roughly west of Trondheim, adjusting his track to arrive during the early hours of darkness, which in early December was at 3:00 P.M. He would then speed up to 29.5 knots and commence his run through the British blockade that stretched from the Shetland Islands to the Norwegian coast near Bergen. When crossing the North Sea, he would again be assisted by picket destroyers and mine warfare craft and another U-boat, which would draw off any would-be pursuers.

Success lay with the visibility. If the weather was poor and Ahrens thought he could make it across the North Sea to the mouth of the Weser, he would do so at maximum speed. If the visibility cleared, thereby increasing the danger of a visual interception by a British warship or aircraft, Ahrens had the option of swinging east into the Skagerrak and entering the Baltic via the Great Belt, then returning to Bremerhaven through the Nord-Ostsee Kanal. To do so, his draft had to be less than thirty-two feet. Ahrens had used that track into the Baltic before and knew he could make it safely in the darkness if he could ensure his draft was shallow enough by deballasting some fresh and feed water tanks. Air reconnaissance would be provided by the Eastern Baltic Air Defense Command based at Cuxhaven if the weather permitted, but only after *Bremen* crossed south of 64 degrees north latitude. Dr. Julius Dorpmüller, the German minister of transport, presented the plan personally to Adolf Hitler, who approved it on November 17, 1939.

On December 1, Attaché Norbert von Baumbach, swearing he would never again ride the Polar Arrow, flew to Murmansk on a courier flight from Moscow to deliver the special communication key, written orders, and updated wartime navigation charts to Commodore Ahrens. The orders called for the preparations for the breakout to begin, but stated that Ahrens was to await an execution order to depart. Two unresolved issues remained with Operation Helene: providing escorting submarines and surface warships for *Bremen's* transit, and tactical air support.

Given the speed advantage enjoyed by *Bremen*, the U-boat command initially felt it unnecessary to provide support. First Officer Eric Warning had argued, however, that it was imperative, since it would remain an option for Ahrens, depending on weather and the tactical situation in the North Sea, to run into the Baltic using the Great Belt. In that case, a well-positioned submarine might provide the crucial deterrent should *Bremen* be pursued by enemy surface combatants. The overtaxed submarine command in Wilhelmshaven finally agreed to assign several precious submarines to assist in security for the transit. One of the several submarines assigned was *U-36*, which would deploy on December 3 and take up a patrol station just south of 64 degrees north to act as a communications relay, initially transmitting a low-power radio beacon for *Bremen* to guide on. When within visual range, she could pass on reconnaissance information by flashing light, and would draw off any pursuing surface ships. Another U-boat, *U-23* if available, would take up a patrol station in the North Sea to draw off any would-be attackers should they be in hot pursuit if Ahrens chose to enter the Great Belt. A third submarine, *U-38*, had been tasked earlier to make a transit through the British exclusion area, northward through the Norwegian Sea, and around North Cape, and to enter the Kola Bay and call in Polyarny, the small fishing village recently converted to a Soviet submarine base.

The German Navy High Command and the Soviet Main Navy Staff had agreed under the auspices of the German-Soviet Nonaggression Pact that Polyarny, located near Murmansk and one of the few Russian ports ice-free year round, might be used as a base by Karl Dönitz's German Submarine Command and possibly armed surface commerce raiders. Grand Admiral Erich Raeder, the Navy commander in chief, had approved the preliminary plan called "Basis North" to provide safe haven in the Murmansk area for German merchant ships evading British warships as hostilities began and unarmed commerce ships fled to safe-haven ports. *U-38* had commenced her transit in mid-November and was scheduled to return in mid-December after reconnoitering Polyarny and meeting with Soviet navy representatives from the Northern Fleet Headquarters in Severomorsk to determine if that port was suitable for German submarines. At the time of departure, Korvetten-kapitän (lieutenant commander) Heinrich Liebe, the command-ing officer of *U-38*, had no instructions in hand regarding *Bremen*, but he was aware the renowned liner was present in the Mur-mansk area.

The U-boat commanders did not like the idea that several of their units would be required to transmit on a prescribed fre-quency to assist *Bremen*'s navigation. To transmit on any frequency at sea was anathema to submariners. They understood that the British high-frequency direction finding capability at Scarborough was deadly accurate even in those early days of the war, and their capability placed additional risk on U-boat security. The sub-mariners were still not keen on the submarine participation in Operation Helene. The Eastern Baltic Air Defense Command, based in Cuxhaven, was ordered to provide seaplane reconnais-sance and antisubmarine warfare aircraft support from 64 degrees south, depending on the weather.

U-36
Weser River–Helgoland
December 2 to December 4, 1939

Unknown to Ahrens and his crew aboard *Bremen*, then still in Murmansk, or to those crewmen who had already made it back safely to Bremerhaven, was that the German submarine *U-36*, a Type VIIA boat, part of the *Saltzwedel* Submarine Flotilla, com-manded by Wilhelm Frölich, slipped from her pier in Kiel on

December 2, made a brief stop for updated orders in Wilhelms-haven, departed that port late Sunday night, and made her way northward, skirting the minefields off the Weser estuary.

U-36's mission as a participant in Operation Helene called for her to conduct a rendezvous seven days later with *Bremen* at 64 degrees north and to act as an armed reconnaissance and visual signal relay.[1] She was one of the assets requested by Commodore Ahrens for Operation Helene, but initially turned down by the German Navy High Command. Operational Type VIIA long-range boats were already much in demand for vigorous attack duty in the North Atlantic. But after the strenuous urging of First Officer Warning, and with the assistance of several of his naval friends and the personal intervention of Transport Minister Dorpmüller, submarine escort had finally been added, however reluctantly by the Befelshaber der Unterseeboote (submarine commander) Wilhelmshaven. That commander would rather have his U-boats hunting British warships, who were now out in full force strengthening their grip around all entrances to German ports, rather than escorting merchant passenger ships, even the famed luxury liner *Bremen*.

HMS *Salmon*
North Sea
December 4, 1939

Not known to Commodore Ahrens and his crew until after the war was that on Saturday, December 2, the British Swordfish-class submarine, the HMS *Salmon*, had left her tender, the HMS *Cyclops*, as a unit of the newly formed Third Submarine Flotilla at Harwich, the North Sea port northeast of London, to patrol in the area north of the German minefields off the Weser estuary. *Salmon's* commanding officer was Lieutenant Commander E. O. Bickford. On this patrol, the thirty-year-old bachelor would catapult his submarine and crew onto the pages of history. Bickford was already well known in the submarine force for once having recommended to Winston Churchill, during a luncheon for submarine officers in Portsmouth, that the Royal Navy submarine force would be better served had they practiced a port and starboard, or two-crew system, to remedy the short supply of boats. This plan could double their at-sea time by returning to sea following a short period of maintenance and embarking a fresh crew, thus minimizing time in port for crew rest and rehabilitation. The suggestion never came to fruition once the war began, and the Royal Navy submarine force began to lose more and more men, rendering the idea totally unworkable due to the shortage of qualified submariners.

While patrolling at periscope depth at 1:30 P.M. on December 4, along the edge of the North Sea minefields, seventy-five miles southwest of Lister Light, *Salmon*'s watch officer, First Lieutenant Maurice F. Wykeham-Martin, sighted what appeared to be a box floating on the surface. "Surface object bearing red two-five," he shouted for the entire watch to hear.

Petty Officer Kenneth Barron quickly scanned his Anti-Submarine Detection Investigation Committee (ASDIC, an anti-submarine sound detection system) on the bearing and immediately detected propeller cavitation. "Hydrophone effects bearing red two-five, possible warship," he shouted on the sound-powered phones.

"Captain to the Control Room. . . . Sound the alarm. U-boat surfacing, sir!" The first lieutenant's cry sent the crew running to attack stations.

Lieutenant Commander Bickford was in the control room in a flash, and after looking briefly through the scope agreed with his first lieutenant; the object was not bobbing with the force three or four seas, but appeared to be heavy, and was tracking on a course of 350 degrees. Bickford assumed the conn. "Ahead full, maximum turns, fire control prepare a firing solution, four-fish spread, forward torpedo room." He did what all good Royal Navy men sought to do in moments of impending contact with an enemy: close the target at full speed.

In seconds, the solution came back from his torpedo officer, "Sir, recommend course one-one-zero, range to contact six thousand yards."

"Very well. Helm, right full rudder, come to course one-one-zero." Bickford was pleased, yet he knew that the distance was just over the five-thousand-yard maximum range for his twenty-one-inch torpedoes. The seconds ticked by as they slowly gained on their prey.

"Sir, range closing, target fifty-five hundred yards, bearing one-one-zero, steady. Set torpedo depth at eight feet, salvo set at seven-second intervals."

U-36
North Sea
December 4, 1939

Wilhelm Frölich, *U-36's* commander, was born in Zeitz and was from the Flensburg Naval Academy Class of 1929. He completed his submarine officers' course at Neustadt in Holstein in 1937. He was one of the senior commanders of the *Saltzwedel* Submarine Flotilla and had a promising career ahead.

Wilhelm Frölich reached the edge of the minefields on the morning of December 4, turned to a heading of 350 degrees, ran near the surface along the minefield boundary with his conning tower awash to make better time and to reach the Fair Island Passage by dark, and then headed toward the Shetland Islands.[2] Frölich stood in the open cockpit atop the conning tower squinting into the spray. He was pleased with his navigation, relieved that they had detected the edge of the minefield. Now his greatest concern was to make maximum headway toward Utsire Light, so as to pass through Norwegian waters under the cover of darkness. He knew the British would be patrolling there. The flotilla intelligence officer at Wilhelmshaven had informed him that there was considerable activity in the mouth of the Skagerrak ever since the sinking of the auxiliary cruiser *Rawalpindi*, and British and Norwegian destroyers were actively patrolling those waters. He again cursed his assignment to transit a hornet's nest of enemy activity just to meet and escort an empty German luxury liner. By running at top speed, he was risking detection due to the cavitation and

surface effects, but he expected no enemy submarines or destroyers to be patrolling this close to the minefields. He passed the conn
to his exec and went below for a midday snack and a glass of tea.

HMS *Salmon*
North Sea
December 4, 1939

Just over three miles astern of Frölich's *U-36*, *Salmon* poured on
the knots, her 1,300-horsepower electric motors now driving her
close to her submerged maximum of 9 knots. "Very good, Number
One," Bickford replied. "Flood tubes one, two, three, and four.
Time to fire?" Bickford was calm, he had full confidence in his
men. Petty Officer William George Taylor, the boat coxswain, was
the helmsman, his hands steady as a rock as he came to the new
course. The control room smelled of diesel fumes and tobacco,
mixed with the strong soap aroma from the wash up in the
scullery, which had commenced following the noon meal. Bickford's boat was reputed as one of the best in the flotilla. His last
boat, the HMS *Odin*, had been the top submarine in the China
Flotilla the year before taking command of *Salmon*.

Bickford glanced at the boat's plaque attached to the control
room bulkhead. Her crest, a salmon saltant proper, had the motto
Fluctibus floreo (I flourish in the waves) emblazoned below it.
What a grand boat and splendid crew! the captain thought, his
heart racing as the tension mounted and the range fell away. This
was what it was all about: combat under the waves—what he had
been bred for. Even the noxious fumes of chlorine and diesel
seemed welcome and cozy to him now. This was his milieu.

The German contact now appeared green in the periscope
and her deck gun was visible periodically as she rode the swells.
Bickford judged she was an oceangoing class, five hundred tons,
outbound using the sanctuary of the minefield to make a good distance at her higher surface speed so as to pass in darkness through
Fair Island passage, which lay in Norwegian coastal waters, where
British and Norwegian ships patrolled.

"Range fifty-two hundred, time to fire, ten seconds," the torpedo officer spoke calmly into the circuit.

"Very good, Number One; stand by for salvo one." Bickford stared at the bulkhead chronometer, calmly watching, then counted aloud, "Stand by all four tubes," and after a pause, "Five, four, three, two, fire one!" The hissing from the forward torpedo room could be heard throughout the boat, which rocked gently as the first torpedo surged from its tube. With the departure of nearly one ton of steel, seawater automatically poured into the compensating Q tank to keep the boat trimmed. Then, at seven-second intervals, "fire two, fire three, fire four!" The first lieutenant had already compensated the trim for the weight of the men running aft to the control room taking attack stations; now he frantically adjusted for the weight of the four torpedoes leaving their tubes. The trim must be kept perfectly, so as not to allow the loss of trim to sink the center below periscope depth, blinding the captain, or by rising, giving away their presence by broaching on the surface. He watched the spirit bubble indicating their trim.

"All torpedoes running, sir," ASDIC operator Barron called.

Bickford stared through the scope. Suddenly, he stiffened as he saw one of his torpedoes, probably the second or third, break the surface briefly in the increased turbulence caused by the close-interval firing. The boat shuddered with each firing, and after the fourth had departed the tube with a hiss and roar, it suddenly bucked upward by the bow, tilted to port, and began an uncontrolled lurch toward the surface. They had lost trim during the firing; the bubble in the spirit level dropped forward in the glass as the bow rose, threatening to broach the boat on the surface.

Bickford reacted immediately. "Ahead one-half," he shouted, "First Lieutenant get her down, man! Get her down!"

Bickford gripped the stanchion by the periscope and hung on tightly as the hull shuddered. He looked at the chronometer; the end of the running time of four and a half minutes, the maximum range of the first torpedo, was still twenty seconds away. He cursed silently, thinking that it had probably missed. The bow gradually came down and the bubble of the spirit level returned to the center position.

The crew of the submarine HMS *Salmon*. (Courtesy of the Royal Navy)

"Rudder amidships," Bickford shouted, as the boat lurched and then slowly picked up speed and swung back on an even keel. "Steady as she goes." Relieved, he looked around at the other faces in the control room. They were ashen white.

Coxswain Taylor smiled, "Good show, eh, sir?"

"Like a carnival ride," Bickford responded, glad for the petty officer's good nature. He waited silently, eyes glued to the periscope as the final seconds of the first torpedo's run ticked by. Then after a crack and reverberation, the target abruptly disappeared into a cloud of dirty gray smoke with fragments rising more than two-hundred feet in the air, followed in seconds by a tremendous shock wave.

"Direct hit, sir, possibly both one and two," the first lieutenant said proudly.

Transfixed by the spectacular scene, the captain paused before saying, "Well done, all hands. Now prepare to surface for survivors."

After a prolonged search around the horizon, *Salmon* slowly surfaced but found nothing but wreckage and oil. Bubbles continued to rise from the bottom for a time, and one body was observed wearing a life belt. Fearing aircraft or another U-boat might be attracted to the scene of the blast, Captain Bickford dived his boat and cleared the area, choosing not to break radio silence to report the encounter but continued on patrol.[3]

The action during which *Salmon* sank the *U-36* was the first of a total of seventy allied submarine attacks against the German submarine fleet during the entire war. Out of a total fifty-one attacks by British submarines, thirteen resulted in sinkings. Bickford's was the first.

German Navy High Command
Berlin
December 4 to December 5, 1939

The German Navy High Command formulated the basis of the secret plan for *Bremen*'s dash home during the first week that First Officer Warning was in Berlin visiting. His personal presence there as *Bremen*'s leading first officer was fortunate, for by that time the ship's name stood out in the forefront, not only in every German newspaper, but in the minds of the navy and all maritime organizations in Germany. Eric Warning, a Naval Reserve Leutnant zur Zee (lieutenant junior grade), had great influence as *Bremen*'s leading first officer on getting the plan developed and put on paper in Berlin by October 25, no easy task in the enigmatic Nazi bureaucracy. Although his naval rank was only Leutnant zur Zee, he carried the designator S after his title, signifying that he was a Sonder Führer (specialist), and experienced in handling deep-draft merchant ships. That designator was highly coveted and carried with it a great deal of admiration among his seagoing navy peers. That title would also make a great difference in the future when Warning would serve as a prize officer aboard the Hilfskreuzer (commerce raider) *Pinguin* in 1940. At that time, Warning was selected by his commanding officer over several senior officers to command the prize *Passat*, the 7,000-ton former Norwegian tanker seized by *Pinguin* in the Indian Ocean, and made a name for himself conducting the daring mining of the channels south of Adelaide, Australia, in 1941.[4]

The *Bremen*'s return plan, code-named "Helene," called for the immediate transport of fifty-seven replacement crewmen (the final total having been decided in Berlin) accompanied by First Officer Warning to Murmansk via the German ship *Utlandshörn* sailing from Stettin to Leningrad. Yet again, the visage of Soviet bureaucracy imposed itself, and, with the men already sitting aboard the ship in Stettin, they were told they must each appear in person at the Soviet passport office in Berlin to fill in the required forms, a process guaranteed to take several weeks at best. In desperation, the German attaché Baumbach sought the assistance of the German ambassador to Moscow, Baron von Schulenburg. Finally, after twenty-four hours of wrangling with the Soviet Foreign Ministry in Moscow, including a personal call to Foreign Minister Vyacheslav Molotov, von Schulenburg and Baumbach managed to obtain group clearance for the replacement *Bremen* crewmen to depart Stettin for Leningrad and their further transport by train to Murmansk in time for *Bremen*'s departure. That date, still undisclosed to the Russians, was to be sometime in early December. After all the red tape, negotiating, and cajoling, however, hostilities suddenly erupted between Finland and the Soviet Union.

Utlandshörn was nearing the Finnish strait en route to Leningrad when the hostilities began, and as a result was ordered to anchor off Tallinn, Estonia, and await Soviet naval escort. When the ship had anchored just off the coast, waiting, Warning had nearly given up hope that the Russians could make anything happen as planned. After a few hours, the first officer was pleasantly surprised to see three Soviet mine warfare craft appear out of the darkness and tie up alongside the steep hull of *Utlandshörn*. Finally they weighed anchor and steamed out of the anchorage and on toward Leningrad.

In Leningrad, the process, which was nearly the exact reverse of their trip with the crewmen going home, had gone quite smoothly.

The replacement crew disembarked from the ship and climbed directly into awaiting railcars parked along the dark quay in the Leningrad wharf area near the Baltic shipyard. After a few more hours of typical haggling over the head count and the mounds of paperwork, the train jerked into motion and the trip north began. There were several long delays as the train lurched along, due to the nearby ground combat the escorts had said, but the train finally arrived in Murmansk. In the early afternoon the crew was allowed to disembark from the train, and, in the already fading light, they made their way through the snow-covered passages between warehouses and climbed onto a darkened ferry, which slowly made its way out to the black harbor.

S.S. *Bremen*
Murmansk
December 6, 1939

Aboard *Bremen* that afternoon Commodore Ahrens sat in his inport salon, smoking his pipe and agonizing over the plans for the run southward. He knew the scheme practically by heart and was only awaiting the arrival of the reinforcements and his first officer before sending the ready signal to the naval attaché Baumbach in Moscow. The long days of waiting had taken their toll. Dark circles edged his eyes, and he had lost weight. The food on board was still plentiful, although mostly canned or frozen, and the security of the port was assumed to be good in the hands of the nervous Russians who ceaselessly patrolled around the foreign ships. The uncertainty was the worst, and it gnawed at his nerves. He had been pleasantly surprised the night before when Soviet liaison officers informed him that a German submarine had arrived the night before and was moored alongside a pier in nearby Polyarny. Ahrens had immediately requested that he be authorized to meet with the commander of that boat. The Soviet officers for once seemed cooperative and later the same day had appeared with the young lieutenant commander Heinrich Liebe. Commodore Ahrens was deeply moved to have the commanding officer of a U-boat in his inport salon, especially one that had already been in combat and had more than 16,000 tons of shipping sunk to its credit.

"Come in and sit down. I'm sincerely glad to see you." Ahrens turned to his mess man, "Bring tea and some schnapps, this is a special occasion." The young submarine officer was clad in a nondescript uniform of khaki trousers, a badly soiled, once-white turtle neck pullover, and a winter sheepskin leather jacket. The sharp-featured young officer carried a well seasoned, white, peaked naval officer's cap under his arm. While sitting on the chair next to him, Ahrens noticed that the submariner exhuded strong smells of diesel fuel, tobacco, and sweat.

"You no doubt welcome the room we enjoy aboard *Bremen* compared with your tight spaces," Ahrens offered in good humor.

"Indeed, sir," Liebe replied, somewhat in awe of the grand nature of the surroundings. "We have become quite used to the confined spaces, sir, but yes, you seem to be well appointed and, I understand, still short of crew."

"Yes, we're expecting reinforcements to arrive anytime now before we . . . " Ahrens stopped in midsentence and turned to the Soviet liaison officer still standing by the door. Ahrens felt uncomfortable being rude to the Soviet officer; nevertheless, he asked if he might meet alone with the German submarine commander. The Soviet officer politely agreed and stepped out of the cabin.

"You see, Captain," Ahrens used the term with pleasure wanting the German naval officer to feel comfortable, "we are nearing the end of our stay and are concerned that one or more of the British merchant ships here since we arrived two months ago might be an intelligence ship waiting to signal our departure to the British." Ahrens leaned forward and lowered his voice. "Soviet authorities banned all communication, as you know, but it would not take much for a enterprising radioman to rig an antenna and to transmit a brief report of our departure. Should that happen we would indeed be forced into a tight situation." Ahrens smiled, "You know, the British would like nothing better than to capture us as a high-speed transport prize, let alone the propaganda effect of owning Germany's top liner."

"I understand, Herr Commodore," Liebe replied. He paused, reflecting deeply for a moment, then continued. " My departure time is pretty much in my own hands as long as I return to Wilhelmshaven by mid-December. I can sortie whenever I desire."

The two officers sipped their tea quietly, as the steward filled two small schnapps glasses. Then, as if both came to the same conclusion at the same time, Ahrens leaned forward and tapped the U-boat commander on the shoulder. "My young man, you may well be able to assist us."

The young officer also leaned forward and smiled. "Indeed, sir, I will time my departure to be the day prior to your release, such that I might ensure there are no, should we say, surprises awaiting you outside of the bay. Of course, only Baumbach, our attaché, will know of our plan. So I need only to confirm your departure date and then I will proceed a day earlier to sanitize your sailing."

Ahrens looked delighted. "Agreed," he replied softly. The submariner stood suddenly, snapped his heels together loudly, and then held out his hand. "Good, sir, I am proud to be able to offer the services of my crew and boat for such a noble ship." The two officers shook hands warmly and Liebe left the cabin, joining the Russian officer in the passageway.

Ahrens remained seated, thinking for a few moments. The presence of *U-38* had certainly been a windfall opportunity for his ship, now if only they would receive clearance to depart soon while the moon conditions were most favorable for sailing in complete darkness. The telephone rang; he leaned forward and picked up the receiver. "Ahrens."

It was the third officer of the watch on the bridge. "Sir, we have a ferry approaching from the town, making our starboard side."

Ahrens grunted, "Have the watch officer meet it at the gangway and see what they have. If it's mail, let me know at once." He hung up the phone. The mail had diminished to a trickle and it was still a mystery whether it was because the Germans were holding it in Bremerhaven or because the Russians were just no longer letting it through. The lack of mail on the one hand was demoralizing, while on the other it signaled to the men still aboard that faint hope that the date of their departure was finally approaching.

After waiting about twenty minutes, Ahrens grew curious and more anxious. He rose and removed his coat from the closet by the door, and was putting it on when a sharp knock stopped him.

"Yes, what is it?" Ahrens opened the door, and there to his great surprise stood his leading first officer Eric Warning with four other officers Ahrens didn't immediately recognize.

"My God," Ahrens said, beside himself, as he seldom registered emotion. But on seeing his chief mate for the first time since his departure in mid-September, Ahrens was truly surprised and relieved.

Warning saluted. "Herr Commodore, Leading First Officer Warning reporting with fifty-seven crew reinforcements, including seven from the Kriegesmarine."

"Come in my friends, we've been waiting for you." Ahrens was truly moved, his eyes glassy, his hands visibly shaking.

The officers entered his cabin, their greatcoats still flecked with frozen spray and beginning to drip. Ahrens suddenly recognized Radio Officer Kurt Gerstung, his cheeks red from the cold and a big smile wreathing his stubbled face. "Ah, now we can hear and speak again. Welcome back, Mister Gerstung." Ahrens shook his communicator's hand warmly.

"Bring tea," Ahrens called to his waiter. Steward Wolfgang Schultz, standing by the door, disappeared in a flash. Acting as the commodore's permanent steward since his promotion and after the majority of the crew had departed in September, Schultz was pleased to be near the action, which enabled him to pick up tidbits of information to pass on in the galley.

"Take off your coats and sit down, gentlemen." Ahrens retreated behind his desk, opened a drawer, and pulled out a bottle of rum. "For this occasion we spice our tea in proper fashion." Schultz quickly reappeared with cups and a steaming pot of tea on a tray and began placing the cups around the mahogany table. Ahrens passed the bottle to Gerstung, who immediately began pouring the dark liquid. Gathered around the table, the officers were genuinely happy to see their skipper in the warm bosom of their ship. Despite being stranded in the dark abyss of the Russian north, the ship still exuded warmth and the genial smells and the feel of home.

Commodore Ahrens began, "Now that you're back we'll set the wheels in motion for our return run." He hoisted his cup, "To Saint Nicholas, the patron saint of all sailors. And our safe return home." It was December 6, St. Nicholas Day, widely celebrated in Germany as the first feast day of the coming Christmas season.

Some of the crew replacements were seasoned *Bremen* sailors who had made the trip south by train in September and returned as volunteers. They were very happy arriving among their old friends and shipmates. Commodore Ahrens had ordered an extra case of wine opened that evening to celebrate their return, and they sat around in the lounge most of the night and into the morning hours. The celebration had been intense, but the next morning all were immersed in preparations for departure.

Commodore Ahrens reported that the ship was ready to depart via the prearranged link to Naval Attaché Baumbach in Moscow. The next day Radio Officer Gerstung's operators received the orders via blind (coded) broadcast that they were to depart at midnight on December 10. Gerstung brought the movement order to the chart house where Warning and two of the naval officers from the high command had gathered. The naval officers were wearing merchant uniforms so as not to cause undue attention from the Russians. They had brought with them the chart overlays for the transit south. These had been carefully spread out on the chart table and appeared to the merchant officers as extraordinarily complex. The senior officer, a Korvettenkapitän (lieutenant commander), began to decipher the symbols and was in the midst of an explanation when Ahrens entered the chart house.

"Gentlemen," Ahrens began, "these next days are key not only for us but for the German people." Ahrens rarely preached, but with outsiders present, he wished to set the stage for the seriousness of the coming transit. "We are in the position of writing maritime history, and although we are neither warship nor Hilfskreuzer, we need naval support to complete this transit. So let's put away our differences and act as though we are wearing the same uniform." He glanced at Warning, who nodded slightly to show his appreciation. Ahrens understood there was friction between his first officer and the naval officers, and it was primarily because, as such a junior reserve officer, Warning carried the coveted S following his naval title of Leutnant zur Zee (lieutenant junior grade).

The group remained in the chart house for most of the evening and finally retired for the night having satisfactorily worked out the procedures for the departure and transit. Ahrens and Warning remained after the others had gone. "Come, follow me," Ahrens said. And the two stepped out onto the wing of the bridge. The night air was cold, clear, and crisp, with bright stars. Ahrens then told Warning about the presence of the U-38 and Heinrich Liebe, which he determined should not be discussed in the presence of any others aboard.

"Liebe will sail after dark on December ninth and scour the channel leading out to the open Barents Sea. If there are any of our former friends waiting there, he will dispatch them in good order, hopefully before they dash off a message of our departure, but no one is to know of his presence." Warning understood.

The two remained on the bridge watching the night sky, and then after a few minutes Ahrens said, "You know, after this, our paths will surely part; you will go one way and I, because of my leg problems, will probably leave the fleet." He shifted uneasily, not used to such frank and personal conversation with one of his officers. "I want you to know that I appreciate your devotion and loyalty and always have, so I say now, whatever happens, I am thankful for your service."

"Thank you, Herr Commodore," Warning replied.

Ahrens was silent again for a time. Then he said to his first officer, "You know Warning, that despite all these plans, code words, rendezvous, and planned air escorts," Ahrens felt in a way as if he were addressing a young boy, "everything really depends on the simple course of the weather. If it is poor and overcast with bad visibility, we stand a fair chance of making it. If, however," and he paused looking up at the stars, "we should have clear horizons, our chances are really minimal for returning home."

Warning looked up in the sky with Ahrens, and after pausing replied, "Yes, sir, I realize that, but in my deepest soul I feel we will make it."

"I feel the same," Ahrens replied, then turned and disappeared into the pilothouse.

Warning remained on the wing of the bridge for some time. When he was about to retire, he was suddenly interrupted by a signalman, who came up behind him and said, "Sir, I have been watching the ship on the other side of the anchorage and they have been sending a flashing light signal to someone located seaward. I can't read the code, it seems not international Morse." Warning thanked the seaman, and stared out into the darkness. "There's not much we can do about that now. If our plan is known, all is now in the hands of fate." He left the bridge and went below to his cabin, where he had not been since the middle of September. He lay down without undressing and fell fast asleep.

As Warning was resting, Ahrens studied his orders for the transit:

1. Check points to be observed but not reported for security.
2. Remain outside of visual range of the Norwegian coast, and do not use the inland waterways due to the size of the ship.
3. Take all measures to sink the ship keeping it out of enemy hands using explosives sent with the crew reinforcements, but doing so only out of visual range from the Soviet coast.
4. The seas between Shetland Islands and the Norwegian coast are under enemy observation. Enemy air surveillance extends to about 64 degrees north. The seas south of 64 degrees north to the Skagerrak must be transited by dark and at highest speed as far to the east as possible, yet keeping well clear of the Norwegian coast. Poor visibility is especially useful for the breakthrough. If clear weather persists, you must delay until more favorable conditions. Weather reports will be sent via blind broadcast for *Bremen* under the same conditions as for German air reconnaissance. The ship must be ready at 64 degrees north by the beginning of darkness in order to

make the middle of the Skagerrak by the next morning. If the weather permits, the ship can proceed south at the beginning of nightfall. It is recommended that you be positioned slightly north of 64 degrees north at nightfall before the southerly run. If the morning finds the Skagerrak in clear flying weather, it would be favorable for German air escort. If security of the ship in Norwegian territorial water is questionable, it is not worth risking the ship to the whims of the Norwegians.

5. Whether to transit through the Kattegat and Great Belt into the Baltic or to transit direct south through the North Sea depends on the situation, and will require full knowledge of safe channels through the minefields.

Caution against surface or aircraft in the Skagerrak is emphasized. Should such threats not materialize, make highest speed and steer zigzag course to avoid submarines.

Friendly air escort is not available north of Lindesnes, therefore air attack there is possible.

Security lies in the absolute secrecy of this event.

The next morning Ahrens invited his first officer to breakfast with him in his inport salon. As Warning ate in silence, Ahrens commented on their orders. "In all cases, I have been assured by the High Command that I alone am personally responsible for the safety of the *Bremen* during this run." He glanced at Warning and smiled, "It's plain as the nose on your face that our navy does not give this venture much chance for success, so they are washing their hands of all responsibility. Why, to me that smacks of what Russians do; cover your ass first and then take a chance."

First Officer Warning was still tired after the good night's sleep, but happy. He had slept little since before they had begun their return journey to Murmansk, but he was catching up. "Yes, Commodore, but they are really quite confident in your capabilities. They told me in Berlin that if anyone can bring *Bremen* home it would be you."

The day after the reinforcements arrived the Russians finally acquiesced to Captain Ahrens's request of three months ago, that some of his crew be permitted ashore in Murmansk to at least see some sights and get a change of scenery from their long confinement aboard. The Soviet naval liaison officer, the political officer from the Northern Fleet Headquarters, the same man who Ahrens and Warning had first met from the team off the old destroyer outside the Kola fjord, grinned like a satisfied schoolteacher informing the mother that some, mind you, only some children would be allowed on a field trip.

Twenty-five of *Bremen's* sailors were allowed to go ashore in a barge provided by the Northern Fleet. They would be taken on a sightseeing tour of Murmansk, no cameras permitted, and then hosted for an evening of entertainment that included dinner at the International Seaman's Club in Murmansk. That club had been opened specifically for the use and enjoyment of foreign sailors. Indeed, the fleet officer announced proudly, there was one of these clubs in every major port of the Soviet Union where foreign merchant ships visited. What the grinning political officer did not volunteer was that use of the club was for foreigners only; Russians were not permitted, that is, except for the club staff made up of men and women working directly under the NKVD—Narodny Kommisariat Vnutrennikh Del (People's Commissariat of Internal Affairs).

Captain Ahrens immediately accepted the invitation and then stepped aside with the first officer. "Select twenty-five of our most deserving from those who have been aboard since arrival. I think most ought to be Chief Müller's engineers, and the quartermasters who have been the busiest."

"Aye, Herr Commodore," Warning replied, smiling. "It's about time."

"Oh, yes," Captain Ahrens added, "there will be no talk of our pending departure whatsoever. I know our men don't know the exact date yet, and neither do the Russians, except for their top people. But give the men a special warning; make sure they are conscious of the importance of impeccable behavior while ashore. You may accompany them along with the chief engineer." The captain smiled, knowing that the engineers were the most like normal sailors aboard other merchant ships, unlike the stewards, cooks, and waiters on liners such as *Bremen* who were selected for their refined manners and quiet nature, which was necessary for sailors that mingle with passengers. The engineers revered their boss, Leading Chief Engineer Frederich Müller, and would certainly tow the line with him present.

The first officer vanished abruptly from the bridge to carry the good news to the men involved and to make the difficult selection. The barge was promised for 1:00 P.M. the next day.

Although the degree may vary somewhat from merchant to naval seamen, there are some aspects universally similar among the world's sailors: the unmistakable desire after long periods of enforced puritanical behavior at sea to make a run ashore, during which they invariably seek out the seediest watering holes to satiate their parched thirst. Now, despite the fact that the *Bremen* crew were permitted beer and sometimes wine with their meals, and on special occasions a festive beer night, they were otherwise not permitted to consume alcohol. And despite the presence in the many passenger bars of hundreds of cases of strong spirits, these were not the property of the ship's company but were strictly for dispensing to the passengers, and therefore kept under lock and key by Chief Purser Julius Rohde. This universal sailors' character includes the congenital tendency, like how water follows the principles of Archimedes, to always seek the lowest standard of public establishment, one of those usually found in the most disreputable sections of the world's ports. So the *Bremen* crew allowed shore leave with the Russians looked forward to the typical liberty in a foreign port. In this case, however, they were sadly disappointed.

After his trips through Russia, First Officer Warning had become sufficiently acquainted with Russian drinking traditions to warn the crew about the manner in which Russians consumed vodka. Therefore, in normal fashion the *Bremen* crew prepared by eating enough greasy food—some of them swallowing spoonfuls of olive oil— to prevent too sudden absorption of the alcohol through the walls of the stomach into the blood stream. Normally this was done by quaffing large quantities of milk before climbing into the liberty boat, but in this case, due to the absence of fresh milk aboard, the olive oil had to suffice.

The Russian barge came alongside on time, which was a surprise, and took the twenty-five crewmen, including Chief Müller, to the subdued city of Murmansk. At the landing they were politely ushered onto a bus, which although it ran them more or less successfully into the town, seemed to the German engineers, who prided themselves on the precision and gleaming appearance of their own machinery, to be in the terminal stages of disrepair. Most of the windows were either cracked or broken, with makeshift patches of wood or cardboard affixed to deter the frigid draft. Nevertheless, the visiting Germans were shown the main section of Murmansk, mostly wooden buildings, and several museums. One was explained to be honoring the accomplishments of socialism, and contained grotesque art and sculpture depicting socialist realism. After the tour of the city, the bus finally jerked to a stop in front of a windowless building made of prefabricated concrete. The *Bremen* crewmen were ushered inside a theater and seated to watch a series of stage shows, including Russian traditional song and dance, with performers dressed in brightly colored native costumes. There was a concert by a *balalaika* group, some opera arias, and finally a rousing chorus of traditional folksongs of Russia's north, which somehow morphed into a crescendo to the tune and words of the *Internationale*. It was entertaining, but by that time the sailors' throats were more than just parched.

Following the concert, the group was taken into an adjoining dining hall, where a large table stood bedecked with food of all types: salads, fish, cabbage, sliced meats, and dark bread. Arranged down the center of the table were bottles of chilled champagne, wine, and vodka. It looked enticing to the men who were used to the fare aboard *Bremen*, which, after three months at anchor without reprovisioning, had grown quite monotonous. They dug into the fare like well-behaved sailors. Although there were only a few Russians sprinkled among the crew, the Germans did their best to keep up with the repeated toasts to mutual friendship between two great nations and that they would remain allies forever in these troubled times. None of those present that evening imagined that, within two years, they would be mortal enemies, tearing one another other apart in vicious combat on the great expanses of the Soviet Union. Thanks to the first officer's caution, none were lost on the way back to the ship. Several engineers, accustomed to the fine art of pilfering from the passengers' fare aboard, managed to filch some bottles of vodka to bring back for their less fortunate shipmates who had not made the cut to go ashore. All in all, the trip ashore was an unusual experience, and one that made the *Bremen* crew thankful to be from a country quite far from Russia. Most important, the Russians had lived up to their promise. The same number of bodies returned to the ship as had departed, and that had made Warning and Chief Müller happy. There were now serious preparations to be made for the trip home.

11

Running for Home

German Navy High Command
Berlin
December 1939

The German submarine disposition at the time of Operation Helene, although not fully known to those aboard *Bremen* when they left Murmansk, included the following U-boats:[1]

North Sea
U-23 — clearing Orkneys to the Shetland Islands
U-20 — off Rattray Head (the easterly point between Moray
      Firth and Firth of Forth)
U-13 — off Firth of Tay (off Dundee)
U-61 — off Firth of Forth
U-57 — off Nordhinder Lightship

Northern Russia
U-38 — Polyarny

The German plan called for a squadron of five German destroyers to take station due east of the channel to Newcastle on the North Sea on December 10, and once *Bremen* passed they were to begin laying mines in that area. The destroyers were backed up by the light cruisers *Nürnberg, Leipzig,* and *Köln.* To the south, the battleships *Scharnhorst* and *Gneisenau* were conducting routine gunnery exercises. During the execution of Operation Helene, some top German warships would be out on preplanned operations, but were informed that *Bremen* would make the break from Murmansk in the early morning hours of December 10.

British Home Fleet
North Sea
December 1939

As *Bremen* prepared to depart Russian northern waters, Lieutenant Commander E. O. Bickford took *Salmon* northwesterly through the North Sea and set up a patrol area just southwest of Stavanger, where he would remain alert for further German contacts breaking out of the Baltic or the Weser estuary.

Admiral Charles Forbes strengthened his watch over the Shetland-Faeroe gap by reinforcing the old cruisers *Caledon, Cardiff,* and *Colombo* with the cruisers *Diomede* and *Dunedin* from the south. The cruisers *Aurora, Edinburgh,* and *Southampton,* escorted by three destroyers, sailed from the Firth of Forth to cover Fair Island Passage, and a fourth destroyer patrolled the Pentland Firth. The cruiser *Glasgow,* escorted by three additional destroyers, cruised off the Norwegian coast should *Bremen* hug the coast as she made the run to the south. During the last week of November, Admiral Forbes himself embarked on the battleship *Nelson,* accompanied by *Rodney,* the heavy cruiser *Devonshire,* and seven destroyers, and set sail from the Clyde, while the cruiser *Aurora* was on alert off Ultshire. Four submarines, *L23, Sturgeon, Thistle,* and *Triad,* patrolled off the Skagerrak, while the submarine HMS *Salmon* and two other submarines from the Firth of Forth and the River Tyne patrolled off Lister.

Murmansk
Saturday, December 9 to Sunday, December 10, 1939

The *Bremen* crew knew the homeward dash was at hand but still remained ignorant of the exact timing of their departure from Russian waters. The British ship *Temple Moat* was reported by Norbert von Baumbach, the German naval attaché, as being an intelligence ship believed to have a clandestine transmitter aboard that was prepared to send notice of *Bremen*'s departure to the British Admiralty. The attaché worked out a plan with the local Russian authorities to have that ship expelled from the harbor before December 1 to ensure she was gone well before *Bremen's* departure, hoping the British would not have sufficient time to replace her with a second intelligence warning ship. Baumbach passed the same information to Heinrich Liebe aboard *U-38*, still moored in nearby Polyarny.

The Russian maritime defense forces, known by the Germans to be part of the NKVD, launched surprise searches of all foreign ships present to prevent the secret raising of transmitter antennae. But the Germans were prepared to overcome their efforts with some ingenuity. Adolf Ahrens planned to depart in the earliest hours of the morning to preclude notice of *Bremen's* absence by the other ships present. With a little luck, they would have one of those blinding December Russian blizzards to cover their departure.

After the reinforcements arrived with First Officer Eric Warning, the entire *Bremen* crew gathered together in the lounge and were told that the new men were aboard specifically to help with the sprint home, which was coming as soon as weather and moon conditions were right. They would use the long December nights much as they had used the foul weather off New York to mask their movements. Two of the crew reinforcements who were naval petty officers held special lookout recognition training for all hands including stewards, waiters, and galley staff. They showed the crew photos and silhouettes of the British merchantman *Temple Moat* that had been in Murmansk when they arrived but had departed and was believed to be lying outside the Kola fjord in international waters watching to report their departure. Several other crew reinforcements had come from the navy *B Dienst* and were assigned to Kurt Gerstung's radio staff as experts in decoding and analyzing British radio traffic. Another group of reinforcements were army engineers sent to instruct the crew in the use of the special pyrotechnics they had brought aboard with them. These were added to the already carefully accumulated piles of combustibles arranged on the promenade deck, in the first-class lounge, and belowdecks in some engineering spaces. All these would be armed with timing fuses, thereby allowing the crew to abandon ship rapidly in case British warships intercepted them. They were allotted exactly fifteen minutes to man the lifeboats, depart the ship, and clear the area before their beloved ship would explode and sink to keep her out of enemy hands. The thought was insufferable.

The excitement among the crew grew daily, especially after the reinforcements had settled aboard. The presence of the additional naval personnel gave the crew somewhat more confidence, although their presence wasn't that obvious because they wore merchant uniforms. Nevertheless, most of the crew knew who they were. The replacement communicators came aboard with the new H key lists needed to mask *Bremen*'s identity as the motor vessel *Helene*. Once the ship was in the Kola channel, the radiomen would transmit a routine report of departure, followed by several coded position reports as they moved south, using the call sign of *Helene* instead of their own. Gerstung's telegrapher had carefully studied the personal traits of *Helene*'s telegraphers so he could mimic them perfectly. Each telegraph operator possessed his own unique characteristics, which monitors studied to determine the true signature. Thus, another major responsibility was placed on Gerstung's men in the radio room, in this case to mask *Bremen*'s true identity. In the meantime, the ship *Helene* herself would remain at anchor in Murmansk Harbor unaware that she was providing cover for *Bremen*'s return dash.

By now *Bremen* had been in Russian waters for more than three months and all aboard were anxious to return home. The approaching Christmas season and the unknown aspects of the war made them even more anxious to get underway. There had been mail deliveries in the early days after arriving in Murmansk, although they had dwindled to few and far between. Most crew had written home and the letters had departed the ship, some in mailbags carried by the large group of crewmembers who had left that dark night in mid-September, and some of those had already been answered. But some letters in the mailbags merely disappeared into the dark bowels of the Russian tender that came every three days to collect mail. Gerstung's radiomen suspected the tender was inspecting them regularly to ensure they were not operating a clandestine radio, as the border guards always snooped around aboard checking into the sealed compartments, where Hanns Tschira had locked his cameras and Gerstung his radio transmitters. The Russians trusted no one.

With the orders now in hand and the operation clearly laid out, Ahrens directed that all hands not on watch assemble in the ballroom. In the past, that space would not have been adequate for all 900 crew members, but now together with the reinforcements, the total crew numbered only 137.

"Comrades," Commodore Ahrens began, "the time has come for us to depart this anchorage." After shifting anchorages a half-dozen times to counter the effects of the strong winds, and often at the request of their Russian hosts for unknown reasons, the captain knew the crew would automatically assume that they were just going to change locations again. But gathering for the Commodore to speak tipped the men that something big was due. To build the drama, Ahrens continued to hold the good news back.

"Yes, we will be hoisting anchor again and our Russian friends will provide escort and tugs. This time we will not only be closer to the shore," he paused again for effect, "but we'll be heading for our own shores." He enjoyed the sudden look of surprise on each crewman's face. "We are heading home for Germany," he burst out with mounting enthusiasm. A spontaneous cheer filled the large room. Ahrens paused, then continued. "We will depart tonight after dark." Then he hesitated again. When the room quieted, he said in a soft voice that each crewman clearly heard, "As I told you before we departed New York last August, we will get through!" Again a cheer broke out and the crew began to sing the national anthem.

Seaman Heinz Slominski recalled:

It was a stirring moment for us. Each of us understood that there was a large chance that we would encounter British warships as the ship neared the blockade between the Shetlands and Norwegian coast. If that happened, we would simply scuttle the ship and man the lifeboats. The thought remained in the back of all our minds but not one word was uttered that evening about the anticipated event. All the preparations had been made, and we avoided looking at the piles of inflammable materials and the red-painted cans of benzene scattered around the promenade deck. To us that eventuality would be met with precision if needed, but we preferred not to think about it. We kept our minds on the immediate task of preparing the ship for the homeward sprint.

Unknown to the *Bremen* crew, with the exception of Commodore Ahrens and Leading First Officer Warning, *U-38* had already quietly slipped her moorings and headed out into the night. The totally darkened U-boat proceeded easterly into the Murmansk fjord, then swung northward past Sayda Bay and into the dark Barents waters. There she would linger with her conning tower awash to monitor surface ships in the vicinity until *Bremen* departed and passed at 27 knots. For Heinrich Liebe, this seemed like the sole opportunity to turn this administrative patrol into a combat hunt.

Getting a 52,000-ton ship underway and steaming the nearly sixteen hundred miles to home waters was a complex matter, especially with a reduced crew aboard. The 137 men set about the preparations with deliberations as if it were a normal sailing, but each man understood the odds were stacked against their returning home safely.

First Officer Warning told the men after the evening meal that the special anchor detail would be set quietly an hour before midnight and the ship would weigh anchor, with the anchor under foot, off the ground but at the water's edge. They would steam north toward the open sea, gradually taking in the anchor as they crept along to keep the sound down. Snow was expected. All were ready and keen to go.

Ahrens grew anxious when, by 9:00 P.M., it still hadn't begun to snow. Then finally at 11:30 P.M. snow fell and gradually increased in intensity. All lookouts watched for the British ship *Temple Moat*, which had departed the harbor the week before and was expected to be lurking outside the fjord. But as the visibility decreased and the wind picked up the crew gradually realized they had nothing to fear; the weather gods were looking out for them as they had in late August when they left New York. With the anchor finally housed, *Bremen* gradually picked up speed and disappeared into the howling winter night.

"Mister Warning," Commodore Ahrens asked in his usual calm voice, "did you ever see such snow?" He was happy to have the serious first officer back on board after his prolonged absence. Ahrens was well aware of his participation in the planning of the departure operation, and he was proud that Warning had made such good allies in the Navy High Command. It was due to his assistance and the persistence of Naval Attaché Baumbach that the plan had finally gained wide support.

Warning smiled as he thought of the near chaos of the early days of loading, the arguments, delays, and cajoling. Now finally the moment of departure had come. In his tidy mind he deplored the ways of the Russians and could hardly wait until they were clear of the harbor, leaving Murmansk and everything Russian behind. The Soviet authorities had been more than cooperative in agreeing to halt sailings of all ships for three days following *Bremen*'s departure, to ensure that no other foreign vessel would quickly depart after noticing the liner's absence and thus be free to transmit a report to the British Admiralty when clear of Soviet waters. In this fashion, if all the ships were kept incommunicado, the escape might go unreported.

The darkness would last until 11:00 A.M. the next day, when a silvery glow would illuminate the sky, but remain without visible sun until about 3:00 P.M. when darkness would quickly descend once again, taking *Bremen* safely into the long winter's night. By the time any observing foreign ship had the chance to transmit a report of their departure, they should be well clear of the coast. But Warning wasn't convinced the Soviet officials were fully effective in carrying out their intentions. He wondered at their seeming incompetence, but they had surprised him before and could do so again. He hoped for the best.

Warning noticed that Ahrens had lost weight since September and appeared gaunt and nervous. He understood the strain on the master, especially since he had been given responsibility for all

German ships in Murmansk, initially numbering eighteen but dwindling by December 10 to half a dozen. The two officers stood quietly side by side in the driving snow, neither wanting to be the first to suggest they should retreat into the wheelhouse to escape the bitter wind. Finally, Ahrens took Warning's arm and side-stepped toward the door. "The weather gods have been good to us again; the visibility is near zero, no need to stay out here and freeze," he said, guiding his first officer into the warmth of the pilothouse. The lookouts huddled on the bridge wings, on the weather decks, on the bow, and high in the mast lookout nest. Since there was little to see, they would have to rely strictly on dead reckoning to make their turn to the west when well clear of the Rybachi Peninsula. For the second time in four months, Ahrens was gripped by fear as he drove his ship into the darkness and uncertainty. He put all thought of failure out of his mind and concentrated on the task at hand. He was sure they would make it home safely, somehow.

U-38
Barents Sea off the Kola fjord
December 10, 1939

Korvettenkapitän (lieutenant commander) Liebe huddled in his sheepskin jacket, leaning on the corner railings of the bridge cock-pit of the conning tower. His two lookouts standing either side of him were straining to see in the darkness. It had not yet begun to snow, yet the air smelled like snow. The seas were confused, run-ning at three feet first from the west then veering to the northwest. The wind was rising and still from the northwest. The barometer was plunging.

"Contact," one lookout shouted. "Light bearing red five-zero."

Liebe swung his Zeiss glasses to port. He saw nothing. "Where away?"

"Sir, it's very faint yellow, I saw it briefly, then it disappeared."

Liebe looked in silence. It was just beginning to snow. He looked at his watch, which glowed green in the darkness. It was past midnight and he knew *Bremen* was already moving slowly toward the fjord. "It's black as the inside of a cow," he muttered. He saw nothing in any direction.

"There it is again, sir, red glow at about red three-zero now. Looks like a cigarette burning."

"I see it," Liebe replied. It was snowing harder now, but the glow grew larger and intermittent. "Right ten degrees rudder, increase speed to ten knots." If it was a lurking British ship, perhaps *Temple Moat*, he would close her and attack while surfaced. "Man the deck gun, sound no alarm; we're too close. Stand by to fire tubes two and four. Number One, firing solution for two thousand meters, ten knots."

It began to snow harder, yet Liebe could just make out the dark form of a ship just over a mile away. Odd, he thought, she must be sitting dead in the water because my sonar has no hydrophone effects of a turning screw. Whoever it was waited in the dark with no way on, that is, standing still. The visibility worsened.

"Tubes two and four ready. Time to fire one minute." The tense voice came over the cockpit speaker.

"Very well. Hold until I say." There was a pause of several seconds, then, "Damn. Can't see a bloody thing up here, visibility is gone completely. Total white out." Liebe knew an attack was now impossible. The wind increased and U-38 disappeared into a total white out. "Shit." Liebe muttered into the voice tube, "Abort the attack, right standard rudder, come to new course zero-five-zero, speed eight knots." Liebe was truly disappointed. He had hoped to put two torpedoes into whomever was lurking as a final tribute to the liner *Bremen* and her courteous commodore. Now the weather had taken over as *Bremen*'s guardian angel. His submarine was useless without any visibility or any passive sonar. The howling and crashing of the wind and building seas had rendered his sonar totally useless. "Prepare to dive. We're going to just sit this out and need to keep from colliding with something in this mess."

The lookouts dove through the scuttle and the gun crew disappeared off the main deck and into the warm stench of the hull. "Dive, dive!" Liebe shouted and dropped through the hatch, pulling it shut with a clang. The main deck slowly descended into the froth and U-38 slipped quietly into the depths, away from the weather and from whatever chance target they had been stalking.

SS *Bremen*
Murmansk fjord
December 10, 1939

It took the sleek liner three hours to clear the fjord. As they entered the open Barents Sea, the snow increased and enveloped her towering bridge in swirling white. They continued north until forty-five miles from the Russian coast, then turned to the west, taking them well clear of the normal shipping lanes and out of the fishing grounds. Despite the poor visibility, Commodore Ahrens carefully followed the track west, clearing North Cape well outside visual range of the coast, then turned south. They saw no surface ships at all. Ahrens wondered whether Heinrich Liebe in his U-38 had been able to spot anything during the heavy snow as they exited the fjord. He had seen no sign of the submarine, yet he had not really expected to. In any case, it had been a splendid experience meeting the skipper of an operational U-boat.

They rounded North Cape at a speed of 27.5 knots and sighted the Anda Light at 1:40 A.M. at a range of twenty-one miles. By first light they would be outside the Lofotons fishing banks. They would be forced to run the strongest area of the British blockade between the Shetland Islands and the Norwegian coast the next day. The snow changed to a heavy rain as the first streaks of silver lit the horizon. They crept south without sighting a single other ship. Ahrens steamed roughly forty miles off the Norwegian coast so as to make use of the loom of navigation aids, when the visibility permitted, yet still too distant for observers to see the gray hull and superstructure.

When *Bremen* reached 64 degrees north, just west of Trondheim, they began watching for the first of several U-boats positioned to relay any sightings to Commodore Ahrens. This information would assist him in deciding whether to dash for the Baltic approaches or to continue south through the North Sea toward Cuxhaven and then south to the Weser estuary.

"Please inform me when we are within twenty-five miles of our line of departure, Mister Warning." Ahrens withdrew from the starboard bridge wing into the chart house, where he had stood for long hours poring over the charts, now overlaid with the track from the Helene operation order. The plot showed the line of departure, which *Bremen* was poised to cross only at twilight on December 11. It was overcast and there was no moon. Again the weather had been in their favor: the wind was from the southwest at just under five miles per hour, the seas also ran from the southwest, and swells were moderate. Ahrens studied the noon estimated position and weather report. The air temperature was six degrees Centigrade and the seawater temperature just two degrees above freezing. He shuddered at the grim prospect of having to scuttle the ship after sighting a British warship. To man the boats with the air and water temperature hovering just above freezing was not a pleasant thought, especially with the seas running at about four feet.

The lookouts sighted Andenes Light bearing 136 degrees at almost twenty-seven miles. That was unexpected but nevertheless welcome, since it was still overcast with light rain falling. The extreme darkness enabled the mast lookout to pick up the loom at that range.

The ship passed the 64-degree line just one hour after full dark at 5:00 P.M. Now the task for all hands was to try to spot the blinking amber light of *U-23*, which was supposed to be lying along their track to relay by flashing light whether any contact lay ahead. The atmosphere was tense. First Officer Warning was in the wheelhouse assisting the other watch officers. The lookouts were quadrupled and standing along the forward edges of the deck as far aloft as the sun deck and atop the bridge. The commodore had ordered that the chief steward serve hot tea and cocoa in the first-class dining room throughout the long night. The provisions aboard were still holding out, although they had long since depleted fresh vegetables, ice cream, and rum. The only alcohol left aboard after the months sitting in Murmansk was a few kegs of draft beer and several bottles of the horrible vodka they had purchased from the Russian chandler, the only staple in plenteous supply besides the dark Russian bread that stayed fresh only hours, thereafter becoming so hard it might be used as a weapon.

"Dim light, three points off the starboard bow!" the cry went up by a lookout standing high above the wheelhouse. "Low on the water."

Warning spun on his heel and drew up his glasses, peering into the rain and darkness. The longer he stared, the more fouled his glasses became. Swearing quietly to himself, he retired into the shelter of the bridge overhang to clean his lenses.

"False alarm!" the cry came back.

"Tell the men to continue to be alert," Warning called out, not about to reprimand the man for the false alarm. It was nearly impossible to find a light on the bobbing conning tower of a Type VIIB submarine in that weather.

The night drew slowly on. Ahrens was beginning to lose hope that there was any possibility to spot a submarine in this darkness and rain. Just as he was about to return to the bridge, the chart house telephone buzzed. Ahrens grabbed the handset, then hesitated before answering. He should have let the quartermaster answer so he wouldn't sound too tense. It was not normal for the master to answer the phone there. But he went ahead. "Ahrens here."

"Sir, we hold a source transmitting on the designated frequency, bearing due south, low power. It could be our submarine contact." Kurt Gerstung was out of breath as he was often when excited. "The signal is weak and intermittent, but it could be her. It's dead on the bearing and I would estimate no more than ten miles ahead."

"Very well, keep me posted." Ahrens was again proud of his radio officer. He had come through before in tense situations, twice off of Halifax, when he picked up the cruisers *York* and *Berwick*, again with the U.S. Coast Guard cutter off St. John, Newfoundland, and now here, where the slightest misidentification of a contact could spell the loss of the ship.

Warning stepped into the chart house. "Sir, I heard Gerstung's men may have the contact."

"Yes, looks that way," Ahrens replied. "If it's her, be prepared to copy her light signal. What she says may determine our fate. I hope there are no contacts; I don't look forward to running in the Great Belt in this weather with our draft so close to the minimum depth there." *Bremen* now was drawing just over thirty feet. It was not possible to reduce the liquid load anymore because they needed all their fuel in case they had to run at full speed, and Chief Frederick Müller had already shifted all the liquid load possible. Otherwise it would have been a simple thing to lighten the ship by dumping fuel for more clearance in the Belt. It was not a pleasant thought, especially after having to pass close aboard the German minefields plotted on his Helene chart overlay. That should be simple enough if the mines were as plotted and had not come adrift.

"Sir, flashing light signal from the contact; it's our submarine," Warning said, grinning widely in the dim light of the chart house.

The message was short as it came via the blinking amber light. The signalman brought it to the bridge where Commodore Ahrens stood next to the first officer and read it under the glow of a red-lensed flashlight:

To: Master of SS *Bremen*
From: *U-23*

Track ahead is clear, weather conditions and poor visibility on your side. No contacts.

Good luck.

Ahrens looked up and out of the wheelhouse windows. The rain was increasing and pounded on the forward windows. "Very well," he said. "Send this answer: 'Your report acknowledged. Thank you for your services. Smooth sailing. Ahrens.'"

The signalman disappeared out the wheelhouse door and made straight aloft for the signal bridge, where the fluttering light could be seen sending the reply, then after the short response, the night closed in again around the sudden light and *Bremen* was again enveloped by pitch blackness.

12

Salmon's *Dilemma* — Bremen's *Escape*

HMS *Salmon*
North Sea
7:30 A.M.
Tuesday, December 12, 1939

Admiral Forbes had ordered the submarine *Salmon* to remain in the patrol area where eight days earlier she had sunk the outward-bound *U-36*. Lieutenant Commander E. O. Bickford was happy to remain at this location. Although it was uncomfortably close to the northern edge of the German minefield guarding the Helgoland Bight approaches to the Weser estuary, it was also a channel frequently taken by U-boats outward bound from Wilhelmshaven and he expected there may be more heading his way. Bickford, a man much stimulated by the proximity of action, had been running *Salmon* on the surface since early that morning following the all-night vigil searching for contacts and, having just completed charging batteries, was preparing to submerge. He climbed up to the conning tower and joined First Lieutenant Maurice F. Wykeham-Martin for a last moment of fresh air and to check the weather firsthand. He noted that the visibility was limited to about four miles in heavy overcast with light southwest winds and seas rolling slightly from the northwest. He enjoyed the early morning air and the gray streaks of dawn. It felt good to be fully charged and ready for what the day might bring. He had just relaxed and began thinking of the next leg of the patrol when his thoughts were interrupted by the lookout's call, "Aircraft, sir, green three-zero, range four miles."

Captain Adolf Ahrens (left) on the bridge wing. (Hanns Tschira—courtesy of Deutsches Schiffahrtsmuseum, Bremerhaven)

Bickford spun around and saw the contact immediately off the starboard bow. It was a seaplane flying low, and before he could guess the type, the lookout shouted, "German Heinkel 70, sir. Heading west."

Bickford ordered the watch to dive, but it was clear they had not been detected, as the aircraft continued heading straight and level. A last glance before he descended the main trunk showed the aircraft turning and taking a reciprocal course. Odd, Bickford thought, why would German aircraft be patrolling this far to the north so early in the day? Something was stirring and he hoped it would herald some new action. He did not have to wait long.

Bickford took his boat down to 150 feet and continued to patrol submerged in a box pattern at 4 knots. The next two hours proved tense but uneventful.

SS *Bremen*
North Sea
9:00 A.M.
December 12, 1939

The lookout watches were still doubled, and as *Bremen* drew closer to the German defensive minefields, every crewman aboard was literally holding his breath. They had made it through the night with only one visual contact: lights from a probable merchant ship heading northeast through the North Sea. It is doubtful the ship had seen the liner, as they passed at about four miles distant without a challenge or the slightest alteration of course or speed. In the morning hours the weather had remained overcast with periodic rain, increasing at times to heavy squalls. Commodore Adolf Ahrens had just returned to the bridge following his brief breakfast in his sea cabin and was stepping out on the wing of the bridge when the report came by telephone from the lookouts aloft on the mast, "Aircraft dead ahead, approaching from the south, range five miles."

Everyone on the bridge who heard the report immediately turned to look ahead with their glasses. "Mister Warning sound the alarm," Ahrens ordered. "It's an airplane all right, coming right at us."

Warning immediately ordered, "Full ahead, Quartermaster, inform the engine room to stand by for emergency speed, aircraft inbound." The tension in his voice was brittle, his enunciation exaggerated; it always was when in extremis. Warning seemed to thrive and grow more deliberate in his actions when sensing danger at hand. The leading first officer had been standing the deck watch since Ahrens had gone below for breakfast, and the first officers from the other two watches were also present in the wheelhouse, adding to the sense of urgency. The small black dot slightly above the horizon began to grow larger. The sea seemed to have belonged to *Bremen* ever since departing Murmansk, and as each hour passed and they grew closer to their goal, time seemed to stand still. Tension heightened. Any suspected or real contact was automatically perceived to be the enemy and to spell instant doom. It is strange how in these situations the worst case is always seized as most probable regardless of the evidence to the contrary. Although Ahrens and the watch officer knew that air escort was expected, the sighting of the first airborne object was still perceived to be the enemy. So works the human mind when ample adrenaline flows.

"Commodore, I recommend we hold this course," Eric Warning said loud enough for Ahrens to hear on the bridge wing. "It offers the least target area if she's hostile." The engine revolutions had increased noticeably, adding to the sensation that the whole mass of the ship was skimming as it rose and fell with growing frenzy. The following seas gave the sensation that the ship was surfing as the stern rose with the swell, then yawed and slid off with the bow pitching downward, sending a wall of white spray in an arc spreading outward in slow motion from the stem. It was a beautiful and powerful sensation.

Another lookout called, "Something's slung below the airplane, looks like a torpedo." The words rang like a shot on the bridge as the tension rose, and all eyes stared at the flying speck.

"Not sure about that," Warning called out loudly. "Could be one of our escorts that Gerstung reported earlier."

"We treat it as worst case," Ahrens replied. "When she passes overhead begin evasive maneuvers; we're approaching thirty knots again. And—"

He was interrupted by another lookout shouting, "Seaplane dead ahead," a pause, then, "looks like . . ." Then another voice broke in, "Sir, it's one of ours, a Heinkel 70 seaplane," a seaman called out.

A nervous shout broke out from the wheelhouse. "It's ours. Look, the black cross!"

"Silence on the bridge!" Warning shouted.

The lookout hesitated and then reported properly, "Sir, contact appears to be a Heinkel, range one mile and closing.

The bridge telephone rang and Ahrens grabbed the handset. "Bridge, Ahrens."

"Sir, Radio Officer Gerstung here, we have radio contact with the escort aircraft," he paused catching his breath, "says they have us in sight. They're making an identity pass and will then patrol ahead either side of our track."

"Ah," Ahrens replied. "Very well, Gerstung, well, done." He was visibly relieved and replaced the large handset into the holder with a loud snap.

SS *Bremen* steaming south toward the Weser River estuary taken from her Luftwaffe escort aircraft on December 12, 1939, the day she passed British submarine HMS *Salmon*. (Courtesy of Wilhelm Bohling)

"Mister Warning she's ours. Slow to twenty-seven and a half again. We seem to be in the capable hands of our Luftwaffe." Ahrens stepped into the wheelhouse and walked through heading for the chart house. He pulled back the curtain and saw that the door was open and three officers standing at the chart table.

"Mark the range and bearing to the minefield entry channel," Ahrens said. "Give the course to the quartermaster."

The navigator and two other officers were hunched over the chart; one was the lieutenant from the naval staff who had brought the extra charts and the minefield details to *Bremen* in Murmansk. There was a delay of a few seconds as the officers measured off the distance with a divider. "Minefield entry channel bears one-six-five at eighty miles, sir."

"Very well." Ahrens thought for awhile and then looked at the gyrorepeater on the bulkhead. "That is dead ahead, but we still have at least three hours before we're safe."

As the ship slowed again most of the crew were all probably thinking the same thing: so close yet so far. But they no doubt felt stronger, because with the airplane they had an extra set of eyes increasing the margin of safety considerably. Yet the prospect of a

British warship appearing out of the mist was still a menacing thought.

Ahrens wiped the rain off his eyebrows, then looked again into the murky distance. The visibility was diminishing again as the rain increased. The sky was brightening to the east as the mid-morning wore slowly on. The tension was palpable through the ship as the crew went automatically about their chores, acting like there was nothing unusual going on, but each took every chance to glance topside to check the weather, the skies, and the seas, as if trying to wish a contact, yet fearing that they might see one. The liner had now been in the area with the highest probability of an encounter with British patrols for almost twelve hours and so far there had been no surface contacts since the one uneventful sighting during the darkness.

HMS *Salmon*
North Sea
9:30 A.M.
December 12, 1939

Lieutenant Commander Bickford sat in the small wardroom with a stack of papers laid out neatly before him and a cup of steaming tea to the side. The tiny wardroom doubled as a battle dressing station during action stations and as his office when he had paperwork to do. It was time for the annual reports of fitness of his four subordinate officers. Most commanding officers dreaded the task, which demanded careful thought and meticulous choice of words, but Bickford looked forward to writing the evaluations. His only problem was finding enough time to sit undisturbed long enough to complete recording his thoughts on paper. He had been blessed with an unusual group of outstanding officers. To the man they were highly motivated and among the very best with which he had ever served. It was not difficult to find the highest praise as he began to choose and jot down the words.

It was 9:30 A.M. as Bickford completed the first glowing report for his first lieutenant, Maurice F. Wykeham-Martin, when the green curtain hanging in the doorway parted and the boat's coxswain, Petty Officer William George Taylor, thrust his head in, smiled widely, and said, "Sir, Petty Officer Barron in ASDIC reports hydrophone effects due north, sounds like a large multiscrew target. Your presence is requested in the control room."

"Very well," Bickford concealed his annoyance at having to scoop up his reports and smiled. "Be right there." He placed the papers in a small tray, shoved it into a drawer, and locked it. Then he slid out of the bench and entered the passageway. As he walked aft to the control room, he noticed there was a tense silence in the space that was crowded with the usual eight men, including the first lieutenant. Bickford stepped toward the forward periscope and noticed Coxswain Taylor looking alert but happy. They were all listening with baited breath for more word from the ASDIC operator. They all knew and respected Kenneth Barron as one of the most capable ASDIC operators in the fleet. He had been right on the button during their last engagement that ended with the sinking of U-36 a week ago, and now, knowing they were in the center of their patrol area, they expected more action. A period of silence followed as the hum of the blowers sang their monotone, the air was warm and fetid, the smell of fuel oil noticeable but less so than normal. The surroundings had not yet grown to its fullest foulness, since they had only been submerged for several hours.

"Sir," the ASDIC operator finally broke the silence, "four propellers, making two hundred rpm." He paused, then continued, "Either two ships at the same speed or one large one with four screws." The men listened intently to Barron's words.

The captain took his usual spot behind the helmsman and slightly to the right of the planesman by the forward periscope. "Very well," he said concealing his excitement. Before he could express that it could possibly be the large passenger ship they had been alerted to look for, his quick first lieutenant said it for him.

"Might be *Bremen*, sir. She's expected to be heading south and has four screws."

"Exactly my thoughts," Bickford said smiling. He could always count on his first lieutenant to be the first to evaluate a situation;

for that reason he valued his presence. Sort of a second brain, Bickford thought.

"Contact making high speed, sir, closing rapidly, estimate at least twenty-five knots, maybe more." Barron's reports from ASDIC were dramatic, as he had a low and resonant bass voice.

"Close the contact," Bickford said curtly. "Pick out an intercept course at six knots. He may have a surface escort in the vicinity."

"The first lieutenant has the conn, right standard rudder, come to course one-three-zero. Bow planes up ten degrees, come to forty feet. Stand by to raise periscope."

Bickford watched the depth manometer spin counterclockwise as the boat rose toward the surface. When the needle passed sixty, the periscope rose and the first lieutenant stepped back, offering the captain the first glance. Bickford stepped forward and opened the hand grips as the scope shuttered to a stop. He spun the handles and focused the lens, then stopped abruptly.

"Right, large passenger ship, high speed, course southeast." He stared through the lenses, then said slowly, "Two funnels, lines of the *Bremen* but she's wearing gray colors." He paused, then stepped back and gave the scope to the first lieutenant.

Bickford called out calmly, "Action stations, prepare to surface, no other contacts, so ahead full! We won't have much time to stop her."

Bickford was keenly aware of the rules contained in the Anglo-German Naval Treaty of 1935 and submarine agreement requiring a submarine to act in the same manner as a surface ship, thus having to surface prior to halting a prize. But Bickford was also aware of the new German order issued on September 4, following the *Athenia* affair, which had stated, "By order of the Führer and until further orders, no hostile action will be taken against passenger liners even when sailing under escort."[1] This order placed passenger ships in a special category of their own, since under international law and the naval agreements, when sailing under escort they could be attacked. Under the Prize Ordinance (the German term for the rules governing submarine warfare), a submarine was authorized to attack a transport or passenger ship if the latter was under escort by warship or aircraft. The ordinance further stated that transports deemed to be on active service with the armed forces could be regarded as warships. Therefore, Bickford's dilemma was how to regard *Bremen*. She was camouflaged. Bickford also knew from British intelligence reports based on intercepted communications that *Bremen* was now under direct orders of the German Navy High Command. Furthermore, he knew of the British Admiralty order of October 1, 1939, for all unarmed British merchantmen sighting enemy submarines to ram them.[2]

The first lieutenant quickly issued the orders to bring the submarine to the surface, and two and a half minutes later he and Bickford stood on the bridge, still snapping on their rain gear. It was heavily overcast and raining. *Bremen* loomed at about four miles, her wake churning white froth. The two officers stared out in the rain.

"Magnificent isn't she?" Bickford said to no one in particular.

"Not zigzagging, sir," the first lieutenant observed, after studying her for a moment. The *Salmon* deck gun crew had scrambled down to the weather deck and was rapidly loading the gun.

"Right, she's not seen us." Bickford quickly barked, "Signal *E*, on the Aldis lamp to stop immediately and keep repeating until she replies." Bickford noticed the large ship was painted entirely gray, from stem to stern and to the top of the formerly yellow stacks, a stark change from her previously black hull, the normal colors of Norddeutscher Lloyd. In fact, she was quite difficult to see and would have been nearly impossible to make out had she been at any greater range. The effect of the gray camouflage was striking.

They watched the passenger ship's towering bow suddenly commence swinging toward them. The large ship appeared to aim directly for the submarine. The signalman sent repeated *E*'s on the Aldis lamp for one full minute, without response. Were the Germans resorting to reciprocal action in response to the Admiralty ramming order to British merchant ships? Bickford wondered as he watched the range beginning to close quickly. After a few seconds they saw the liner abruptly reverse her rudders and begin swinging away.

"Roger, she sees us and is ignoring." Bickford stared out through his glasses. "She's either cutting to run or is commencing a zigzag course." He paused again, leaning hard against the side of the steel conning tower rail as the boat rocked in the swell.

"Right, put a round across her bow," he shouted down through cupped hands to the gun crew. The trainer responded by raising his arm, and tapping the second gunner on the head.

Bickford watched as the gun crew swung the gun out, training the muzzle just forward of *Bremen*'s bow. They had only seconds to act, as the liner was pouring on the steam and was already approaching 30 knots. Just as the loader pushed the round home, slamming the breech, and the trainer squinted through the sights, the first lieutenant barked, "Aircraft, red two-zero, two miles coming straight in!"

SS *Bremen*
North Sea
9:30 A.M.
Tuesday, December 12, 1939

Radio Officer Kurt Gerstung was suddenly jolted out of his concentration. The monitor listening in on the escort aircraft circuit burst into life. The radio alarm rang and crackled a few moments and then the key operator began to copy the Morse coded message. Gerstung heard it the same time the young operator with the log had and sprang to his feet. The monitor was so startled he dropped his log to the deck then lifted one of his headphones, but they were not necessary as the circuit was being piped into a speaker for Gerstung to monitor with him. There was a crackling of static again and then the unmistakable beat of the signal tapped out on the telegrapher's key in clear German text. Within seconds, a breathless signalman in dripping rain gear entered the radio room with the same message scrawled on a wet piece of paper.

"Sir, our aircraft just sent this by flashing light," he said while handing the soggy paper to Gerstung.

"Very good," said the radio officer. "We just received the same via wireless."

"Sir," the telegrapher stopped typing and read his message still on the roll. "Aircraft reports submarine sighting! Four miles, port quarter. He's heading in to check it out."

Gerstung's knees suddenly went weak, but he recovered. He grabbed the phone and dialed the bridge. "Captain please, emergency!" he shouted at the seaman who answered.

Then seconds later the calm voice of the commodore. "Ahrens here."

"Sir, our escort aircraft has just reported sighting a submarine on the surface, four miles astern in our wake. He's going in for identification."

"Right, Gerstung, thanks." Ahrens slammed the phone into the holder and stepped back to the front of the wheelhouse. "Mister Warning, sound the alarm and commence steering zigzag course either side of base course one-four-zero, come to full ahead. Ahrens walked across the wheelhouse, "Our air escort sighted a submarine. We'll show him our stern. Have all hands scour the bearing for torpedo wakes."

Ahrens walked over to the window, picked up the phone, and rang main engine control. "Ahrens here, give me Chief Müller."

There was a pause. The leading chief engineer was on the upper level of number three reduction gear, going around with the watch checking the temperature on the main bearings of number three shaft, which had been running high. The leading engineer preferred to spend his time roaming among his engineers in the four large engine rooms, surprising them with his visits and making the rounds with each member of the watch. The messenger found him down in the main shaft alley behind the reduction gear shining a flashlight on a temperature gage with the young watch stander holding a clipboard. "Sir, the captain on the horn, wants to speak to you now.

"Aye, one moment, I'll be there." The engineer sprang like a man half his fifty-five years, vaulting over the railing onto the catwalk, trotting along the gratings, and scampering up the ladder to the main control area. He took the phone held out by the top watch engineer.

"Müller here."

"This is Ahrens. We need all you can give us, Chief. There's an enemy submarine nearby and we're making a run for it. Fuel is no longer the issue. Give me all you can."

"Aye, Herr Captain, been waiting for this!"

Ahrens smiled as he replaced the handset. He was fond of his leading engineer and he knew that Frederich Müller would get the best and the most out of the plant. The engineers aboard *Bremen* had always been superior and trustworthy. The time in Murmansk had been difficult for them because of the necessity to conserve fuel as well as having to be ready to use the main engines at the spur of the moment because of the rapid requirement to shift the anchorage due to the weather and the unpredictability of the Russian harbor master's demands to move the foreign ships around the harbor with no apparent reason. For that reason, the engineers had run a constant watch with a steam blanket on the turbines and ready steam to the main throttle for almost three months straight, and they were worn to a frazzle.

Ahrens walked to the starboard bridge wing and looked aft through his glasses. The visibility was so poor he could not make out the airplane, but was able to hear the aircraft's droning engines. The rumble of *Bremen's* engines accelerating could be felt through the soles of his feet from the deck as the wake churned up astern. Ahrens glanced inside the wheelhouse at the log and saw it was reading 29.5 knots, and it still felt as if they were accelerating. He looked at Warning, who appeared dour and serious as always, and smiled. "Ever gone this fast, Mister Warning?"

They had actually done 30 knots when trying to outrun the aged Russian destroyer before sailing into the Kola Bay three months ago, when they had thought it might have been British.

The first officer merely looked at the log and shrugged. "No sir, I was not aboard during the trials." It was a well-known legend among the crew that during *Bremen's* sea and engineering trials in 1928, she had allegedly exceeded 32 knots for short bursts during a full-power run. That fact had been kept secret on the orders of the Norddeutscher Lloyd engineering staff, which claimed their

extreme capabilities, such as top speed, fuel and feed water con-
sumption rates, and true horsepower were a national security matter and would be fudged downward in maritime magazines.
Bremen's and her sister *Europa*'s wartime roles were specified as
high-speed transports, and they already had the basics for rapid
conversion into armed transports. There were two base rings for 88
mm gun mounts already installed in place between the stacks on
the sun deck level, one forward and one aft. There were also ver-
tical shafts adjacent to each mount location for the installation of
ammunition hoists connecting to now-empty voids that would
become magazines on the E deck level. Therefore, the accurate
knowledge of their top speed was known solely by those who had
served aboard during the trials and witnessed the high-speed runs.
Yet it was widely known among the crew that they had surpassed
30 knots. It was a sight to behold with the 52,000 tons shooting
through the waves at that speed, with dishes, silverware, and bar
glasses vibrating as the engines whined at a thrilling rpm.

"Well, sir, we need all Müller can give us now." The stern rose
on the crest of a swell and then slid off in a cushion of spray and
foam. The feeling of the ship shuddering and plunging gave the
sensation that they were skimming rather than steaming.

HMS *Salmon*
North Sea
10:00 A.M.
December 12, 1939

Bickford turned and saw the lumbering Dornier 18 reconnaissance
and submarine hunter seaplane coming straight and low at his conning tower. He could make out the black cross on the wings and
the glass-enclosed cockpit with two helmeted heads inside. He had
never before seen such a close-up view of German aircraft, and it
was a frightening image. The first contact had been a Heinkel 70.
It was daunting that *Bremen* had more than one escort.

"Emergency dive," Bickford shouted as he grabbed the lookout's arm and pushed him toward the scuttle. The first lieutenant
followed. The captain stepped back and waited until the gun crew

jettisoned the three shells over the side, vaulted up to the conning tower, and disappeared down the scuttle. Before following, he stopped to glance once more at the aircraft and then at *Bremen*. Even in her new drab camouflage paint she looked elegant, crouching like a large cat preparing to spring as she picked up speed, her high stern churning out white foam and swinging as she altered course rapidly on her zigzag.

Salmon had definitely been spotted, but its form must have been difficult to make out in the poor light. Bickford was certain the aircraft would not yet open fire or drop a weapon until it had a positive identification. Yet, perhaps they were already sure *Salmon* was not one of theirs. It was still early in the Atlantic war, but the news of the destruction a week ago of *U-36* not far from here had certainly put the Germans on edge. They knew a British submarine was in the area. Just how important was the liner *Bremen* to these navy ships? Bickford wondered as he slid smoothly down the ladder. The lookout had stepped off the ladder and was poised to pull the hatch shut as soon as the captain had passed him. As Bickford slid by the young lookout, he smiled but said nothing. Bickford was sure the young man was afraid, but so was he.

This had been the second enemy aircraft sighted in the area within the past three hours and it meant the Germans were throwing a lot to protect the huge liner. Bickford wondered if the *U-36* encounter a week ago had been related to the superliner's transit.

Bickford took *Salmon* down to a hundred feet, then ordered, "Stand by to fire numbers one and two. Torpedo Officer, firing solution?"

With the target that large it would be an easy shot, but after opening the outer doors and flooding the tubes Bickford paused and thought, I cannot fire at her. She is apparently not armed, she is escorted by aircraft but still remains as far as we know unarmed, and I have no orders to sink her. He repeated his thoughts out loud, and all in the control room looked at him. Had she in fact seen their warning to stop? The signalman had repeated the letter *E* for a full minute, and the liner, although not answering, had begun to zigzag. Was that a result of the aircraft sighting and report or *Salmon*'s signal to stop?

"Sir, contact at four thousand yards and opening. She'll be out of range in two minutes." The torpedo officer repeated the range as it opened. "Range forty-five hundred, five thousand, sir, max range six thousand yards."

Bickford was perspiring heavily even though it was not that warm in the control room. The pressure was terrible. He knew exactly what the stakes were. So far since the war had broken out in September the British had nurtured the hope that the Germans would still not slip into the unrestricted warfare mode of the last war. The naval treaties were designed to prevent that, and despite the sinking on September 3 of *Athenia*, the naval leadership in Britain had hoped the slowly spiraling war, called the Sitzkrieg in Germany, or phony or twilight war in Britain, would not deteriorate into an all-out, shoot first, query second, war at sea. Bickford knew that his decision in the next few minutes, even seconds, could become a precedent-setting act, and, whether he fired or held his fire, his actions would be dissected in detail for a long time to come. It was entirely too late to send signals home for guidance, for despite the efficiency of the wireless, it took hours, sometimes days, to get a signal out and receive a response. Bickford knew his orders and they said nothing about firing at a passenger ship. He could not confirm visually that she was armed, and although daylight, he could not determine whether she was running with or without lights, and while under air escort she was not necessarily an armed ship. Or was she? He must decide immediately.

Bickford thought quickly, and then looking at his first lieutenant said firmly, "We'll let her go, Number One."

Lieutenant Wykeham-Martin immediately nodded. "I agree, sir."

"Take us deep, two hundred feet, and slow to two knots." Bickford felt strengthened by his Number One's concurrence. "Those aircraft are her escorts. Who knows what others she has riding shotgun?"

As *Salmon* turned away and went deep to avoid being attacked by the aircraft, Bickford drafted a brief signal to send when they

ZEC

Navy Allows Bremen to Escape for Reasons of International Decency!

"International Decency My Blind Eye!"

Daily Mirror, December 14, 1939.

could return to periscope depth. Bickford handed the signal to Coxswain Taylor, "Here, give this to Sparks. Have him send it as soon as we return to periscope depth."

As far as Bickford could fathom, he had done the correct thing; he could not torpedo an unarmed passenger ship, whether she had passengers aboard or not, and she appeared to him, except for the colors of her hull, superstructure, and funnels, exactly as she had been when he had ridden *Bremen* to New York and back to Southampton six years earlier. One does not forget the graceful beauty of a ship like that, Bickford thought. (In Lieutenant Commander Bickford's patrol report, he claimed he had traveled aboard *Bremen* to the United States and back to Southampton while on leave in 1933.)

Salmon continued deep until 10:15 A.M., when she returned to periscope depth and streamed an antenna. Bickford sent the following HF signal on the main aerial:

> Bremen has passed me in position 57 degrees 00 minutes north, 5 degrees 45 minutes east, steering 130 degrees, screened by aircraft. Time of origin 0945/11.[3]

Bickford passed some anxious moments after filing the report. First of all, it was risky to transmit in those waters in case he was intercepted. Then, his decision to let *Bremen* pass was certainly going to be judged by his seniors. Should he have swallowed his feelings and fired? The range had been extreme, but he could have blasted two torpedoes away in time before she had passed beyond the maximum range of six thousand yards. Had he given her ample warning; should he have risked his boat to stop this symbol of German maritime power? Bickford was an experienced officer. He had made the decision while under the threat of attack by an enemy aircraft, yet there was the gnawing doubt that perhaps he should have been more ruthless. He had read the intelligence reports about the sinking of the liner *Athenia* in September. He had also seen the press reports and how the British media had bewailed the fact that a German submarine had apparently attacked the liner without warning, killing passengers including women and children. Bickford was certain he had done the correct thing. He also knew of the German post-*Athenia* sinking order to refrain from firing at passenger ships and the order in October rescinding that and allowing German submarines to attack liners after a warning, if showing no lights. He was also aware of the Admiralty order for all merchant ships sighting U-boats to send the SSS signal requesting armed assistance, and the German response, that all merchantmen using radio to request assistance could be attacked without warning.

Nevertheless, Bickford experienced several anxious moments. Three hours later, while still at periscope depth, *Salmon*'s radiomen intercepted a signal from the Admiralty telling his squadron commander, Submarine Squadron Three aboard HMS *Ursula*, that "*Bremen* was not a target." He was greatly relieved that he had made the correct decision.[4]

SS Bremen
North Sea
December 12, 1939

After receiving Gerstung's report from the aircraft, Commodore Ahrens stood fixed in place on the starboard wing of the bridge. Only a few of the crew knew what was going on as they had seen the German aircraft fly over and circle over a spot in the ocean the ship had passed moments earlier. What gave away the fact that something was up was the sudden increase in speed and the commencement of the zigzag steering. It was impossible not to notice. Even the engineers in the black holds sensed something was up. Chief Engineer Müller sent a runner up the port escape trunk to see what was happening.

Only Able Seaman Heinz Slominski, who was on the sun deck watching the airplane, had seen what he said was the conning tower of a submarine several miles on their quarter and had reported it to First Officer Warning. By that time, the crew had felt the ship increasing speed. Leading Chef Hans Künlen had become irate when the cake he was baking collapsed after the first sharp course change at the increased speed. The cake was to be in commemoration of their triumphant return. Now it was a complete loss and he had to start all over again. "Liners are not to be driven in such reckless manners!" Künlen shouted, his men standing quietly by, gaping at their irate chief. He had been on edge ever since leaving Murmansk and was to be given wide berth. He had insisted on staying aboard when the majority of his men had gone back to Germany with the first group in September. He had refused to go himself, claiming that as long as there were any crewmen to feed on the ship his duty was to ensure they were properly fed. Those who stayed aboard had been relegated to eating mostly preserved foods, canned hams, salt pork, and canned fish. But Künlen took great pride in his fabulous pastries, which he had baked each day, and still had an abundance of flour in his stores. The only catch was that the yeast had long since given out and he was baking unleavened bread and making thin Russian-style pancakes he called *blini*. In any case, the crew were happy to get freshly baked goods each day, even though they longed for fresh vegetables and meats. The only drink left aboard were a few cases of Rhine wine the crew had enjoyed during the evening meal each day, so they could hardly complain.

Slominski had been assigned lookout duties on the sun deck level and marveled at how beautiful the scene was: the clouds had finally parted and blue sky was visible for the first time in months. The seas had abated and there was the feeling that somehow they were going to break through after all the months of waiting. But on the bridge it was still tense.

After an hour steering the zigzag course at high speed, Gerstung appeared on the bridge again, breathless with another message from the aircraft sent out by telegraph key backed up by Aldis lamp. "Sir," he puffed, "the submarine has broken off and gone deep. The threat believed ended for the moment. The aircraft is expecting two more to relieve him before he breaks off."

"Very well," Ahrens responded, not fully relieved at the report. How much could he trust those airplanes? Did they really have a full handle on the situation? Although simple mathematics showed that if the submarine was still on the surface making his maximum speed of say, 14 knots, *Bremen* was already well outside of deck gun and torpedo range. With the liner's speed advantage of at least 16 knots, the submarine was falling back at more than four miles every fifteen minutes and was no longer a threat. But what lay ahead? There were still no more contacts reported by lookouts and Gerstung's radio direction finders were silent. The weather was now clearing and the visibility had improved to well over ten miles. If Ahrens was to cut and run for the Great Belt into the Baltic, it was now time. As they steamed at high speed, however, there seemed to be no glaring reason to do so. With another ten hours to steam, they would be well past the German minefields, through the Helgoland Bight, and into the approaches to the Weser River estuary. So Ahrens kept the speed on but ceased steering the zigzag course. Now steaming at a straight 140 degrees, they were making excellent time, especially since the hard pounding into the seas had stopped. The crew began to feel a flood of relief.

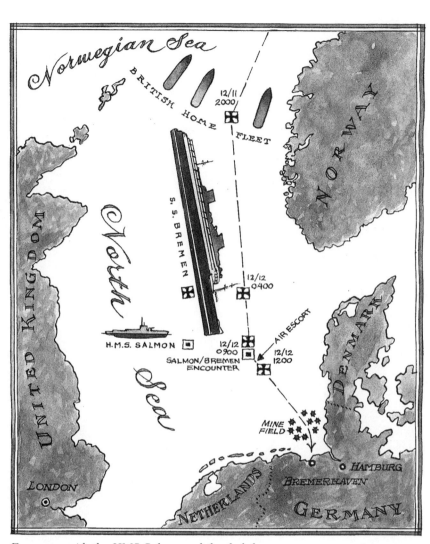

Encounter with the HMS *Salmon* and the dash home.

Suddenly, the aloft lookout cried, "Contact, masts off the port bow on the horizon!" All eyes swung to port. Then a few seconds later, again the voice from aloft, "Possible warship masts, two points off the port bow."

Warning was back on the signal bridge just reading the last visual signal from the single aircraft still orbiting ahead of them. He spun around on hearing the lookout's shout, and, unable to comprehend the words in the wind, dashed to the wheelhouse.

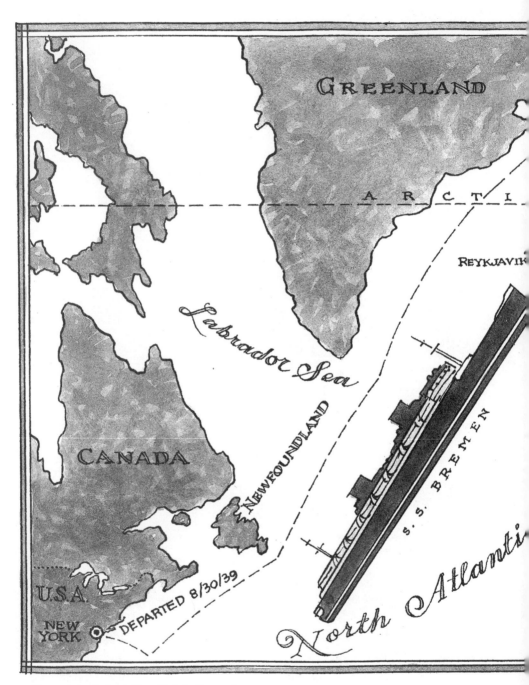

Bremen's track from New York to Bremerhaven.

NORWEGIAN Sea

CIRCLE

ICELAND

BRITISH HOME FLEET

NORWAY

SWEDEN

FINLAND

RUSSIA

MURMANSK
ARRIVED 9/6/39
DEPARTED 12/10/39

U.K.

BREMERHAVEN
ARRIVED 12/13/39

ean

The third mate repeated the message, and Warning quickly ran to the captain's side.

"Why isn't the aircraft reporting if there is a contact there?" He asked no one in particular.

"Perhaps he hasn't seen it yet." Ahrens responded, peering through his binoculars.

"How the hell can that be? I can just make out the masthead, has left bearing drift," Warning muttered.

The bridge watch stood silently, as if nothing untoward was going on. Ahrens marveled at how stoic his men were after all the months of uncertainty. Then it became obvious the contact, whatever its identity, was not going to close them, if indeed they had been sighted. Either it was a merchantman heading in toward the Great Belt and had not seen them or it didn't care and was on its merry way. The contact was opening again and Ahrens breathed a sigh of relief. It was now 3:00 P.M. and beginning to get dark. If they could survive the next two hours, the chances were good that they would make it home.

The proximity of the minefield began to bother Ahrens, while the first officer remained mostly in the chart house with the navigator and the naval liaison officer, who had brought the current minefield channel plots with him. They were locked in a conference, bending over the chart and looking more and more cheerful. The clearing skies had made it possible for the navigator to get a good sun line at noon for the first time since leaving Murmansk and they had also been right on their track based on the looms of the last two Norwegian lights. The ship was still more than forty miles from the coast but the looms were visible and easy enough to shoot a general bearing on.

Ahrens was getting more and more anxious as the daylight began to wane, but began to realize it looked as if they were going to make it now, provided no mine had drifted off from the field. How awful it would be to have made it this far only to hit one of their own mines, after all the steaming they had done. Ahrens began to realize that it was next to impossible now to be picked up by a British submarine unless it had wandered inside the lanes of the minefield. Highly unlikely, he thought.

13

Cheers and Retribution

SS *Bremen*
Weser River estuary
Wednesday, December 13, 1939

Darkness finally came and with it a great feeling of relief. The *Bremen* crew knew it was virtually impossible now for a British warship to be in these German-controlled waters. The bridge watch finally sighted a dim form approaching, and they were certain it was the pilot boat with whom radio contact had already been made an hour earlier. After evading all other ships for so long, it was still ominous to see the form come closer. Finally an amber-lensed signal light began to blink.

The third mate was on the signal bridge and read the coded groups of the challenge out loud. "It's ours," he finally grunted and ran forward to inform the bridge. The approaching contact turned out to be a German torpedo boat, part of the German Vorpostenkette, or seaward screen of early warning ships. As it made the liner's starboard side, the bosuns dropped a ladder for the pilot to climb. "Seeing another German craft sent a welcome feeling through all of us," Heinz Slominski remembered.

When the pilot reached the top of the ladder, he shook hands with Eric Warning and then said loudly so the crewmen standing around could hear, "Congratulations, you've made it through!" Those were welcome words the *Bremen* crew would hear repeated time and again over the next days and even weeks.

As soon as the pilot arrived on the bridge and met Commodore Adolf Ahrens, the tall liner began to creep toward the Weser estuary. After a few hours of steaming, it was with great relief that they

Bremen entering port along
the Weser River estuary
on December 13, 1939.
(Courtesy of Wilhelm Bohling)

sighted the islands west of Cuxhaven. Then, as the ship entered the
Wesermünde, the watch noticed that the navigation lights, which
had been extinguished since the outbreak of hostilities on September 3, were turned on for their benefit and orientation. To port they
sighted the familiar Rotesand Lighthouse, and to starboard the light
on Wangerooge—their first visible greetings of home.

First Officer Warning was the first to sight the outer German
sea buoy and knew immediately they were finally in home waters.
The joy was infectious. Ahrens conned the ship to a holding place
to the side of the estuary and stopped all engines. It was dark but
the crew's spirits were light as feathers. They had made it!

At evening meal, Hans Künlen broke out an extra case of wine
the crew didn't know was still left. He opened a half-dozen bottles
at the mess table and then brought in his cake. It was slightly lop-
sided because it had been baked during the zigzag portion of their
breakthrough, but no one complained. The captain came below

Commodore Adolf Ahrens (second from left) with *Bremen* officers in the ballroom on December 13, 1939. (Courtesy of Deutsches Schiffahrtsmuseum, Bremerhaven)

and drank a toast with the crew while First Officer Warning remained on the bridge waiting for the pilot boat to bring more welcomers from Norddeutscher Lloyd.

As the proud ship neared the pier at Columbus Quay, looking rather scruffy in her hastily applied gray paint, a group of several hundred men stood waiting on the quay—the shipmates who had left them in Murmansk in September. Many had already been inducted into the army and were not there to greet the returning liner. Regardless, it was moving for those aboard to see so many of them again after saying good-bye in the darkness of Murmansk Harbor.

Shortly after the ship was tied up, Commodore Ahrens called all personnel to the ballroom. After assembling, the crew listened to Norddeutscher Lloyd director Rudolf Firle's stirring address. He had brought with him the blue-and-white Norddeutscher Lloyd Commodore's House Flag and handed it to Ahrens, who gave a moving speech. He ended the talk by repeating the words of Norddeutscher Lloyd passenger director, John Schroeder, in New York, when he had said on August 30, "Captain Ahrens, *Bremen* will come through!"

British Home Fleet
North Sea
Wednesday, December 13, 1939

At 10:45 A.M. December 13, as *Bremen* was sailing triumphantly up the Weser River, British submarine *Salmon's* crewmen sighted a large formation of German warships including the battleships *Scharnhorst*, *Gneisenau*, and *Hipper* with three German cruisers. This formation was deployed both as a fleet exercise and as an elaborate ruse to draw units of Admiral Holmes's Home Fleet. At first sighting, it appeared the cruisers would pass at a considerable range, when a sudden course change turned them directly toward *Salmon*. Bickford fired a spread salvo of five torpedoes at eleven-second intervals. At that moment the cruiser *Leipzig* was on a 90-degree track, range five thousand yards. At exactly 10:40 A.M., the cruiser took a direct hit amidships. The remaining two cruisers, *Nürnberg* and *Köln*, turned hard into the source of the torpedo but not soon enough as one of the torpedoes blew a large portion of the stem off *Nürnberg's* bow.

Bickford quickly went deep to evade the destroyers sent in to attack and eluded a lengthy depth charging that inflicted no damage. Thus, Bickford and his *Salmon* crew had vindicated their failure to stop the prize *Bremen* by heavily damaging two cruisers. *Leipzig* was so badly damaged that for the remainder of her life she was limited for use as a training ship. A few days later, London's *Daily Mirror* splashed the headline: HE SAW *BREMEN*, SANK CRUISER AND U-BOAT. The *New York Times* pronounced: BRITISH SUBMARINE THAT SPARED *BREMEN* SAID TO HAVE SCORED TWICE.

After returning to base, three of HMS *Salmon's* officers, First Lieutenant Maurice F. Wykeham-Martin, Torpedo Officer Lieutenant R. H. M. Hancock, and Warrant Engineer O. F. Lancaster, were awarded the Distinguished Service Cross. Seven *Salmon* ratings were awarded Distinguished Service Medals and Commanding Officer E. O. Bickford was promoted to the grade of full

Three of *Salmon*'s officers were awarded the Distinguished Service Cross: (left to right), Lieutenant R. H. M. Hancock, Lieutenant Maurice F. Wykeham-Martin, and Warrant Engineer O. F. Lancaster. (Courtesy of the Royal Navy)

commander and awarded the Distinguished Service Order. After their rewards for sinking *U-36*, sighting and challenging *Bremen*, and severely damaging two German cruisers, *Salmon* returned to sea and made several more combat patrols. She was lost in July 1940 off the coast of Norway with all hands, suspected a victim of a mine.

In the endorsement to Lieutenant Commander Bickford's December patrol report, his senior commander of the Third Submarine Flotilla wrote:

> This patrol must surely be unique in the annals of the submarine branch. In the short space of ten days, Salmon destroyed an enemy submarine, attacked the German Fleet with success possibly destroying one if not two cruisers and last but not least spared the Bremen, a more than valuable asset for propaganda.[1]

Bremen, Germany
Tuesday, December 14, 1939

The day following *Bremen*'s return, Dr. Julius Dorpmüller, the German minister of transportation, hosted a reception at the ornate Bremen headquarters of Norddeutscher Lloyd in honor of Commodore Ahrens and his crew. The German press and several select American journalists attended.[2] A few days later, Captain Ahrens was widely quoted in British, American, and German newspapers giving an account of the voyage from New York and the escape through the British blockade:

> The *Bremen* was already zigzagging. The great ship was swinging first to the port and then to the starboard, then to the port again. Alarm signals shrieking throughout the vessel called all hands to the lifeboats. Only the men in the engine room stayed below. We searched meanwhile, with binoculars for the submarine's periscope, which was spotted shortly sticking above the water. At full speed one of the German flying boats dove down on the submarine. We on board spent several moments at the highest tension. But even before the plane could attack, the submarine had already submerged. It was evident that the British commander gave the order to dive as soon as he saw the plane approaching.
>
> The periscope disappeared beneath the water, and the submarine vanished somewhere into the depths. The Britisher had not been able to complete his well prepared attack on the *Bremen*. He had been forced [to go] deep by the German plane.
>
> The full alarm stage was maintained on board for some time. The German plane kept circling the spot where the submarine had disappeared. Finally the pilot flashed the message "Attack need not be feared anymore."
>
> From the bridge came the order, "All men return to their posts." Our engines slowed to normal speed. The danger was past, the British attack having been warded off.[3]

In this first concrete German confirmation of *Bremen*'s escape to pass German censors, the German Propaganda Ministry predictably scorned the British claim that the commander of *Salmon* had correctly refrained from firing at the fleeing liner in deference to the naval treaties that forbid attacking merchant ships without warning.

British Admiralty
London
December 1939

British Admiralty officials studied Ahrens's account of the confrontation with the British submarine HMS *Salmon* in detail. Ahrens had confirmed that *Bremen* had an armed Luftwaffe escort during her final dash through the Shetland-Faeroe gap and that her run from Murmansk had been part of an elaborate military plan and supported actively by the Soviet government. Officials in London raised the question again whether the Royal Navy would have been correct in attacking *Bremen* nonetheless, since she was under escort by military aircraft and could have been interpreted as being in a military convoy, thereby exempting her from protection of the London Naval Treaty.

The question remained: If Lieutenant Commander Bickford had managed to fire one or more warning shots, and *Bremen* had ignored them, would the submarine commander have been justified in firing at her to stop and sink her? That question is rendered moot by the fact that by the time *Salmon* had submerged after being seen by the German aircraft, it is questionable whether it was physically possible for her to get off a torpedo, given the speed advantage of the liner. *Salmon*'s top submerged speed was limited to short bursts of about 10 knots. Records show that at that time *Bremen* was still steering a zigzag maneuver at nearly 30 knots. It is clear from Bickford's patrol report that he had decided not to sink the liner after he was forced to submerge and that the subsequent signal he received from his commander confirmed that *Bremen* was not a target.

World Press
Berlin, London, and New York
December 15, 1939

The furor in the world press continued unabated especially when news of Bickford's continuing success aboard *Salmon* broke the day after his encounter with the liner. *Bremen* stole the headlines in German newspapers: WHERE ARE ENGLAND'S GENTLEMEN OF THE SEA?; BRITISH PURSUER FLEES; and *BREMEN*'S RETURN—A WORLD SENSATION.

The British press headlines read: SHE GOT AWAY AGAIN; *BREMEN* REACHES GERMANY AT MERCY OF BRITISH SUBMARINE; and *BREMEN* SIGHTED ON VOYAGE WITHIN TORPEDO RANGE.

The *New York Times* announced: BREMEN OUTWITS FOE TO REACH HOME; PLANES SAVE LINER, ESCORT FORCED A BRITISH SUB-MARINE TO DIVE; LONDON CITES WAR RULES; and NAVAL COM-MANDERS UNDER ORDERS NOT TO SINK MERCHANT SHIPS WITHOUT WARNING.

Quite predictably, Joseph Goebbels's Propaganda Ministry treated the British version of failing to stop the liner with contempt, saying that *Bremen*'s successful dash through the blockade was merely proof that British claims of maritime superiority were a sham.

North Atlantic
December 20, 1939

After *Bremen* had returned to Germany and had been feted by the homeport and the Propaganda Ministry, the world was stunned by the loss of a major German naval combatant and successful surface raider. The liner's triumphant return was soon eclipsed by the news of the scuttling of the German pocket battleship *Graf Spee* on December 17, outside Montevideo Harbor. A running battle with the British cruisers *Exeter, Ajax,* and *Achilles* on the River Platte ended with commanding officer Captain Hans Langsdorff's decision to abandon and then scuttle the trapped battleship outside the neutral harbor, thereby causing the German navy to call a moratorium of several months in the actions of all surface raiders. Three days later, the German liner SS *Columbus* was lost. The *Bremen* crew were deeply affected by this news because they had come within a hair of being forced to meet the same fate.

Ironically, on the same day that Commodore Ahrens was quoted concerning the incident with the HMS *Salmon, Columbus* was reported as having obtained clearance to depart from Veracruz Harbor and was expected to make her dash for freedom, close on the heels of the sensational story of *Bremen*'s successful escape. Just as *Europa, Bremen,* and other German ships had prepared to scuttle themselves in the event of encountering British combatants, so, too, had *Columbus,* the third Norddeutscher Lloyd express liner.

On December 20, as the *Bremen* crew were still basking in their victorious return, the news arrived of the fate of their comrades aboard *Columbus* after a complex odyssey. She had reached New York on August 18 from the West Indies and sailed again the next day with 727 passengers, first to Jamaica, then to Haiti and Puerto Rico. Her master, Captain Wilhelm Daehne, had received the QWA 7 message broadcast to all German ships to return to Germany or seek a neutral port, so she skipped St. Georges, Grenada, which was British owned, and reached Curaçao on August 26 to fuel. On Sunday, August 27, he was ordered to "Land passengers, proceed to Haugesund, Norway and to enter a U.S. port only in extremis." Captain Daehne turned around and sailed for Aruba on August 28, the day *Bremen* had entered New York. While in Aruba, he was ordered to return and land passengers in New York, then on August 31 he was told to cancel New York and land passengers in Havana instead. The ship proceeded to Cuba, where the passengers disembarked and were returned to Florida aboard the steamer *Florida*. *Columbus* then headed for Veracruz and subsequently moved to safer anchorage in Antonio Lizardo, fourteen miles south of Veracruz. There she took on twenty-five thousand barrels of fuel and painted herself gray for camouflage. Norddeutscher Lloyd tried quietly to sell the ship to German citizens in South America in order to obtain foreign registry, thus avoiding seizure on the high seas. Captain Daehne protested to Berlin via the German consulate in Veracruz and the German embassy in Mexico that any attempt to break out would be futile. Nevertheless, perhaps because of *Bremen*'s success, Berlin ordered him to try to evade.

On Wednesday, December 20, the 35,000-ton *Columbus* slipped out of the darkness of Veracruz Harbor. Declared for Oslo, Norway, it was fully loaded with sufficient fuel and provisions for a fifty-day voyage. Her crew had placed inflammable material on the promenade deck ready to be doused with gasoline. In this case, however, *Columbus* was unlucky after being sighted and trailed by the Norfolk-based cruiser USS *Tuscaloosa*. She was sighted by two British destroyers that took chase. *Tuscaloosa* joined the fray and

The crew of *Columbus* in lifeboats as their ship burns off Norfolk, Virginia.
(Courtesy of Deutsches Schiffahrtsmuseum, Bremerhaven)

when *Columbus* stopped, the crew abandoned ship after setting her afire. *Columbus* burned and sank just outside neutral waters of Cape Hatteras. The entire crew was taken aboard the American cruiser and into Norfolk, where they were interned until the end of the war.

AFTERWORD

After returning to Bremerhaven, the liners *Bremen* and *Europa* were used as troop accommodation ships. Both were hurriedly refitted in Hamburg with 88 mm antiaircraft weapons, modified to carry tanks, and painted an interrupted black, white, and shaded gray camouflage. Large loading doors were cut in the sides to handle military cargo for fifteen thousand troops. The ships were prepared for Operation Sea Lion, the invasion of England, which never came about. There were also some reports of a plan to use the two grand liners as decoy ships to run a high-speed feint toward Norway, drawing off British warships while the main German landing forces would land on the East Anglian coast of England. The Germans also had contingency plans to strip the ships down to the main deck and convert both with their excellent engineering plants into aircraft carriers, which also never happened.

On a quiet Sunday afternoon, March 16, 1941, as *Bremen* lay moored to the Columbus Quay in Bremerhaven, a fire erupted in the Hunting Salon on A deck. The ship's master, the firefighters, and most of her crew were ashore. The ship burned furiously, and after battling the fire for hours, firefighters watched in bewilderment as the proud liner listed heavily to starboard, finally collapsing as a tired prizefighter against the pier. She died a slow death, her remaining burned out steel hulk fed piecemeal to the starving Ruhr factories as the war ground to an agonizing end. To this day, her rusting lower deck skeleton can be viewed at low tide in the murky waters in the shallows of the Weser estuary off Bremerhaven at a place called Blexen Reede (Rude).

Bremen following the fire in July 1941. (Courtesy of AGW Archives, Bremen)

Months following the fire, a former *Bremen* seaman named
Gustav Schmidt, a longtime shipmate in Heinz Slominski's deck
force, who had been missing since the fire, was apprehended
while serving on a merchant ship in the Black Sea port of Con-
stanta. He was overheard boasting of igniting the fire that destroyed
Bremen. The sailor was arrested and, following intense interroga-
tion by the Gestapo, confessed to lighting the fire just to see how
fast his shipmates could run. Even though witnesses claimed that
two foreigners had been seen giving Schmidt more than 300,000
reichsmarks to do the job, the murky Gestapo trial never really
proved the alleged culprit was guilty. Regardless he was summarily
executed.

The U.S. Navy took *Europa* following the war and used her to
return troops home as transport USS *Europa* until transferring her
to France as compensation for the disastrous loss of the liner *Normandie* in New York in February 1942 to a fire caused by a care-
less welder while the Navy was converting her into a transport.

Europa was then renamed *Liberté* by the French and served on Atlantic duty, surviving two ignominious collisions and one sinking. She was salvaged and refitted in 1950, and continued to serve the post-war French passenger fleet until she was sold as scrap to an Italian firm at La Spezia in December 1962.[1]

Commodore Adolf Ahrens retired from maritime service due to medical problems following the *Bremen*'s victorious return to Bremerhaven in December 1939. The long career of standing watches on pitching decks had taken its toll on his legs. He was awarded a Gold Medal by the city of Bremen for his exemplary seamanship and after the war was elected to the West German Bundestag as a representative from Bremen.

Leading First Officer Eric Warning reverted to the grade of Kapitänleutnant (lieutenant junior grade) (S) in the German Navy, served as a prize officer aboard the commerce raider *Pinguin*, and was lost at sea when that ship was sunk by the British cruiser *Cornwall* in May 1941.

Waiter Ernst Henningsen served in a German navy tug in the Mediterranean and was captured by Allied troops during the liberation of Naples. He was subsequently shipped to Georgia as a prisoner of war where he served for two years picking cotton, then returned to work at the American Officers' Club in occupied Bremerhaven.

Apprentice Wilhelm Bohling served in the German army ending his wartime career in the German 325th Parachute Division in France. In 1944, during the opposition to the Allied Normandy landings, he was wounded in action and survived to return to the ships of Norddeutscher Lloyd.

Able Seaman Heinz Slominski served in the German Navy as a tug crew member in Hamburg, was jailed by the Gestapo toward the end of the war as a smuggler, and survived to work for the Americans in Bremerhaven during the occupation.

It is reasonable to summarize, having followed this story by hearing and reading the poignant words of the *Bremen* crew, that this grand ship played a major part in their lives. To German citizens of that era, just emerging from the devastation of a lost war, coping with the humiliation of the treaty that followed, weathering a major economic depression, and dealing with and the failure of the Weimar democratic experiment, the superliner *Bremen* represented the reemerging hope not only in the maritime world, but also as their optimism for the new Germany itself. The severe bitterness and pain at seeing their pride and joy go up in smoke just eighteen months following her breathtaking dash through the blockading force of the world's mightiest navy was in a way symptomatic of the feelings by so many as they watched their hopes of a new Germany hijacked by a dictator who spawned an ideology so horrible that it is still largely taboo to reminisce and record stories of German successes during the Nazi times.

Until recently, it has been considered distasteful to record and publish accounts of the most notable events involving German citizens and how so many suffered misery and sorrow under the same tyranny, only because they were under the identical flag as the perpetrators. Their suffering was eclipsed by the larger shadow of those many millions of others less fortunate. Furthermore there were the 1945 sinkings by Soviet submarines in the Baltic of the cruise ships *Wilhelm Gustloff,* with a loss of more than seven thousand civilian refugees; *Steuben,* with a loss of at least thirty-five hundred refugees and wounded German soldiers; and *Goya,* with the loss of five thousand refugees. Only the really terrible stories like what happened at Auschwitz, Dachau, and the other horrible sites of death and suffering have been considered worthy wartime subjects to relate.

But who can deny that it is high time the rest of the stories of the losses and anguish suffered by Germans be told? Their stories are devastating, too. For example, it is still not known how many Germans were lost in the Baltic maritime tragedies in the last months of the war, during the flood of refugees from the eastern front, or during the severe firebombing raids that finally precipitated the end of the war. The loss of the superliner *Bremen,* although paling in comparison with the devastating loss of life in the other tragedies of the war, is perhaps more a metaphor for the failed hopes of Germans than for their actual suffering of the flesh.

While researching this story, I encountered in and around Bremen and the port of Bremerhaven a lingering pride in the grandeur of that famous liner, its accomplishments, its dash to safety, and eventually its ignoble loss, more a tragic loss of symbol than of blood. This was brought home by the fact that the two former *Bremen* commanders, Leopold Ziegenbein and Adolf Ahrens remained outspoken anti-Nazis and, through their persistent strength of character, never succumbed to the popular Nazi Party ideals. It is also noted that both Ziegenbein and Ahrens flew the old German tricolor from their home flagstaffs throughout the war, with impunity due to the respect they commanded, and that Ahrens later held elective office in the new West German Bundestag.

There are those who portray the German people of the 1930s and 1940s as unfortunate misguided followers of a wayward leader, but I do not wish to be included in that group. I think the Germans still bear full responsibility for electing and following Adolf Hitler and sharing in the collective guilt for the atrocities committed under his rule. But their own stories must also be told.

NOTES

INTRODUCTION

1. John Malcolm Brinin, *The Sway of the Grand Salon*. New York: Delacorte Press, 1971.

2. Thomas Siemon, *Ausbüxen, Vorwärtskommen, Pflicht erfüllen: Bremen Seeleute am Ende der Weimarer Republik und im Nationalsolzialismus, 1930–1939*. Bremen: Staatsarchiv Bremen, 2002, pp. 163–165.

3. Ibid., pp. 202–203.

4. Ibid., p. 209.

5. *New York Times*, September 17, 1935, p. 14.

1. UNCERTAIN CROSSING

1. The struggle was not so much centered around the leader of the onboard SA personnel minders, but rather with the Nazi officials who traveled as passengers and tried to spread their party ideas and propaganda to the other travelers.

2. DEBEG was the telecommunications organization founded in the 1920s called Deutsche Betriebgesellschaft fur drahtlose Telegraphie m.b.H. Berlin. It was placed aboard all German passenger ships, tankers, freighters, and other ships with special tasks. DEBEG also provided broadcast telegraphers aboard the airships *Graf Zeppelin* and *Hindenburg*.

3. See Jochen Brennecke, *Die Deutschen Hilfskreuzer im Zweiten Weltkrieg*. Herford, Germany: Koehlers Verlagsgesellschaft, 1958, pp. 107–115.

4. FDR memorandum to Acting Secretary of Treasury, August 25, 1939, FDR Library, Hyde Park, New York.

5. Converting Merchant Ships to Auxiliary Raiders—NID 24/T165/45, Center for Naval History, Navy Yard, Washington, D.C., 1945.

6. Treasury Department, Memorandum for Assistant Secretary Herbert Gaston, August 28, 1939, FDR Library, Hyde Park, New York.

7. Treasury Department, U.S. Coast Guard Memorandum for Assistant Secretary Herbert Gaston, August 28, 1939, FDR Library, Hyde Park, New York. This report of a false swimming pool bottom was no doubt an anti-Nazi hoax.

2. ROOSEVELT'S NEUTRALITY

1. David Kahn, *Hitler's Spies: German Military Intelligence in World War II.* New York: Macmillan, 1979, p. 328. Herman Lang worked by day as a machinist, draftsman, and assembly inspector at Carl Norden in Manhattan, while at night he did his espionage copy work under the code name Paul. Lang smuggled blueprint copies of the Norden bombsite to the Luftwaffe aboard the cruise ships *Bremen* and *Reliance*. He received payment of $3,000 from the German government. He was eventually betrayed by a double agent, arrested by the FBI, tried, and convicted as one of the "Nazi Nineteen" in a sensational spy scandal and sentenced to eighteen years.

2. William Breuer, *Hitler's Undercover War: The Nazi Espionage Invasion of the USA.* New York: St. Martin's Press, 1989, pp. 28–29.

3. Letter from Edwin Drechsel, son of William Drechsel, to the author, July 2, 2003.

4. Ibid.

3. OBFUSCATION AND DELAY

1. The following were taken verbatim from the transcripts of the telephone conversations between officials in the Treasury Department, the White House, the State Department, and the Customs Office in New York. From the FDR Library, Hyde Park, New York.

4. INTO OBLIVION

1. The full text of Captain Ahrens's speech appeared in newspapers throughout Germany and was reprinted in the *New York Times*, September 18, 1935, p. 17.

5. RUNNING NORTH

1. Treasury Department Memorandum to President Roosevelt from Acting Secretary John W. Hanes, September 1, 1939. From the FDR Library, Hyde Park, New York.

2. From a letter written by John S. Conaghan, October 18, 1981, quoted in the *Nautical Research Journal* 31, no. 4 (December 1985): 176.

7. RUNNING FOR REFUGE

1. Clay Blair, *Hitler's U-Boat War: The Hunters, 1939–1942.* London: Modern Library, 2000, pp. 67–79.

2. In a major diplomatic blunder, a German surface raiding party including the pocket battleship *Deutschland* (later renamed Lützow) and a U-boat cap-

tured *City of Flint* and had a prize crew take it to Murmansk. Later, while attempting to escape to Germany through Norwegian waters, *City of Flint* was captured by Norwegians and returned to her American crew.

3. Admiral Karl Dönitz testified during the International Military Tribunal in Nürnberg and defined in his memoirs the conditions under which German submarine commanders were permitted to attack merchantmen. See Karl Dönitz, *Memoirs: Ten Years and Twenty Days*. New York: Leisure, 1959, pp. 8–10.

4. German Sink on Sight Policy, Section 24-5/C-100 NID 24/T7/45, February 7, 1945, World War II German Files, Navy Historical Center, Navy Yard, Washington, D.C.

5. Clay Blair, *Hitler's U-Boat War: The Hunters, 1939–1942*. London: Modern Library, 2000, p. 96.

6. Ibid., pp. 700–702.

8. Soviet Support

1. George F. Kennan, *The Marquis de Custine and His Russia in 1839*. Princeton, N.J.: Princeton University Press, 1971, p. 55.

2. Adolf Ahrens, *Die Bremen: Geschichte eines Schiffes*. Essen: Verlag von Reimar, 1956, p. 136.

3. Edwin Drechsel, *Norddeutscher Lloyd Bremen, 1857–1970*. Vol. 1, *History, Fleet, Ship Mails*. Vancouver, B.C.: Cordillera, 1995, p. 420.

4. William Shirer, *Berlin Diary*. New York: Book of the Month Club, 1940, p. 254.

5. Elbert Post, a Dutch seaman serving aboard *Bremen* as a cook, wrote an account of *Bremen*'s run from New York to Murmansk when he had returned home in October. The article was printed in the Amsterdam newspaper *Het Volk* and reprinted in the *New York Times*, October 15, 1939, p. 2.

6. It is now known that of the 619 passengers returned to Belgium, France, and Holland, an estimated 260 died in extermination camps.

9. Plotting Escape

1. The *Het Volk* article was repeated in part in the *New York Times*, October 15, 1939.

2. From Adolf Ahrens's letter, November 2, 1939, to the German Navy High Command. Bundesarchiv-Militärarchiv, Freiburg, Germany, RM 7, file 843.

10. *Salmon* Bags a U-Boat

1. From the Navy High Command, Berlin, Operation Order NR 364/39, November 21, 1939.

2. Lawrence Patterson, *Second U-Boat Flotilla*. Barnsley: Leo Cooper, 2003 p. 28.

3. This account is based on the very detailed *Patrol Report of HMS Salmon Dec. 3–16, 1939*, December 17, 1939, No. 0808, obtained from the Submarine Museum and Archives Gosport, Hampshire.

4. See Brennecke, *Die Deutschen Hilfskreuzer im Zweiten Weltktieg*, pp. 107–115.

11. RUNNING FOR HOME

1. From the German Navy High Command War Diary, KTB, Kriegstage-buchs Microfilm Publication T1022. Dr. Timothy P. Mulligan composite records relating to U-boat warfare 1939–1945, guides to the microfilm records of the German Navy, NARA, Washington, D.C., 1985.

12. *SALMON'S* DILEMMA — *BREMEN'S* ESCAPE

1. Dönitz, *Memoirs*, p. 10.

2. Ibid., p. 11.

3. *Salmon* patrol report of December 17, 1939.

4. Ibid.

13. CHEERS AND RETRIBUTION

1. From the endorsement (Captain S) No. 0848/1 to Patrol Report by commanding officer, HMS *Salmon*, Lieutenant Commander E. O. Bickford, dated December 17, 1939, from British Submarine Museum, Gosport, Hampshire.

2. In his book *Berlin Diary*, p. 257, William Shirer complained bitterly that the German Propaganda Ministry pitted Jordan Max of NBC, Shirer for CBS, and, Nazi favorite, American author Lothrop Stoddard to broadcast an interview with Commodore Ahrens, finally choosing Stoddard. The process so infuriated him because, Shirer claimed, being forced to fight over the broadcast rights played into Nazi hands and he rejected the proposal in advance, thus dashing the chance for CBS.

3. Summarized and translated from the article "Ich komme durch," *Nordwestdeutsche Zeitung, Bremerhavener Zeitung, Wesermünder Tageblatt, Unterweser Zeitung*, December 15, 1939, p. 1.

AFTERWORD

1. From Edwin Dreschel's letter to the author, dated November 4, 2004. (Edwin is the son of the late Captain William Dreschel.)

BIBLIOGRAPHY

PRIMARY SOURCES

Interviews

Bohling, Wilhelm. Former *Bremen* steward. Interview with the author in Bremerhaven, June 4 and November 11, 2003.

Drechsel, Edwin. Son of the former New York marine superintendent William Drechsel. Letter to the author, July 2, 2003.

Ebeling, Maris (née Warning). Daughter of Leading First Officer Eric Warning. Interview with Imke Schwarzrock, Bremen, January 23, 2004.

Harms, Horst, Dipl. Ingenieur. Son-in-law of Julius Hundt, *Bremen* chief engineer from construction through July 1939. E-mail interview August 6, 2003.

Henningsen, Ernst. Former waiter in *Bremen*'s first-class dining room. Interview with the author in Bremerhaven, June 5, 2003.

Slominski, Heinz. Former deck seaman aboard *Bremen*, April–September 1939. Interview with the author in Bremerhaven, November 11, 2003.

Wilm, Renata (née Ahrens). Daughter of Adolf Ahrens. Interview with Imke Schwarzrock, Bremen, January 23, 2004.

Documents

Admiralty Files 53/107740 and 107741. Logs of HMS *Berwick*, August 30–September 6, 1939. National Archives, Kew, Richmond, Surrey TW9 4DU.

Admiralty Files 53/111293. Logs of HMS *York*, August 30–September 6, 1939. National Archives, Kew, Richmond, Surrey TW9 4DU.

Admiralty Files 173/16506. Logs of HMS *Salmon*, December 1–31, 1939, Naval History Branch, Ministry of Defense, Room 303, 3-5 Old Scotland Yard, London, SW1A HW.

Ahrens, Adolf. Letter (secret) report to the German Navy High Command, November 2, 1939, discussing requirements for reinforcing the crew for the voyage from Murmansk to Bremerhaven. Bundesarchiv-Militärarchiv, Freiburg, Germany, RM 7, file 843.

————. Letter (secret) report to the German Navy High Command, December 14, 1939. Bundesarchiv-Militärarchiv, Freiburg, Germany, RM 7, file 228.

ALUSNA (American Legation U.S. Naval Attaché) Berlin War Diary, November 15, 1939, reporting that Danish fishermen had sighted *Bremen* in camouflage paint standing south off the Jutland coast.

ALUSNA Berlin War Diary, EF30/A12-1, December 6, 1939, reporting the arrival of *Bremen* in Murmansk on December 6 following a false report of her capture off Lisbon on September 3, 1939.

ALUSNA Berlin War Diary, December 18, 1939, reporting that HMS *Salmon* sank one U-boat and torpedoed *Leipzig* and a Blücher-type light cruiser at the mouth of the Elbe on December 14.

ALUSNA Berlin War Diary, December 20, 1939, report stating that *Bremen* arrived safely in Bremerhaven on December 13 according to German radio broadcasts and British boasting that their submarine had let *Bremen* pass either because the submarine missed her shot or because German planes forced her down.

ALUSNA London Report Number 799, August 30, 1938. Office of Naval Intelligence, Navy Department, Washington, D.C., 1947. Naval Historical Center, Navy Yard, Washington, D.C.

Assistant secretary of commerce. Cable, August 21, 1939, alerting New York to enforce clearance procedures.

Baumbach, Norbert von, naval attaché, German embassy in Moscow. Letter (secret) to Adolf Ahrens, November 8, 1939, discussing details of the pending transit from Murmansk to Bremerhaven. Bundesarchiv-Militärarchiv, Freiburg, Germany, RM 7, file 843.

Bickford, E. O., lieutenant commander. Patrol report, December 17, 1939. Submarine Museum, Gosport, Hampshire, PO12/2AS.

Bremen. Log of the last voyage. Deutsches Schiffahrtsmuseum, Bremerhaven, Han-Scharoun-Platz 1, D-27568.

Cairns, Huntington. Transcript of telephone conversation with John W. Hanes, August 29, 1939, 4:01 P.M., about the thirty *Bremen* men, saying State and Immigration claim it is up to Commerce and asking if FBI officials are satisfied with the departure of the thirty.

Durning, Harry, New York collecter of customs. Transcript of telephone conversation with John W. Hanes, August 29, 1939, talking about withholding tugs and having a Coast Guard cutter ready up river to block *Bremen* if she tries to depart without clearance and the apparent equal treatment of French *Normandie* and *Transylvania*.

————. Transcript of telephone conversation with John W. Hanes, August 29, 1939, 4:50 to 4:57 P.M., about trouble holding the *Bremen* talks concerning the thirty technicians and physicians on the pier, since they are not passengers, and having the FBI check them out.

————. Transcript of telephone conversation with John W. Hanes, August 29, 1939, 4:09 P.M. saying Customs is at the end of its rope and can't hold *Bremen* any more and says it will clear her that evening at 5:00 P.M.

Feis, Herbert, Department of State advisor on international economic affairs. Memorandum to Secretary of State Cordell Hull, August 29, 1939. FDR Library.

————. Transcript of telephone conversation with John W. Hanes, August 29, 1939, about continuing the delay of *Bremen* by showing some confusion and sleight of hand. (Refers to British note in the press.)

————. Transcript of telephone conversation with John W. Hanes, August 29, 1939, 3:24 to 3:28 P.M., discussing the removal of seventeen crewmen from *Bremen* and taking them to Ellis Island.

————. Transcript of telephone conversation with John W. Hanes, August 29, 1939, 3:16 to 3:20 P.M., describing *Bremen* taking on thirty men as crew and discussing the legal implications. Describes the discovery of a three-inch gun mount emplacement and ammunition hoist underneath but no gun and no ammunition.

Feldkamp, Ursula. "Tintoretta und der Reisenden-Sonderdienst des Norddeutschen Lloyd 1931–1939." *Deutsches Schiffahrtsarchiv* (1995).

Führer Conferences, on matters dealing with the German navy 1939. U.S. Navy Historical Center, Navy Yard, Washington, D.C. German Foreign Ministry Correspondence, Series D.

Hanes, John W., assistant secretary of treasury. Memorandum for President Franklin D. Roosevelt, August 24, 1939, reporting on the alert to Department of Commerce in New York of irregularities in clearance and departure of foreign vessels and directing immediate detention, interception, and retention in custody of belligerent vessels in territorial waters.

————. Transcript of telephone conversation with Harry Durning, collector of customs, New York, August 25, 1939, talking about the president's desires to hold the other German ship *New York* in New York and reporting the pending arrival of *Bremen* and *Europa*.

————. Transcript of telephone conversation with Frank Murphy, August 25, 1939, about the legality of holding German ships in ports.

————. Transcript of telephone conversation with Herbert Feis, August 29, 1939, 10:45 A.M.

————. Notes, August, 29, 1939, informing of *Bremen*'s arrival, unloading, and request for immediate departure and denial of clearance. Also reports the thirty physicians and technicians who were signed on as crew. FDR Library.

————. Memorandum for the files of conversation with General Edward Watson, August 30, 1939, 11:20 to 11:23 A.M., reporting the status of *Bremen* in New York for the president. FDR Library.

————. Memorandum September, 1, 1939, referring to the amount of fuel *Bremen* took aboard in New York.

Hull, Cordell, secretary of state. Memorandum of conversation with Dr. Hans Thomsen, German chargé d'affaires, and Adolf Berle, August 30, 1939, concerning holding the SS *Bremen*.

Kriegstagebuchs, KTB, German Navy War Diaries, Microfilm Publication T1022, NARA, College Park, Maryland.

Mulligan, Dr. Timothy P. Composite Records relating to U-boat warfare 1939–1945. Guides to the microfilmed records of the German navy, Washington, D.C., NARA, 1985.

Murphy, Frank, U.S. attorney general. Letter to President Franklin D. Roosevelt, August 28, 1939, approving the legality of seizing German and Italian vessels in territorial waters following a declaration of war. FDR Library.

———. Memorandum to the Treasury Department, August 26, 1939, authorizing the Coast Guard the use of all necessary force within territorial waters to compel compliance of maritime law. FDR Library.

Navy High Command, Berlin. Operation Order (secret, only by officer) Nr. 364/39 Gkdos. Chefs, November 21, 1939, detailing the measures for bringing in the steamer *Helene* (code name for the express liner SS *Bremen*). Bundesarchiv-Militärarchiv, Freiburg, Germany, RM 7, file 843.

———. Operation Order (secret) Nr. 461/39 Gkdos. Chefs, December 7, 1939, detailing the measures to bring in the steamer *Helene*. Bundesarchiv-Militerarchiv, Freiburg, Germany, RM 7, file 843.

———. Operation Order (secret, officer handling only) from Marine-Gruppenkommando Ost, B. Nr. 323/39 Gkdos. Chefs, December 9, 1939, to Befehlshaber der Sicherung der Ostsee (Commander of Baltic Security East) Berlin, Befehlshaber des Marine-Gruppenkommandos West (Commander Naval Group West) Wilhelmshaven, and Befehlshaber der Unterseeboote (Commander Submarine Forces) Wilhelmshaven. Subject: Weisung Gruppe Ost fur die Einbringung des Dampfers *Helene*. (Directive for bringing in the steamer *Helene*.) Bundesarchiv-Militärarchiv, Freiburg, Germany, RM 7, file 843.

Nixon, Irving F., Commissioner of field services and labor. Transcript of telephone conversation with John W. Hanes, August 29, 1939, 3:30 to 3:32 P.M., discussing the status of the thirty men signing on as crew members since *Bremen* cannot carry passengers. They are all American citizens. No one of interest to the FBI.

Rohwers, J., and G. Hummelchen. *Chronology of the War at Sea 1939–1945*. Translated from the German by Derek Masters, Vol. I: 1939–1942. London: Ian Allan, 1973.

Roosevelt, Franklin D. Memorandum to John W. Hanes, August 25, 1939, ordering the withholding of clearance papers from all ships suspected of carrying armaments until a complete search has satisfied that no armaments are aboard.

————. Transcript of telephone conversation with John W. Hanes, August 28, 1939, reporting *Bremen's* arrival off Sandy Hook headed into New York Harbor, also telling Hanes to take his time inspecting and holding *Bremen* until Wednesday. (Roosevelt calls *Bremen* a "dangerous ship to have loose.")

————. Memorandum to John W. Hanes, August 25, 1939, directing the withholding of clearance papers of all ships suspected of carrying armaments. Stating he has reason to believe the possibility that merchant ships are carrying armament to be mounted at sea converting them to raiders. FDR Library.

Ruck-Keene, P., commander of the Third Submarine Flotilla HMS *Cyclops*. Endorsement to the HMS *Salmon* patrol report, December 17, 1939. Submarine Museum, Gosport, Hampshire, PO12/2AS.

Rückkehr des Schnelldampfers Bremen (Return of the express liner *Bremen*). Report (secret) of the commanding officer's debriefing by Fregatten Kapitan Stange, German Navy High Command, December 20, 1939, Bundesarchiv–Militärarchiv, Freiburg, Germany, RM 7, file 228.

Siemon, Thomas. *Ausbüxen, Vorwärtskommen, Pflicht erfüllen: Bremen Seeleute am Ende der Weimarer Republik und im Nationalsolzialismus, 1930–1939.* Bremen: Staatsarchiv Bremen, 2002.

Treasury memo based on cabinet meeting, August 25, 1939, to all collectors of Customs to enforce certain rules against foreign belligerent ships in territorial waters.

Tschira, Hanns, *Bremen* photographer. Personal notebook, 1941. Deutsches Schiffahrtsmuseum, Bremerhaven.

U.S. Coast Guard. Memorandum to Assistant Secretary Herbert Gaston, August 28, 1939, informing him of *Bremen's* scheduled arrival in New York on August 29, 1939, and the German liner *New York's* departure.

————. Memorandum, August 28, 1939, reporting the intercept of German communications from DEBEG (Berlin) to an unknown ship to remove telegraph equipment when the vessel is changed to a man-of-war.

————. Memorandum to Assistant Secretary Herbert Gaston, August 30, 1939, discussing a report from the U.S. Coast Guard District Headquarters in San Francisco of a false bottom in *Bremen's* swimming pool for war supplies and her anticipated rendezvous with a submarine for special equipment.

————. Log from cutter *George W. Campbell*, August 30–September 3, 1939. National Archives, 11E4/22/07/04 Box 458 in two volumes.

Wachtel, first officer of *Bremen*. Report (secret), December 16, 1939, of *Bremen's* voyage from Murmansk to Bremerhaven and endorsement. Anlage (1) to Nebenstelle Bremen Abwehr I/Marine B. Nr. G. 12370/39/Ima5,v.16.12.1939. Bundesarchiv-Militerarchiv, Freiburg, Germany, RM 7, file 228.

Watson, E. M., Memorandum of telephone conversation with John W. Hanes, concerning holding *Bremen* for fortyeight hours as directed per instructions.

————. Memorandum to President Franklin D. Roosevelt, August 29, 1939, informing him that *Bremen* applied for clearance late August 28 but was refused, and *Bremen* would depart without clearance and tugs were withheld to prevent her departure.

Memoirs

Ahrens, Adolf. *Die "Bremen" schlägt sich durch: Die Heimkehr des grössten deutschen Handelsschiffes*. Berlin: Steiniger, 1940.

————. *Die Bremen: Geschichte eines Schiffes*. Essen: Verlag von Reimar, 1956.

————. *Die Siegesfahrt der "Bremen."* Berlin: Steiniger, 1940.

Ferber, Gertrude, *Acht Glas*. Berlin: Steiniger, 1940.

Post, Elbert. Account printed in Amsterdam newspaper *Het Volk* and reprinted in the *New York Times*, October 15, 1939. Post was a Dutch seaman who served aboard *Bremen* as a cook.

Renneberg, Walter. "Ich war dabai" (I was there). Erinnerungsbericht an die letzte Fahrt der Bremen am (Reminiscing the last voyage of *Bremen*), August 22, 1939.

————. "Twenty Nine and One Half Knots through the English Blockade." A personal written account by former *Bremen* crewman Walter Renneberg of the voyage of *Bremen* to Murmansk in August–September 1939 and the return trip by crewmembers from Murmansk to Bremerhaven by Soviet rail and the German transport *Sierra Cordoba* by way of Leningrad. From the archives of the Deutsches Schiffahrtsmuseum, Bremerhaven.

Ricklefs, Hermann. "Die Letzte Bremen Fahrt miterlebt." *Niederdeutsches Heimatblatt*, no. 207 (March 1967). Ricklefs was the first officer during *Bremen*'s last voyage.

Ritter, Nikolaus (cover name Dr. Rantzau). *Die Aufzeichnungen des Nikolaus Ritter, Offizier im Geheimen Nachtrichtendienst*. Hamburg: Hoffman and Campe, 1972.

Tschira, Hanns. *Die Bremen Kehrt Heim: Deutscher Seemannsgeist und Deutsche Kameradschaft retten ein Schiff*. Berlin: Verlag Hermann Hilger K.G., 1940.

SECONDARY SOURCES

Bartlett, Ruhl. *Policy and Power: Two Centuries of American Foreign Relations*. New York: Hill and Wang, 1963.

Bishop, Beatrice, and Travis Beal Jacobs. *From the Papers of Adolf A. Berle*. New York: Harcourt Brace Jovanovich, 1973.

Blair, Clay. *Hitler's U-Boat War: The Hunters, 1939–1942*. London: Modern Library, 2000.

Blum, John Morton. *From the Morgenthau Diaries*. Vol. 3, *Years of Urgency, 1938–1941*. Boston: Houghton Mifflin, 1965.

———. *Roosevelt and Morgenthau*. Boston: Houghton Mifflin, 1970.

Braynard, Frank D., and William H. Miller. *Fifty Famous Liners*. New York: Norton, 1985.

———. *Lives of the Liners*. New York: Cornell Maritime Press, 1947.

Brennecke, Jochen. *Die Deutschen Hilskreuzer im Zweiten Weltkrieg*. Herford, Germany: Koehler, 1958.

———. *Ghost Cruiser HK33*. London: Kimber, 1954.

———. *Luxusliner Bremen Brennt!: Letzte Fahrt Bremen—New York*. Herford, Germany: Koehler, 1973.

Breuer, William. *Hitler's Undercover War: The Nazi Espionage Invasion of the USA*. New York: St. Martin's Press, 1989.

Brinin, John Malcolm. *The Sway of the Grand Salon*. New York: Delacorte Press, 1971.

Burns, James MacGregor. *Roosevelt, the Soldier of Freedom*. New York: Harcourt Brace, 1970.

Churchill, Winston S. *The Gathering Storm*. Cambridge, Mass.: Houghton Mifflin, 1948.

Cole, Wayne S. *Charles A. Lindbergh and the Battle against American Intervention in World War II*. New York: Harcourt Brace, 1974.

Coleman, Terry. *The Liners: A History of the North Atlantic Crossing*. New York: Putnam, 1985.

Costello, John. *Days of Infamy*. New York: Pocket, 1994.

Daily Mirror (London) "Another Liner Safely Home," December 14, 1939.

Dallek, Robert. *Franklin D. Roosevelt and American Foreign Policy, 1932–1945*. New York: Oxford University Press, 1979.

Davis, Kenneth S. *Franklin D. Roosevelt into the Storm, 1937–1940: A History*. New York: Random House, 1993.

Drechsel, Edwin. *Norddeutscher Lloyd Bremen, 1857–1970*. Vol. 1, *History, Fleet, Ship Mails*. Vancouver, B.C.: Cordillera, 1995.

Farago, Ladislas. *The Game of the Foxes*. New York: Bantam, 1971.

Feis, Herbert. *The Road to Pearl Harbor*. New York: Princeton University Press, 1950.

Ferris, Theodore E. naval architect and marine engineer. Interview in "Express Liners." *Marine Engineering and Shipping Age* (July 1930): 350–355.

Freidel, Frank. *Franklin D. Roosevelt: A Rendezvous with Destiny*. Boston: Little Brown, 1990.

Hinsley, Francis H., et al. *British Intelligence in the Second World War*. 3 vols. New York: Cambridge University Press, 1979–1983.

Hughes, Tom. *The Blue Riband of the Atlantic*. New York: Scribners, 1974.

Ickes, Harold L., *The Secret Diary of Harold L. Ickes*. Vol. 3, *The Lowering Clouds, 1939–1941*. New York: Da Capo, 1974.

Kahn, David. *The Codebreakers*. New York: Macmillan, 1967.

———. *Hitler's Spies: German Military Intelligence in World War II*. New York: Macmillan, 1979.

Kennan, George F. *The Marquis de Custine and His Russia in 1839*. Princeton, N.J.: Princeton University Press, 1971.

Kimball, Warren F. *Churchill and Roosevelt: The Complete Correspondence*. Princeton, N.J.: Princeton University Press, 1984.

Kludas, Arnold. *Das Blaue Band des Nordatlantiks. Die Geschichte eines internationalen Wettbewerbs*. Hamburg: Koehler, 1999.

———. *Die Geschichte der deutschen Passagierschiffahrt, 1850–1990*, five volumes. Hamburg: Ernst Kabel, 1986.

———. *Die Schnelldampfer Bremen und Europa. Höhe-punkt und Ausklang einer Epoche*. Hereford: Koehler, 1993.

Lash, Joseph P. *Roosevelt and Churchill, 1931–1941: The Partnership That Saved the West*. New York: Norton, 1976.

Marine Engineering and Shipping Age. "The *Bremen*." July 1930.

Marine Engineering and Shipping Age. "Express Liners: An Interview with Theodore E. Ferris." July 1930.

Maxtone-Graham, John. *The Only Way to Cross*. New York: Collier, 1978.

Miller, William H. "Memories of Long Ago Southampton." *Marine News* 6 (1985): 331.

Napier, Rob. "The North German Lloyd and Bremen (IV) 1929." *Nautical Research Journal* 31, no. 4 (December 1985).

Nixon, Edgar B. *Franklin D. Roosevelt and Foreign Affairs*. Cambridge, Mass.: Harvard University Press, 1969.

Persico, Joseph E. *Roosevelt's Secret War: FDR and World War II Espionage*. New York: Random House, 2001.

Randall, J. G., and David Donald. *The Civil War and Reconstruction*. Boston: Heath, 1961.

Rauch, Basil. *Roosevelt from Munich to Pearl Harbor*. New York: Creative Age, 1950.

Reynolds, David. *The Creation of the Anglo-American Alliance, 1937–1941*. London: Europa, 1981.

Rohwer, J., and G. Hummelchen. *Chronology of the War at Sea, 1939–1940*. Vol. 1, *1939–1942*. London: Ian Allan, 1954.

Roskill, S. W. *The War at Sea, 1939–1945*, Vol. 1, *The Defensive*. London: Her Majesty's Stationary Office, 1954.

Salewski, Michael. *Die deutsche Seekriegsleitung 1935–1945*. 2 vols. Frankfurt am Main: Bernard & Graefe, 1970.

Sherwood, Robert E. *Roosevelt and Hopkins*. New York: Harper, 1948.

Shirer, William. *Berlin Diary*. New York: Book of the Month Club, 1940.

———. *The Rise and Fall of the Third Reich: A History of Nazi Germany*. New York: Simon and Schuster, 1960.

Tansill, Charles C. *Back Door to War*. Chicago: Henry Regency, 1952.

The Shipbuilder. "The Atlantic Liner *Bremen*." Quarterly: October, November, December 1930.

Tschira, Hanns. "Die Kühne Heimfahrt unserer *Bremen*." *Das leben im Bild* (Berlin), Nr. 4, 1940.

———. "Ich war auf der *Bremen*," *Der Angriff* (Berlin), Nrs. 305, 306, 307, December 20.

———. "Ich war auf der *Bremen*," *Westfällischer Kurier*.

———. "Ich war auf der *Bremen*," Der kühne Durchbruch unseres schönsten Schiffes." *Hessische Landeszeitung* (Darmstadt), Nr. 56, February 24, 1940.

———. "Wie die *Bremen* es schafft." *Das Illustrierte Blatt*.

———. "Wie die *Bremen* sich durchschlug." *Berliner Illustrirte Zeitung*. Nr. 51, 1939.

Völkischer Beobachter. "Die Bremen wieder in der Heimat." (Berlin) Nr. 348, December 14, 1939.

Von der Porten, Edward. *The German Navy in World War II*. New York: Galahad, 1969.

Witthoft, Hans-Jurgen, and Ludwig Dinklage. *Die deutsche Handelsflotte, 1939–1945*. 2 vols. Hamburg: Nikol Verlag, 1992.

———. Norddeutscher Lloyd: Bremen. Hamburg: Seehafen Verlag, 1984.

Index